AF541913

A PLAIN, BLUNT MAN

A PLAIN, BLUNT MAN

THE ESSENTIAL SARDAR VALLABHBHAI PATEL

edited by

URVISH KOTHARI

ALEPH

ALEPH BOOK COMPANY
An independent publishing firm
promoted by ***Rupa Publications India***

First published in India in 2023
by Aleph Book Company
7/16 Ansari Road, Daryaganj
New Delhi 110 002

ISBN: 978-93-93852-78-6

1 3 5 7 9 10 8 6 4 2

Printed in India.

For
My daughter, Aastha

CONTENTS

TIMELINE OF PATEL'S LIFE

1875: Vallabhbhai Patel is born to Ladba and Jhaverbhai Patel in Nadiad, a western Indian town in Kheda district, at his mother's parental home. His actual date of birth is not registered; 31 October is an adopted birth date.

Spends his childhood in Karamsad, where he also completes his initial schooling.

1891: Goes to Petlad, a nearby village, to study English in the fourth and fifth standards.

1893: Marries Jhaverba from Gana, a nearby village.

1897: Passes his matriculation exam from a high school Nadiad.

1900: Passes the district pleader exam and begins practising in Godhra.

1902: Moves from Godhra to Borsad in Kheda district.

1903: A daughter, Manibehn, is born to Vallabhbhai and Jhaverba.

1905: A second child, a son, is born to the couple. He is named Dahyabhai.

1909: Jhaverba Patel passes away in Mumbai after an intestinal surgery.

1910: Vallabhbhai goes to England to fulfil his dream of becoming a barrister. He enrols at Middle Temple.

1913: Returns to India as a barrister and settles in Ahmedabad.

1915: Enters public life as a member of the Gujarat Sabha.

1916: Comes into contact with Mohandas Karamchand Gandhi as a member of Gujarat Sabha.

Attends the annual session of Congress in Lucknow.

1917: Becomes active in public life after getting elected as a member of the Ahmedabad Municipality. Appointed chairman of Health Committee and leads plague relief efforts in Ahmedabad.

Appointed as a secretary of a committee of the Gujarat Provincial Conference; Gandhiji is the president of the conference.

1918: Becomes Gandhiji's deputy during the Kheda Satyagraha.

1919: Becomes the chairman of sanitary committee of Ahmedabad Municipality. Starts movement against the Rowlatt Bills.

1920: Indian Nation Congress wins a decisive victory in the Ahmedabad Municipality elections under his leadership.

1921: Abandons Western attire and adopts khadi. Collects Rs 10 lakh as Gujarat's contribution to Tilak Swaraj Fund. Appointed the chairman of the reception committee in the thirty-sixth annual session of Congress held at Ahmedabad.

1922: Travels up to Burma and successfully collects ₹10 lakh for Gujarat Vidyapith established by Gandhiji.

1923: Leads the Nagpur Flag Satyagraha and Borsad Satyagraha.

1924: Is elected the president of Ahmedabad Municipality where he introduces a khadi uniform for the employees of Ahmedabad Municipal Corporation.

1927: Takes on flood relief work in Gujarat and manages his duties exemplarily.

1928: Resigns as the president of Ahmedabad Municipality.

Leads the Bardoli Satyagraha where he earns the loving title 'Sardar'—leader.

1929: Is appointed the president of the Maharashtra Political Conference.

1930: Is arrested for the first time at Raas, a village in Kheda district, and jailed just days before the beginning of the historical Dandi March by Gandhiji. He would be jailed multiple times this year.

1931: Is elected president of Congress and presides over the annual session at Karachi.

1932: Sentenced to a jail term of sixteen months. Imprisoned at Yerawada Jail along with Gandhiji and Mahadev Desai.

Ladba, Sardar Patel's mother, passes away.

1933: Vitthalbhai Patel passes away in Geneva. Sardar Patel refuses to accept conditional parole to attend the last rites of his elder brother.

1934: Travels to many parts of the country to campaign for elections. Appointed the chairman of the Congress Parliamentary Board.

1935: Takes up plague relief work in Borsad taluka.

1936–37: Congress, under the leadership of Jawaharlal Nehru and Sardar Patel, wins in the provincial elections and forms governments in eight provinces. Patel actively guides the state governments.

1938: Becomes the president of the Kathiawad Political Conference.

Plays a key role in the success of the annual session of Congress organized at Haripura in southern Gujarat.

1939: Friction with Subhas Chandra Bose on ideological issues within the party.

1940: Is once again arrested for taking part in individual satyagraha and sent to Sabarmati Jail. He is shifted to Yerawada Jail later.

1941: Undergoes treatment for serious intestinal issues.

1942: Arrested following Quit India Movement along with the entire leadership of Congress and imprisoned at Ahmednagar Fort Jail from 1942 to 1944.

1944: Shifted from Ahmednagar to Yerawada Jail, Pune.

1945: Is released from Yerawada. Takes part in parleys with Viceroy Lord Wavell for the freedom of India.

Is put in charge of the election management of Congress for the central and provincial assembly elections.

1946: Meets the Cabinet Mission along with other leaders at Shimla.

Joins the Viceroy's Executive Council and heads the departments of Home Affairs and Information and Broadcasting in the Interim Government.

Becomes part of the Constituent Assembly formed to prepare the constitution for a free India.

1947: Supports the resolution of partition of the country.

State department is created under his leadership; they aim to tackle the complicated issue of the merger of the princely states with the union of India.

Becomes deputy prime minister. He would also hold portfolios of Home and Information and Broadcasting.

The efforts of the Nawab of Junagadh to merge his state with Pakistan fail and the the army of the provisional povernment of Junagadh, formed in Bombay, take Junagadh.

1948: Owing to Patel's efforts, most princely states are merged with surrounding regions to form unions that eventually become new states. He is ably supported by Viceroy Mountbatten and Political Reforms Commissioner V. P. Menon.

Hyderabad becomes part of India after his firm police action.

Bans RSS for six months in the wake of Gandhi's assassination.

1949: British India and princely states become one united independent India due to the untiring efforts of Patel and his trusted lieutenants.

1950: Issues a warning about China's dangerous intentions and the importance of maintaining Tibet as a buffer zone between India and China.

Passes away on 15 December in Mumbai after a heart attack. His body is cremated at Sonapur crematorium in the presence of President Rajendra Prasad, Prime Minister Nehru, and many other leaders.

INTRODUCTION

Sardar Vallabhbhai Patel's life and work have attracted much less study compared to that of Gandhi and Nehru—the two other leaders of the swaraj-troika. He is either discounted as a right-wing leader who gained acceptance in the Congress because of Gandhi's support or simply hailed as the Iron Man who achieved the integration of India. Critics label him as an anti-Muslim, pro-RSS fanatic, and leaders dealing in the politics of minority-bashing claim him as 'one of our own'.

Sardar Patel was right of centre when it came to his political views and was a staunch Hindu. However, he was, above all, a follower of Gandhi who believed in the Congress party's inclusive philosophy. He did not, at any time, subscribe to what is now known as Hindutva. Indeed, he said unambiguously, 'The duty of Hindus is to fully help the Muslims…' and 'The State must exist for all, irrespective of caste and creed.' He did not go the lengths of Gandhi and Nehru in taking care of the sentiments of Muslims. At the same time, he did not approve of the crimes of Hindu communalists and, most importantly, did not engage in majoritarian politics and politics fueled by hate and suspicion.

His assertive nature, biting tongue, and iron willpower were community characteristics to a large extent. His closeness with Gandhi pushed him to defy many stereotypes. Unlike most members of his caste, he abandoned his caste identity and plunged into the freedom movement leaving behind a life of luxury. He had remarkable administrative abilities, uncommon for a farmer at the time.

Yet, he proclaimed himself a farmer and remained one at heart, hiding his barrister avatar. He was not interested in literature or literary pursuits, nor did he have any time for empty speeches or political punditry. He did not have high regard for any sort of ideology. He believed in concrete action. Gandhi's lack of verbosity, fearlessness, and action-oriented programs made a deep impression on him and brought him to the movement for Indian independence.

He did not think he had anything to offer to the world in terms of original thinking or political theory or a model of movement. He wanted to serve his country with dedication and found Gandhi's way most aligned to this goal, and so he was quick to learn from Gandhi. He had no qualms in saying that he was not a Mahatma and he had a party to run, without being disrespectful or sarcastic to Gandhi.

Known for creating a well-oiled party machine and election strategy with a strong, bordering on autocratic, party high command, he did not use power to serve or consolidate his selfish interests. He had many industrialist friends. But he did not use their money to propagate his personality cult. He never thought of toppling Prime Minister Nehru after withdrawing his candidature for the top job at Gandhi's suggestion. Violence during partition and the complex process of integration of the states were two enormous, almost existential challenges for independent India. Sardar Patel dealt with both with varying degrees of success. On many other issues, Patel advised and expressed nuanced opinions with utmost clarity.

Even though he was rightly hailed as the architect of the unity of India, his memory faded from public life rather quickly, only to reemerge a couple of decades ago as those with vested political interests tried to revive it. He had no disciples; many of his close associates from the Congress saw the advancement of their political careers by inching closer to Nehru after the Sardar's death. His son Dahyabhai left Congress after accusing the leadership of shelving his father's memory and ignoring his huge contribution. Maniben, Sardar Patel's daughter and close associate, chose to stay in Congress till it was split by Indira Gandhi in 1969.

∽

The first biography of Sardar Patel, in two parts, was written by a fellow Gandhi associate, Narhari Parikh, in Gujarati. The first of the two parts was published during Patel's lifetime in 1950. Parikh's compilation of Patel's speeches from 1918 to 1947 was also an early important document. His phenomenal work during the crucial years of the transfer of power and integration of the states was documented in V. P. Menon's detailed accounts of both events in the first decade after Independence.

Ten volumes of Sardar Patel's correspondence, edited by Durga Das, and a compilation of his speeches and letters in his birth centenary year by Maniben Patel and G. M. Nandurkar were a rich addition to the literature on this great leader. V. Shankar, a civil servant and the personal secretary of Sardar Patel during his last years wrote his memoirs in two parts, in 1974 and 1975.

Rajmohan Gandhi's biography of Sardar Patel in 1991 was the first well-researched, complete biography that had the length and depth to set many records straight. Lately, the publication of *The Collected Works of Sardar Vallabhbhai Patel*, edited by Dr P. N. Chopra, has provided readers with a collection of letters, speeches, and writings of Sardar Patel along with newspaper coverage, official documents, and reports.

This volume is a selection of his best and most representative works—speeches, articles, and letters that highlight various aspects of his life and work. Some of the material, especially from the early phase of his life, has been translated from the original Gujarati by the editor. Newspaper reports and government reports are not included in the volume. I have tried my best to avoid selections that could further a biased and incorrect representation of one of our founding fathers and have instead tried to provide a nuanced selection of Sardar Patel's ideas and thoughts in the hope that this volume might lead to further reading and study of Patel's life and work.

Urvish Kothari
Mahemdavad, Gujarat
January 2023

SARDAR PATEL: A LIFE SKETCH

The Charotar region of the Kheda district (formerly known as Kaira district) in Gujarat was well known for its fertile land and resourceful cultivators. Among the different classes of cultivators, the Kanbis or Patidars—owners of the pati (land)—were 'the best farmers', described as 'sober, quiet, industrious, and except on such occasions as marriage, thrifty'[*]. They numbered 20.32 per cent of the total Hindu population of the district.[**] Vallabhbhai Patel's father Jhaverbhai was a Leva Kanbi (Leva being a dominant subcaste of Patidars in Gujarat).

Vallabhbhai was the fourth among five sons and one daughter of Jhaverbhai and Ladba Patel. Viththalbhai Patel was the eldest. Vallabhbhai was born in Nadiad at his maternal uncle Dungarbhai Desai's place. He admitted to his biographer Narhari Parikh that his date of birth 31 October 1875 was not accurate and was decided 'according to his own fancy'[***] as there was no record of the real date of his birth. Jhaverbhai was a religious man. Inspired by his father, Vallabhbhai fasted twice a month till the age of seventeen or eighteen while he was at Karamsad. He did not show any religious inclination and never indulged in such rituals after that period.

Sending children to school was not the norm at that time. According to the 1872 census, out of 1.43 lakh Hindu boys up to twelve years of age in the district, only 6.36 per cent were able to read and write or were going to school.[****] Vallabhbhai was one of those lucky boys; he studied until the seventh standard in the Gujarati medium. Later, he studied in the English medium at schools in Karamsad, Petlad, Nadiad, and for some time at Baroda. He became proficient in the English language.

***Gazetteer of Bombay Presidency*, Vol. III, Bombay: Government Central Press, 1879, p. 31.

**Ibid.

***Narhari Parikh, *Sardar Vallabhbhai Patel Vol. 1*, Ahmedabad: Navjivan Publishing House, 1953, p. 8.

*****Gazetteer of Bombay Presidency*, Vol. III, p. 134.

His leadership qualities also came to the fore during his school days once he became a student leader. On one occasion he mobilized his fellow students for the election campaign of one of his teachers who was contesting a municipal election. The rival candidate bragged that he would shave off his moustache if he lost. After his teacher emerged victorious, Vallabhbhai along with some fifty students and a barber, went to the defeated candidate's home and asked him to fulfil his promise. Considered headstrong by some of his teachers, young Vallabhbhai had a tender side too. While staying at his friend Kashibhai's place at Nadiad, he cared for a young child.*

Vallabhbhai passed his matriculation from Nadiad high school at the age of twenty-two. He wanted to begin earning as soon as possible to fund his law studies in England and so did not choose the L.L.B. course that would take six long years. He opted for the district pleader's examination, prepared for it while staying at home, and cleared it at the end of three years. His elder brother, Viththalbhai, who was already practising as a pleader, suggested that they work together in Borsad. But Vallabhbhai chose to start his independent practice in Godhra in 1900.

Vallabhbhai married Jhaverba in 1893 at the age of eighteen. After spending two years in Godhra, he moved to Borsad, a town in the Kheda district that had the dubious distinction of having the largest number of criminal cases in the Bombay Presidency. Vallabhbhai soon established himself as a successful criminal lawyer. Yet, he had not forgotten his dream of becoming a barrister all this while.

Just when Vallabhbhai had saved enough money to pursue his legal studies abroad and secured the necessary travel documents as V. J. Patel, Viththalbhai expressed his desire to avail the opportunity to become a barrister in England. Without demurring, Patel handed over his documents and savings to his sibling. It would take him five more years to save the amount of money he needed to fund his studies and become a barrister.

---

*This was the son of Dungarbhai, a friend of Kashibhai's father. His wife died young, and so Kashibhai's mother brought the child to her (Kashibhai's) home and raised him. Vallabhbhai was staying there for his studies.

Patel remained largely untouched by the first Swadeshi Movement in 1905 and other activities of the Indian National Congress as also political developments of the time. His focus was on having a successful career and a good life. When he set out for England in 1910, he was already thirty-five, had two children—Maniben and Dahyabhai—and had lost his wife who died of medical complications after an operation. He entrusted his children to a British governess in Bombay before leaving for England. He wanted them to be fluent in English.

His tenure at Middle Temple was marked by extraordinary educational achievements. Short on funds and in a hurry to complete the course as fast as possible, he studied hard, keeping away from the pleasures of English life. His singlemindedness of purpose bore the desired result. He completed his course in 1912 securing the first rank in his cohort and also got an exemption from two terms along with a prize of fifty pounds. At the age of thirty-seven, Vallabhbhai had no time to waste, and soon returned to India in February 1913. He had the option to work in a government job in Bombay. But he was more inclined to set up his own practice.

∽

Vallabhbhai chose Ahmedabad as his base, just a year and a half before Gandhi would return to India from South Africa and decide to settle in Ahmedabad. He quickly became known for his fierce demeanour, sharp arguments, biting sense of humour, and ability to secure the acquittal of his clients. Smoking a hookah and playing bridge at the Gujarat Club with fellow lawyers such as G. V. Mavalankar were his favourite activities outside the court. Young lawyers like Mahadev Desai and Narhari Parikh, who used to attend the court proceedings, were impressed by the performance of Barrister Vallabhbhai. They nicknamed him 'a young lion'.*

There was an understanding between the Patel brothers that the elder one would plunge into public life and serve the nation whereas the younger one 'had to commit all the sins' and perform the inferior

*Parikh, *Sardar Vallabhbhai Patel Vol. 1*, p. 42.

task of earning for both.* As a result, Vitthalbhai entered political life in Bombay Presidency. Vallabhbhai was not interested in the political activities of that period which were largely based on petitions and appeals. He did, however, join the Gujarat Sabha, a local civic organization, and went to attend the Congress session at Lucknow in 1916. It did not impress him; he was averse to verbose, lengthy resolutions and long speeches.

When Gandhi came to the Gujarat Club to make a speech to the assembled lawyers, Vallabhbhai showed little interest in him even though he was famous for his work in South Africa. He did not even care to stop his game of bridge, instead mocking his lawyer friend Mavalankar for his keenness to listen to Gandhi. Gandhi's ideas of simplicity, labour, and brahmacharya appeared absurd to Vallabhbhai and, at the time, he was not inspired by the practices Gandhi observed at his ashram.

The newly appointed Municipal Commissioner J. A. Shillidy's 'rather arrogant and self-opinionated manner'** was instrumental in pushing Vallabhbhai into active public life. Many of Vallabhbhai's friends thought and insisted that only he, with his fearlessness and sharpness, could tackle Shillidy.

Vallabhbhai did not disappoint his friends and well-wishers. After getting elected to the municipality, he waited for an opportunity. When he found a solid case against the commissioner, he studied the details thoroughly and made a strong brief against him. Even pro-British members were left with no other option but to vote in favour of Vallabhbhai's resolution; the resolution criticizing the English commissioner was passed with a majority vote. The bureaucracy was shaken by this unprecedented turn of events. When Shillidy was called back due to many other accusations, it was seen as a victory of Vallabhbhai's leadership. There were many such incidents when Vallabhbhai defied convention and fiercely opposed British civil servants.

Even after getting involved in public affairs at the municipality level, Vallabhbhai had no political inclination or appetite for wider

---

*Ibid., p. 22.
**Ibid., p. 27.

political involvement. Also, he was duty bound to earn for two families. However, Gandhi's satyagraha at Champaran changed his views on nationalist politics. He was attracted to the direct approach of Gandhi. He saw in Gandhi fearlessness, firm resolve, lack of verbosity, and a willingness to sacrifice himself in the interest of India and Indians.

The first Gujarat Political Conference was convened at Godhra under the auspices of the Gujarat Sabha in 1917 after Gandhi became the president of the Sabha. Vallabhbhai was appointed secretary to an executive committee formed by Gandhi.

When Gandhi proposed to take up the cause of the farmers of Kheda who were unable to pay their land revenue due to heavy rainfall resulting in crops getting washed out, many members of the Gujarat Sabha were apprehensive. Gandhi asked for the assistance of experienced hands to conduct the satyagraha, not by majority vote, but only after securing support from all the Sabha members. Vallabhbhai lost no time in offering his services. Gandhi was forty-nine and Vallabhbhai was forty-three, much past their youth, when their association began.

~

The 1918 Kheda Satyagraha against oppressive structures of land revenue had Gandhi and Patel on one side and Frederick Greville Pratt, the commissioner of the Northern Division, on the other. Pratt and Patel had a somewhat acrimonious history due to the former having imposed two English officers—a municipal engineer and a health officer—on the Ahmedabad municipality, much to the dissatisfaction of the elected representatives. Patel had had heated arguments with Pratt over the incompetence of the appointed municipal engineer.

The satyagrahis of Kheda demanded the postponement of land revenue due to washed-out crops. After much coercion and threats, the satyagraha ended in a lukewarm settlement, with the government proposing that if those who can afford to do so remit the land revenue, it would be postponed for the rest. Though it was for the first time that the government had to take into consideration public grievance, Mahatma Gandhi did not think this end was entirely satisfactory. Nonetheless, it cemented the bond between Gandhi and Patel—a development that had significant implications for the nation.

Gandhi called Patel his 'deputy commander' and admitted in a public meeting:

> When I met Vallabhbhai first, I could not help wondering who this stiff-looking person was and whether he would be able to do what I wanted. But the more I came to know him, the more I realized that I must secure his help. Vallabhbhai too has concluded that although he has a flourishing legal practice today and is doing very important work in the municipality, he must become a whole-time public worker and serve his country. So he has taken the plunge.... If it were not for his assistance, I must admit that this campaign would not have been carried through so successfully.*

Patel also accompanied Gandhi in his unusual recruitment campaign for the British army during World War I. Both Gandhi and Patel believed military training would be beneficial in fostering courage amongst the locals of Kheda. Gandhi, though he believed in non-violence, was willing to become a recruiter for the army for the greater good. His recruiters were not supposed to fight or kill. In a letter to the Viceroy, he wrote, 'I recognise that in the hour of its danger we must give, as we have decided to give, ungrudging and unequivocal support to the Empire of which we aspire in the near future to be partners in the sense as the Dominions overseas....'** In this quest, Patel became Gandhi's 'recruiting sergeant'. Both leaders had a tough time convincing people to fight for the British. They bore many hardships and tasted the indifference of the same people who hailed them as leaders during the Kheda Satyagraha, yet were able to recruit almost 100 men.

The year 1919 saw the imposition of martial law in Punjab and the looming implications of the oppressive Rowlatt Acts. Gandhi declared countrywide satyagraha against the Acts. He was joined by Patel, who signed the pledge drafted by Gandhi at Sabarmati Ashram. The Non-cooperation Movement and Khilafat Movement brought the country's political temperature to a boiling point. In 1920, the Gujarat Sabha

---

*Ibid., p. 89.

**M. K. Gandhi, *The Story of My Experiments with Truth Vol. II*, p. 459, available at www.gandhiheritageportal.org.

was brought into the fold of the Indian National Congress, emerging as the Gujarat Provincial Congress Committee (GPCC). Patel was elected the president of GPCC in 1921.

Patel started wearing khadi in the summer of 1921. Along with his foreign clothes, he also abandoned his legal practice and adopted a lifestyle more suited to an ardent Gandhi disciple. He was often criticized as Gandhi's blind follower. But, in reality, Patel was a fiercely independent thinker, and Gandhi was well aware of this quality. In fact, Patel never became an ashramite and often made fun of the rigidities of some of the ashram dwellers. A straightforward personality with forthright opinions, ideological discussions held little interest for Patel. He wholeheartedly accepted Gandhi as his leader in the quest for swaraj. However, when Gandhi supported the Khilafat Movement (1919–24), an agitation led by Indian Muslims to oppose Britain's breach of promise and the harsh treatment meted out to the Ottoman Empire after World War I, Patel was sceptical. He could not comprehend why Indian Muslims should be supported in their advocacy of protecting the Caliphate—a political-cum-religious organization with its figurehead, the Caliph, based in Turkey. Nonetheless, he soon joined Gandhi in support of the Khilafat Movement as it was a significant stepping stone in achieving Hindu–Muslim unity.

When Gandhi announced the Tilak Swaraj Fund of ₹1 crore, Vallabhbhai collected ₹10 lakh as Gujarat's contribution and enrolled 3 lakh members into the party. He was elected chairman of the Reception Committee for the annual session of the Congress held in Ahmedabad in 1921. He ensured simple yet tasteful arrangements for the event. The delegates were given a khadi bag at a nominal price so they could safely store their footwear and not have to worry about them being stolen. Tents and pandals made of khadi were erected. An exhibition of swadeshi goods was organized.

Patel managed things so efficiently that when the accounts for the sessions were closed, there was enough money left to build the Congress House in Ahmedabad. In due course, he acquired the land on which the session had been conducted, and it became the site of the V. S. Hospital which was built with the help of local donations. Both buildings were Patel's contributions to Ahmedabad.

~

In February 1922, the violence at Chauri Chaura proved to be the proverbial last straw for the Non-cooperation Movement. Gandhi suspended the satyagraha in Bardoli, disappointing most leaders who thought the movement had gained excellent momentum and was successfully exerting heavy pressure on the British rulers. After Gandhi's arrest under sedition charges, Patel continued to spread his message, occasionally writing for Gandhi's Gujarati weekly *Navjivan*. He was one of the trustees of Gujarat Vidyapith, established by Gandhi in 1920 to promote national education. He actively collected funds for the organization and travelled to Rangoon (Burma) to gather aid when Gandhi was in jail.

Patel was well established as Gandhi's lieutenant in Gujarat. But the 1923 Nagpur Flag Satyagraha made him a well-known figure beyond Bombay presidency. It began with the district magistrate prohibiting the flying of the National Flag on the municipality building in Jabalpur. The ban was extended to display the national flag on public roads and especially on the road going through Civil Lines. After the police brutalized members of a procession carrying the flag at Jabalpur and Nagpur, the Congress Working Committee decided to start a satyagraha in Nagpur. Jamnalal Bajaj took the lead. Patel was tasked with mobilizing resources and volunteers from Gujarat. After Bajaj's arrest, the All India Congress appointed Patel as the leader of the satyagraha. He firmly believed that Gandhi, who was imprisoned and unable to provide guidance, had already shown the path and it was up to his followers to walk on it. Gandhi's absence did not prove to be a hindrance for Patel; he did not feel limited. The British government was prepared to crush the satyagraha. They attacked and arrested hundreds of satyagrahis, keeping them in Nagpur jail in pathetic conditions. Yet, the will of the Congress workers to court arrest and bear police atrocities without indulging in counter-attack was exemplary. Vitthalbhai, Patel's elder brother and an assembly member, tried to assist from within by consistently pressuring the government. The combined efforts of Congress workers and Vitthalbhai resulted in a victory.

Vitthalbhai's intervention was noteworthy because of the ongoing tussle between the 'pro-changers' willing to attend the assembly and the 'no-changer' Gandhians opposed to the idea of joining legislatures as a part of non-cooperation. Vallabhbhai was a prominent no-changer. Jamnalal Bajaj, C. Rajagopalachari, Rajendra Prasad, and Dr M. A. Ansari formed an informal group with him. On the other hand, pro-changers like Vitthalbhai, C. R. Das, and Motilal Nehru formed the Swaraj Party. Vallabhbhai never shied away from criticizing his elder brother's political views. But he abided by Gandhi's decision and did not oppose the resolution that allowed members of Congress to contest elections and vote.

The success of the Nagpur Satyagraha was followed by a satyagraha at Borsad, Patel's home ground. The government had imposed a punitive tax on all residents above the age of sixteen, accusing them of sheltering outlaws. The tax was required to maintain an additional police force. Locals believed the police were in collusion with the outlaws. Patel took up the cause on behalf of the provincial Congress committee and laid the conditions of the fight before the people of Borsad. He explained the rationale behind the satyagraha—it was not only about resisting taxation, but for raising their voices against injustice. He also outlined the dangers of joining a non-violent fight and the atrocities they might have to bear.

Patel had already obtained a detailed report from two colleagues and cross-examined them. Once he was satisfied with the preparation of the people, he took the lead and camped at Borsad. The satyagraha lasted for five weeks. Government officials tried to crush the movement by seizing property in lieu of the punitive tax. But under Patel's inspiring leadership, the people courageously faced the British officials and upheld the principles of non-violence. Ultimately, the government conceded and announced that the costs of the extra police force would be financed from the general revenue. Patel declared the abolition of punitive tax as a triumph of truth, non-violence, and penance.

While the Nagpur and Borsad satyagrahas highlighted Patel's leadership as a fighter in the Gandhian mould, his involvement with the Ahmedabad municipality revealed his administrative capabilities as a competent public servant. His tenure as an elected member of the Ahmedabad municipality began in 1917 as an elected member. In the 1920 municipal elections, he led Congress to a grand victory. He was elected the president of the Ahmedabad municipality twice, in 1924 and 1927.

Patel contributed significantly to the betterment of Ahmedabad and set an example of leadership in the institutions of local self-governance. Not to be cowed down by English civil servants and their Indian counterparts, Patel's style was to take the bull by its horns. He was able to collect multiple long-pending taxes from the cantonment area. He organized a parallel education infrastructure with the help of the citizens of Ahmedabad when the government stopped disbursing grants for municipal schools. Patel achieved all this even before he became the president. He was committed to ensuring the city's cleanliness which was largely made of 'poles', congested and old residential areas known for their insanitary environment. Patel involved both elected representatives and the locals to execute this unprecedented task. During his tenure as the president, his daily schedule always included moving around in the city so he could familiarize himself with the issues faced by the locals. He envisaged and initiated many schemes for the development of Ahmedabad that his successors later completed.

In 1927, many areas in Gujarat including Ahmedabad and Kheda district were devastated by heavy rainfall. Patel took charge of relief activities and engaged volunteers without waiting for assistance from the government. His organizational skills were in full display, from effectively securing and disseminating relief material to collecting funds from the people and the government for the rebuilding of ravaged villages. He adopted a cautious approach to ensure the affected population did not become heavily reliant on external aid for prolonged periods. When Gandhi asked him if his presence was needed, Patel wrote back saying that if he wanted to check whether Gujarat had learned the lessons he taught, he should not come. Both Gandhi and Viceroy Lord Irwin praised Patel's effective management.

Despite a remarkable display of public work, Patel continued to face several restrictions from the government and rival factions in the Ahmedabad municipality. His second innings as the president ended abruptly in 1928 when he resigned as a mark of protest against the appointment of the Chief Officer Ishwarlal Bhagat. By then, the stage for the most memorable satyagraha of his life was set.

~

Bardoli, a taluka in southern Gujarat, was to be the starting point of a nationwide satyagraha in 1922. Unfortunately, it had to wait for six more years after Gandhi postponed the movement. In 1928, the scenario changed. The issue was now local. The government had declared a 22 per cent increase in the taluka's land revenue. After a careful study of the issue, Patel took the lead. Gandhi chose to be a witness, assuring Patel of his presence whenever required.

Quoting the correspondence between Patel and the government, Gandhi wrote, 'Vallabhbhai is not unknown to fame or the Government. They have been obliged to acknowledge his worth as a public worker of great capacity, integrity, and industry. They have acknowledged his great work in the municipality of Ahmedabad. Only the other day he received unstinted praise for his philanthropic services in connection with the floods in Gujarat. But his work seems to have counted for nothing when they found him engaged in an activity calculated to cause them embarrassment and possibly loss of prestige....'*

Patel's abilities as an organizer of a large-scale satyagraha were tested. He received help from well-known figures, many even senior workers. Women, including his daughter Maniben, were active participants. He assigned his associates to different camps in the taluka and released pamphlets. His fiery speeches in Gujarati were generously sprinkled with rustic humour and proverbs, establishing a close connect with the masses. He travelled from village to village, training people to maintain their composure even when government officers confiscated their farms and cattle. He assured them that their confiscated land would return. Several local officials and Indian members of the legislature resigned in support. The satyagraha lasted from February to August 1928. As it progressed, the story of people's courage and Patel's leadership spread across the nation.

---

* *The Collected Works of Mahatma Gandhi*, Vol. 36, pp. 88–89, available at www.gandhiheritageportal.org.

Bardoli was nicknamed Thermopylae, and the phrase 'Bardolization' came into currency. Patel, a man with a self-professed brutally honest attitude, took no prisoners when it came to reminding both the government and the people of their responsibilities. He reproached citizens for their lackadaisical approach to fighting injustice. Gandhi was prepared to take the lead when the possibility of Patel's arrest was looming large. But the government avoided arresting him.

The satyagraha reached a successful conclusion under Patel's leadership. The increase in revenue was slashed marginally. Apart from the monetary gain and a temperamental change in the people's attitudes, an additional outcome of the satyagraha was a loving title for Patel: 'Sardar of the Farmers'. Soon, it was popularized as 'Sardar'.

The next landmark arrived in the form of the Dandi March in 1930. Gandhi led a protest to oppose the unjust tax levied on a commodity as basic as salt. It was an issue concerning the poorest of the poor. Patel took an active part in deciding the destination of the march. He was even prepared to carry on the satyagraha in the event of Gandhi's arrest. But five days before the Dandi March, Patel was arrested for allegedly violating an order and giving a speech at a gathering. This was the first instance of Patel's imprisonment. He was fifty-five.

During his detention at Sabarmati Jail, Patel maintained a diary for some time. But he wasn't a man with a literary bent of mind. Instead, he was interested in taking up issues, explaining complex themes in plain language, and engaging in action. He was arrested two more times in the same year, but imprisonment could not dampen his spirit and sense of humour. There are many stories of him taking care of his fellow satyagrahi prisoners.

After the 1928 Bardoli Satyagraha, Patel emerged as a natural choice for the presidentship of the Congress party. But following Gandhi's unwillingness for the post and Patel's withdrawal of his candidature, Jawaharlal Nehru was elected unopposed. Patel was elected to the top post in 1931. It was a stormy year. The youth was agitated by the hanging of Bhagat Singh, Sukhdev, and Rajguru. Gandhi, Patel, and Nehru admired the patriotism and courage of the revolutionaries but fundamentally differed from the martyrs when it came to their use of violence to achieve freedom. This resulted in demonstrations against Gandhi and the new Congress president, Vallabhbhai Patel.

On 5 March 1931, Gandhi and Viceroy Lord Irwin signed a significant political agreement known as the Gandhi–Irwin Pact. Its primary motivation was to convince Gandhi to participate in the second Round Table Conference in England (the leadership of the Indian National Congress had refused to attend the first conference). But young leaders like Jawaharlal Nehru and Subhas Chandra Bose were against this decision. Heated discussions ensued at the Congress session, and Patel bore the brunt of the criticism. In his concluding speech, he appealed to his critics to be patient, not resort to hasty measures, and follow the terms of the pact. Patel tried his best to restore faith and conserve the inner strength of the people through constructive programmes, at one point saying, 'Gandhiji is now almost 63 years old. I am 56. Should we—the old—be anxious for independence or you—the young? (Nehru and Bose were fourteen and twenty-two years younger than Sardar respectively.) It is true that the government has given us plenty of cause to be angry. Do not get your weapon rusted. Keep it bright and shining. You have before you plenty of work—Khadi, prevention of alcoholic drinks, and self-purification. All these activities increase the strength of the people to an incredible extent.'*

Unfortunately, the presence of too many dissenting factions caused the second Round Table Conference to conclude on an unsatisfactory note. Moreover, when Gandhi was in London for the meetings, the British government under the new viceroy, Lord Willingdon, adopted an aggressive approach and issued multiple ordinances. Gandhi was arrested soon after his return. All organizations and institutions related to Congress were banned. Both Gandhi and Patel were sent to Yeravada Jail in January 1932. Patel was later shifted to Nasik Jail after spending sixteen months at Yeravada.

∽

*Narhari Parikh, *Sardar Vallabhbhai Patel Vol. 2*, Ahmedabad: Navjivan Publishing House, 1953, p. 55.

Mahadev Desai, one of Gandhi's closest aides, joined Patel and Gandhi at Yeravada after two months, where he witnessed their activities, discussions, and characteristics and made detailed notes in his diary. Gandhi paid rich tributes to his fellow inmate. He wrote, 'I have the jovial company of Sardar Vallabhbhai here and he makes me laugh heartily several times a day with his fine humour.'*

While referring to a book, Gandhi asked Patel what the term 'British Bible' denotes. Sardar instantly replied, 'Pound, shilling, and pence, what else?' The book did say so. A newspaper article used the phrase, 'Gandhi's constructive vacuities'. When Desai asked Patel what it meant, the latter answered, 'Your overcooked and burnt dal was one.' Someone asked Gandhi in a letter, 'When we walk with our three-storeyed human body, several ants get crushed beneath our feet. How can we avoid this violence?' Sardar suggested, 'Ask him to carry his feet above his head.'**

According to Desai, Patel lost his humour when Gandhi went on to a fast until death to protest against separate electorates for the depressed classes (dalits) in 1932. He only regained the spark after the fast ended. When Patel took too many towels for a sponge bath, Gandhi remarked how he would have to take stock. Patel replied, 'We have not maintained any accounts. We had almost lost you. We did not expect you to come back and take the stock.'***

Patel also changed his food habits and quit drinking tea. When Mahadev Desai asked him about it, he replied, 'I do not feel like having tea when I am staying here with Bapu. I have decided to eat what Bapu eats. I have given up rice and I eat only boiled vegetables. I take roti with milk for my meals twice a day, because Bapu eats roti.'**** While in prison, Patel learnt Sanskrit and new skills like book-binding and making envelopes from used paper.

Patel's caring intimacy touched Gandhi. In a letter to Srinivas Shashtri, he wrote, '…I had known him [Sardar] for his unmatched

---

*Ibid., p. 91.

**Ibid.

****Mahadevbhaini Dayari Vol. 2*, Narhari Parikh (ed.), Ahmedabad: Navjivan Prakashan Mandir, 1949, p. 101.

****Ibid.

courage and flaring patriotism, but the sixteen months I have spent with him in jail are unique. His overwhelming love for me used to remind me of my mother. I never knew he was so motherly. He would be alert to my most silent movements at night and ensured personally that the smallest of my needs are satisfied....'*

Patel lost three family members during this jail term: his aged mother, son's wife, and elder brother. The government offered Patel conditional release to attend Vitthalbhai's funeral. Patel refused firmly. 'I cannot purchase my liberty at the sacrifice of my honour and self-respect even on an occasion when my presence outside is necessary.'**

The satyagraha movement was on a low ebb when Patel was released from Nashik Jail in 1934. Gandhi expressed his desire to leave Congress because he felt the party's intellectual members did not have faith in his programmes centred around khadi and spinning wheels. Despite being an ardent disciple, Patel did not try to persuade Gandhi. He endorsed the view that if Congress did not want to walk in Gandhi's footsteps, it should be made clear. To pretend otherwise would be an insult to Gandhi.

Patel too faced hurdles in the Gujarat Provincial Congress Committee. His presidentship had become a source of dissatisfaction among some of his colleagues. The development disturbed him. In a letter to Dinkarrai Desai of Bharuch, dated 31 December 1935, he expressed his anguish, 'It is obvious that holding a position is reason enough for creating malice and misunderstanding.... I feel things will be easy if I leave. There seems to be no other way to eliminate the misunderstanding about me. I left the [Ahmedabad] Municipality the same way and I can serve it better now. I intended to leave [the presidentship] but only after making it easy for Chandubhai [Dr Chandubhai Desai]. I wanted to ensure that he gets maximum cooperation. But he took it otherwise....'***

---

*Parikh, *Sardar Vallabhbhai Patel Vol. 2*, p. 127.

**Ibid., p. 147.

***Ibid., p. 190.

He also narrated his state of mind to Dr Chandubhai: 'I am disturbed by the poison created in the public life of Gujarat.... I am disillusioned. I can see that I should keep away from Gujarat. People will find what is right when they start seeking their paths.... The only sad part is the environment will be polluted and people will distrust one another. I am unhappy that efforts to make all unite have failed. If my presence suffocates the environment of Gujarat, I should make the path clear.'* After a few such exchanges and episodes which further created a feeling of distrust, the environment stabilized and Patel continued as the president of GPCC.

Plague relief work at Borsad once again exhibited Patel's service-oriented leadership. The disease surfaced in 1932 and spread year after year. In March 1935, Patel sought a detailed assessment of the situation, the scientific steps required to combat the plague, and the available resources from Dr Bhaskar Patel. Once satisfied with the data, he camped at Borsad. A pandal erected under a tree became his office. He directed and coordinated all aspects of the relief operations, personally visiting the affected villages, recruiting volunteers, educating them about the risks involved, arranging hospital beds, conducting cleanliness drives, preparing pamphlets for the villagers, etc.

At a time when family members were not ready to treat patients of the plague, local leaders and volunteers joined Patel. He was accompanied by his close associate, Darbar Gopaldas, and later joined by Gandhi and Mahadev Desai, who stayed at Borsad. Groomed in the Gandhian school, Patel's courage in the face of adversity and enthusiasm for public service even after gaining fame inspired the volunteers.

Following the failure of the second Round Table Conference, Patel was imprisoned for two years and upon his release in 1934, he found many dissenting groups within Congress, including members of the liberal faction who wanted a revival of the Swaraj Party.

Dissatisfied with the party's policies, a group of young socialists led by Jayaprakash Narayan and Acharya Narendra Dev formed the Congress Socialist Party in 1934. They considered Patel as a conservative, right-wing, anti-revolution leader and were upset with

*Ibid., p. 190.

his bitter criticism of socialists and communists. In reality, Patel wasn't ideologically motivated. No 'ism' fascinated him, not even Gandhism. As a leader, he was aware of his limitations. He saw his role as an individual responsible for running the party machinery effectively, with strict discipline and respect for Gandhi's political authority.

Patel, a man of action and implementation, saw socialists as daydreamers who indulged in debates on social change but had no concrete plans. He always considered himself a farmer who knew how to cater to the interests of the agricultural community and asserted that India needed to look after them. Socialists accused him of being pro-capitalist. Patel would not hide his friendship with G. D. Birla and his closeness with many businessmen. He collected lakhs of rupees for the party but led a simple and frugal life.

~

After Gandhi's declaration of discontinuing civil disobedience in 1934, doors of entry into legislatures opened. Patel was unhappy with the discordant notes among Congress leaders. He asserted the authority of the Congress Parliamentary Board on the provincial and central Congress organizations, which helped create a system of central high command in the party. He was entrusted with the responsibility of collecting funds for the upcoming central legislature elections. The 1937 elections in eleven provinces with nearly 3.5 crore voters presented a substantially bigger challenge.

For the first time, Nehru's popularity and Patel's organization skills in electoral politics were on full display at a national level. With Patel as its chairman, the parliamentary sub-committee of Congress had two other important members: Maulana Azad and Rajendra Prasad. But it was Patel's responsibility to select the candidates and secure resources. He proved to be a master electioneering organizer, balancing principles with pragmatism and unfazed by the pressures of those seeking candidature.

Considerations of electability and caste of the candidates crept in, admitted Rajendra Prasad. Many leaders and workers presented their claims for their candidature. Sadly, many were asking for a price for their services to the nation. Gandhi was not in favour of such an election campaign. Patel and Nehru were keen for Congress's victory and both travelled widely and campaigned with full force.

Congress secured a spectacular victory, achieving a clear majority in many provinces. Patel, in a statement after the win, praised the inspiring leadership of Jawaharlal Nehru and the cooperation of other leaders, including Rajendra Prasad, Govind Vallabh Pant, and Bhulabhai Desai, as important factors behind the electoral victory.

Patel's style of governance irked many. It came under sharp attack, particularly in two instances. Controversy erupted when Patel chose B. G. Kher as Bombay's premier (present-day chief minister) over the popular Parsi leader K. F. Nariman. Nariman accused Patel of harbouring a grievance against him. One of the reasons was his alleged role in the defeat of Patel's close associate and the Congress candidate in the 1934 election, K. M. Munshi. Even so, Patel could not ignore Nariman's popularity in Bombay. In 1937, he gave him a ticket in the elections but was unwilling to appoint Nariman as the head of the Congress ministry in the province.

Nariman and the Parsi newspapers went wild. Sardar was accused of influencing the votes of elected candidates in favour of Kher and being unfair to Nariman because he was a Parsi. Patel had no tolerance for disorderliness and wanted to run the party according to his understanding of discipline. Nonetheless, it was absurd to suggest that he discriminated against Nariman as he was a Parsi.

As the dispute continued, the issue reached Gandhi. He requested a Parsi barrister Bahadurji to look into the case. After a careful study and detailed statements of eighty-three people, Bahadurji opined that the charges against Nariman in the 1934 incidence appeared true whereas those against Patel in 1937 were not proven.

Dr Khare's case was different. But it bore similar results for Patel. Dr Khare was appointed as the premier of Central Province. He displayed gross indiscipline and complete disregard for the party administration. Subhash Chandra Bose, the then president of Congress, tried to persuade Dr Khare, but to no avail. When Dr Khare was debarred from holding any position in Congress, he started a vitriolic campaign against Patel. Newspapers and critics of the party joined the bandwagon.

Subhash Chandra Bose issued a detailed statement refuting Dr Khare's charges. Gandhi wrote an article in his English weekly *Harijan*. But Dr Khare was adamant. His actions resulted in his dismissal from Congress. Even in this episode it was Patel who had to bear most of the abuses and accusations. Nariman returned to Congress a decade later, apologizing for his previous conduct, and Patel accommodated him. But Dr Khare chose to join the Hindu Mahasabha.

~

1939 saw an epic clash in the history of Congress—a significant fissure had emerged between the right wing and the left wing. Before delving deeper, a detour is required to highlight Patel's exceptional management skills. The occasion was the Congress session in Haripura, near Bardoli, in February 1938. Patel had secured 500 acres of land from three villages and an adjoining jungle to create 'Vitthal Nagar'. Half the land was given by Muslim landowners. Patel specifically mentioned this in his concluding speech. The newly created temporary town had a sewage system, waterworks, a printing press, 500 cows for milk and butter, and a provision to feed and host approximately 75,000 people from all over India every day. There were thousands of daily visitors. Bose, the Congress president, was given an enthusiastic welcome in Haripura.

By that time, Bose and Patel were already at loggerheads due to an issue in Vitthalbhai Patel's will. Vitthalbhai died in Vienna in 1933. Bose, who was also there, took great care of Vitthalbhai in his final days and arranged to send his embalmed body to Bombay as per the latter's wishes. Sardar, imprisoned in Nasik Jail at that time, wrote an affectionate letter thanking Bose. Later he discovered a provision in Vitthalbhai's will that gave away a major portion of his assets to Bose 'for the political uplift of India and preferably for publicity work on behalf of India's cause, in other countries'. Sardar had doubts about the authenticity of the will.

Bose thought he was the unconditional and rightful owner of the said amount. G. I. Patel, the executor of the will, did not agree with that interpretation. He saw Bose as a trustee and not the owner of the assets. Patel cross-examined the executor during their first meeting.

Once he was convinced, he assured the executor that he would abide by the latter's interpretation, and in case of a court verdict making the will void, he would form a trust to execute the wishes of his elder brother. Patel secured the written consent of all the heirs. He also offered to hand over the amount to the Congress Working Committee and form a committee of Congress leaders for its use. But Bose did not agree with Maulana Azad's suggestions of names for the committee.

As a last resort, G. I. Patel took the matter to the Bombay High Court in 1939. The court decided that the will did not give any absolute estate to Bose. Dissatisfied with the judgment, Bose appealed but was dismissed with costs. This turbulent episode coincided with a serious rift in Congress when Bose sought presidentship for a consecutive second term. It was not customary for Congress to reappoint the same president.

The differences between the right and left factions were continuously widening. Bose, twenty-four years younger than Sardar, was a left-wing leader, and they did not share cordial relations. Nehru, who became Congress president in 1936, was eight years older than Bose and sympathized with the left wing and tried to strike a balance. Right-wing leaders like Patel, C. Rajagopalachari, and Rajendra Prasad resigned, objecting to President Nehru's preaching and support of socialism.

Gandhi persuaded them to withdraw their resignation. He too was unhappy with Nehru's behaviour. He wrote to Nehru that his critics (Patel and others) might be guilty of intolerance, (but) 'you have more than your share of it. The country should not be made to suffer for your mutual intolerance'.* In 1939, Gandhi tried to convince Maulana Azad to be Congress president. After he refused, Pattabhi Sitaramayya was chosen as the candidate with Gandhi's support. Bose was unwilling to withdraw, citing nominations for his name from several provinces and the backing of both socialists and non-socialists for his re-election.

Bose believed that the presidential election should be fought based on specific problems and programs. One of his major contentions was the 'prospective fight over federation'. The Congress Working Committee (CWC) consisting of Patel, Rajendra Prasad, and others

*Rajmohan Gandhi, *Patel: A Life*, Ahmedabad: Navjivan Publishing House, 1999, p. 255.

issued a joint statement that reasserted how previous presidential elections have been unanimous. Moreover, the Congress's ideologies, policies, and programs were not decided by the presidents but by the CWC.

Bose refuted both claims and said that in the past, there had been re-elected presidents as well as those who won by contesting elections. He cited the adoption of the new constitution of Congress in 1934 and said CWC visualized the Congress president as a constitutional monarch, whereas his role is akin to that of the prime minister. He accused, 'It is widely believed that there is the prospect of compromise on the federal scheme between the right wing of Congress and the British Government during the coming year. And that the right wing does not want a leftist president who may put obstacles in the path of negotiations.... It is imperative, in the circumstances, to have a president who will be anti- Federationist to the core of his heart.'*

In another statement, he pointed out that although the Congress resolution on federation was one of uncompromising hostility, the fact remains that influential Congress leaders had been advocating the conditional acceptance of the Federation Scheme both publicly and privately. He went further, quoting 'general belief' that the prospective list of ministers for the Federation Cabinet had been drawn up already. He was willing to withdraw 'if a genuine anti-federationist is accepted as the president'.

In an atmosphere rife with bitterness, Bose won comfortably. He received only 5 out of 105 votes in Sardar's Gujarat but secured 404 votes out of 483 votes in Bengal. The right-wing leaders, including Patel, resigned from CWC on the pretext of giving Bose space to appoint members of his choice. But in the long run, it became difficult for Bose to move ahead without the cooperation of Gandhi and his loyal associates. The conflict resulted in his resignation in April 1939. Bose formed a new party called Forward Bloc.

---

*P. N. Chopra, *The Collected Works of Sardar Patel Vol. 8*, New Delhi: Konark Publishers Pvt Ltd, 1996, p. 29.

Congress revised its policy of non-interference in the princely states at the 1938 Haripura Session. Gandhi, Patel, and other leaders began taking an interest in the popular movements and the people's demand for a responsible government. Rajkot, Gandhi's home ground, became the battlefield of an inglorious fight.

Rajkot had been witnessing a struggle against rampant taxation and oppressive rule of Dharmendrasinhji and his dewan Virawala for quite some time. After Patel's intervention, the ruler Dharmendrasinhji agreed to form a ten-member inquiry committee to investigate and offer reforms to solve the crisis. Three members were to be appointed by him and seven names were to be nominated by Patel.

Influenced by his dewan Darbar Virawala, Dharmendrasinhji renounced the agreement. Patel tried to persuade him to abide by the arrangement, but he was unsuccessful. The state machinery came down heavily on local leaders and workers. They were beaten, tortured, and jailed. Kasturba Gandhi and Maniben, Patel's daughter, were detained for participating in the satyagraha. Even after Gandhi's indefinite fast and the viceroy's intervention, Darbar Virawala remained adamant. He even successfully instigated some Muslims and bhayats (local chiefs) against Gandhi. Patel was portrayed as a villain by the dewan and his supporters. The charged atmosphere led Gandhi to withdraw the satyagraha.

The Rajkot Satyagraha disappointed Patel. But Bhavnagar, another important princely state of Kathiawad, posed a threat to his life. Patel was to preside over the People's Conference on 14 May 1939. When his car was heading from the railway station as a part of the procession, it was attacked by some Muslim miscreants. Patel was safe, but others were wounded, and two succumbed to their injuries. In a statement issued soon after the incident, Sardar urged people to remember that many Muslim leaders were associated with the conference and had cooperated by participating in the procession.

In a meeting that sought to raise a memorial for the two workers killed in the assault, Patel said he dreamt of achieving unity among all the communities. But it was necessary to find the culprits to gain unity in its truest sense. He was adamant not to let the matter slide until the attackers were punished. He warned people against those who sheltered such antisocial elements. If any local Muslims were not involved in the crime, it should be easy for them to prove the same.

This was the time when Jinnah was successfully establishing himself as the leader of the Muslim community with the help of sympathetic British rulers. Both were hostile towards Gandhi and the Congress. The beginning of World War II and Britain's autocratic decision to involve India in the war without seeking the consent of Indians posed challenges for Congress leadership.

Patel, alongside most Congress leaders and Nehru, was prepared to extend cooperation to the British if they declared their war aims and assured India of an effective transfer of power. Gandhi saw a breach of non-violence in such an offer. But he did not impose his views on Patel and the rest of the party. It was one of those rare occasions when Patel chose to openly differ with Gandhi, because the Mahatma left it to the leaders to choose the path ahead. Patel, Nehru, and most prominent Congress leaders thought it fit to offer conditional support to Britain.

Britain did not accept the offer. In October 1939, provincial Congress ministries resigned from their respective governments in protest. The stage for the next fight was set and the program of individual satyagraha began, wherein a person would declare themselves a lone satyagrahi. After their arrest, another takes their place so that the protest is registered without putting the government machinery in fix. Patel also participated in an individual satyagraha and was arrested.

Patel was released from prison due to a severe health condition. He had a longstanding intestinal problem that worsened during his jail term. Gandhi took care of him and applied his natural remedies but could not heal Patel completely. When Sir Stafford Cripps came to India, Gandhi and the entire Congress leadership summarily rejected his offer that comprised a dominion status of sorts. Dominion status would mean Indians would still pledge allegiance to the Crown.

The proposal sent via Sir Cripps created suspicion and hostility towards the British government in the minds of Congress leaders. The final call for non-cooperation and a decisive fight for freedom were imminent. Under Gandhi's leadership, Congress decided to launch the Quit India Movement when they realized all hopes of achieving independence from the British through debate and deliberation were lost. Patel was highly supportive of Gandhi's 'Quit India' call.

It was the largest nationwide movement yet and was joined by the youth and elderly alike. The government lost no time in making arrests to crush the agitation. Gandhi was arrested and sent to Aga Khan Jail in Poona. Senior Congress leaders like Patel, Nehru, Maulana Azad, and Jivatram Kripalani were sent to Ahmednagar Fort Jail. They were accompanied by two socialists, Narendra Dev and Asaf Ali.

Not much in the form of future plans or policy discussions transpired collectively among the top leaders during thirty-four months of imprisonment at Ahmednagar Fort from August 1942 to June 1945. They had a routine life, including playing bridge. Nehru wrote *The Discovery of India* during that period. As the length of imprisonment was unspecified, it seemed endless, especially to Patel who was the oldest and nearing seventy. In letters to his daughter, he often expressed his preparedness to welcome death with the satisfaction that he served India in whatever way he could.

Gandhi was released early due to health concerns. When the remaining prisoners of Ahmednagar came out of jail, they faced big changes. The activities and influence of the Muslim League, already on the rise thanks to British support, had increased sizeably in the absence of Congress leadership. The League had become an essential presence in any discussions for the transfer of power with the British.

~

In 1945, Viceroy Lord Wavell invited leaders from different parties to Shimla to discuss the future of India. The talks failed as Jinnah insisted on the League being the only party sending Muslim representatives. Congress, claiming to represent all Indians, could not accept that.

Clement Attlee, the newly elected British prime minister from the Labour Party, announced the creation of a Constituent Assembly in India to frame the constitution and declared elections for the central and provincial legislatures. Maulana Azad was the Congress president at that time. Like in previous elections, Patel was in charge of raising funds and choosing candidates. The Muslim League posed a formidable challenge for the seats reserved for Muslim candidates. Gandhi warned Patel not to rely on the power of money. But Patel did not want Congress to lose the elections for the lack of funds.

Congress faced mixed results. They secured a majority in eight provinces, but the Muslim League won most Muslim-reserved seats except in the North-West Frontier Province. It strengthened the League's claim as the only party representing true Muslim interests. Patel accepted that his party had not made enough attempts to secure Hindu–Muslim unity.

The trial of the Indian National Army's officers at Red Fort raised the political temperature in the country. The disappearance of Subhash Chandra Bose, chief of the INA, and an open trial of a Hindu, a Muslim, and a Sikh officer of the INA became rallying points. It was followed by a revolt of the Royal Indian Navy, triggered by incidents of racial discrimination towards Indian officers.

The revolt started in Mumbai and spread widely, resulting in civil disturbances in many cities. The Communist Party supported it. Neither Congress nor Muslim League extended political support to the revolt. Patel took an active part in convincing the Indian Navy men. He wrote, 'Discipline in the Army cannot be tampered with.... The Naval ratings may have their grievances but they should not be allowed to be exploited by political parties nor should their grievances be mixed up with politics.'*

When Patel met Viceroy Wavell for the first time in January 1946, he made a strong impression. Wavell found him 'not an attractive personality and uncompromising, but more of a man than most of the Indian politicians....' Patel told Wavell that there could not be any settlement between the Hindu and Muslim communities as long as the British were in India. They should leave Indians to sort out their matters themselves.

The Cabinet Mission arrived in March 1946 and brought new proposals and plans to form a representative interim government. This was the time when Patel's clarity of thought and courage, combined with his sharp manoeuvring skills, were much needed. The Cabinet

---

*'A Letter to T. Vishwanathan', *The Collected Works of Sardar Patel Vol. 10*, p. 197.

Mission proposed an Indian Union with two autonomous groups of federations: one group consisting of the Hindu majority provinces and the other with a dominant Muslim population. Jinnah was sceptical of accepting this arrangement and sought the right to secede after five years. As Patel and his colleagues refused to accept this demand, Sir Stafford Cripps came up with the May 16 Plan.

Without going into the complexities of the Cabinet Mission's original proposal and the May 16 Plan, it would be sufficient to say that Patel weighed different options very carefully to prevent the party from conceding to any unreasonable offer extended by the British. He was distrustful of Jinnah's intentions and was not ready to accept his demand for a separate Pakistan. The plan had two problematic aspects: the provision for the provinces to secede and a weak central government. Such considerations made Patel oppose the plan. Instead of an immediate response, he decided to defer the decision. Muslim League had not declared its decision either.

Keeping the deadlock as it was, the Cabinet Mission announced a council of fourteen leaders with their names as ministers: six from the Congress, five from the Muslim League, a Sikh, a Parsi, and a Christian. It was named the June 16 Plan. Previously, Viceroy Wavell had offered five positions each to Congress and the Muslin League. But the former rejected the proposal. In the new offer, Congress was given another seat. But all ministers named by the Cabinet Mission were Hindu: Nehru, Patel, Rajendra Prasad, Rajagopalachari, Hare Krishna Mehtab, and Jagjivan Ram. Although Gandhi wanted to reject the offer, Patel was willing to accept the revised plan.

The situation changed soon as Jinnah raised unreasonable demands, and Viceroy Wavell accepted them. He was given a veto on every major communal issue and a say in the appointment of the three non-Muslim members (Sikh, Christian, and Parsi) if any of the suggested names refused to join. Moreover, Congress could not replace any of the suggested candidates with a Muslim leader. Patel and all other leaders who were opposed to Gandhi's stand of rejecting the offer were on back foot.

To push them further, the June 16 Plan said that if any of the two major parties were unwilling to join the coalition by not accepting one of the two plans, the viceroy would continue forming an interim government. It effectively meant that if Congress did not join the government, the viceroy would proceed with interim government with only Muslim League members.

Patel fully understood the stakes and verified the complexity of the situation through discussions with Indian officials in the British administration. He was left with only one choice. He had to accept the original May 16 Plan with all its limitations while ignoring Gandhi's objections. He was not keen on its implementation, but its acceptance would provide him a window to manoeuvre and make adjustments for the time being.

Congress accepted the May 16 Plan and intimated the viceroy. Forming a government with the Muslim League was a compromise in many ways. Congress's acceptance meant that at last, the party had accepted Jinnah and the Muslim League as the representative of Indian Muslims. These developments were contrary to Gandhi's position. But Patel, Nehru, and most Congress leaders thought they averted a full-fledged disaster of a Muslim League-only government.

~

In the meantime, the appointment of the next Congress president was due. Maulana Azad, who had remained the president for six years because of World War II, Quit India movement and subsequent imprisonment of Congress's top leadership, wanted an extension. Gandhi discouraged him and expressed a preference for Nehru. While twelve out of fifteen provincial Congress committees suggested Patel as the next president, Gandhi's wish prevailed. Patel withdrew his candidature to facilitate Nehru's election again, knowing the new president would become India's first prime minister.

Congress President Nehru's declaration on 7 July 1946 that the party was not bound to accept the May 16 Plan infuriated Jinnah. He declared 16 August 1946 as 'Direct Action Day' to rally aggressively for a separate Muslim homeland. Patel agreed with Nehru. But openly announcing this would be a strategic blunder. It should be noted that Patel never used any occasion to belittle Nehru in public. He usually defended Nehru before party leaders without denying his limitations.

Nehru was not in favour of joining the viceroy's Executive Council, a precursor to the Indian ministries. He resented the viceroy's absolute power. But Patel disagreed and decided to put all his weight into joining the government. It was not about seizing power. Patel saw this as an important step in the direction of preparing for independence and did not want to let it go to waste. The interim government was formed on 2 September 1946. Nehru was the head of the council of twelve ministers. Patel was allotted the Home and Information and Broadcasting ministries. Muslim League refused to join the body.

During this period, Viceroy Wavell came to think of Patel as the most impressive of the Congress leaders. Patel was a tough negotiator. He was driven more by pragmatism rather than idealism and believed in seizing opportunities. When Wavell invited the Muslim League to join the government arbitrarily even if it had not accepted any of the two plans, Patel did not want Congress ministers to resign and leave the reins of government in the League's hands.

After the Muslim League entered the interim government, the issue of allotting portfolios arose. Finance and Home Affairs were the two most important positions. Considering the communal violence engulfing various areas after Direct Action Day, Patel was not willing to give up the Home Affairs portfolio. He threatened to resign if it was given to a member of the League. Nehru backed him.

Communal riots in Noakhali and Bihar presented a grave situation for the government. Patel was in charge of Home Affairs, but the final power rested with the viceroy. Patel travelled to some of the riot-ravaged areas with a minister from the Muslim League. Barring such exceptions, he found it almost impossible to work with them. It was this experience that prepared Patel to accept the impending reality of the country's partition.

The British kept putting their weight on Jinnah's side, accepting his claim that he represented all Indian Muslims. In light of the League's recent electoral success, such claims could not be discounted. The British decided that the constitution for independent India could not be prepared without the Muslim League and the princely states. Their absence during the Constituent Assembly's first meeting on 9 December 1946 created a deadlock.

Patel enjoyed a good rapport with V. P. Menon, the viceroy's reforms commissioner. Menon devised a scheme that proposed a dominion status for India and partition of the country to create a separate Pakistan. Patel remained hesitant about the partition, but after weighing the pros and cons, he gave in. Patel and Menon agreed that the acceptance of dominion status would secure British cooperation during the transfer of power while the creation of Pakistan would pacify Jinnah.

~

British Prime Minister Atlee's announcement of quitting India not later than June 1948 changed the situation. Patel realized it was important to hold the ministries when the actual transfer of power took place and abandoned the thought of resigning in protest even if he found it difficult to work with the League members. Menon's proposal was sent to London with a vague assurance that Patel would ensure its acceptance by Congress. Nehru and most Congress leaders supported Patel. Moreover, the communal riots in Punjab were seen as one of the reasons to support the partition of the country.

The British administration supported Patel's pragmatism rather than Gandhi's idealism. Gandhi was completely opposed to the idea of a partition. After the arrival of Viceroy Lord Mountbatten in March 1947, Gandhi tried sincerely to avoid the division of India. However, Patel saw it as their only option and most Congress leaders including Nehru agreed.

Though Patel accepted the partition as a less damaging solution to the communal conundrum, he always declared that Congress was in favour of a united India. It was the Muslim League who was adamant. Later he clarified in no uncertain terms that if the Muslim League wanted partition, the provinces of Punjab and Bengal will have to be partitioned too. This further enraged Jinnah who wanted the whole of Punjab and Bengal in his proposed scheme for Pakistan.

Accepting dominion status after demanding complete independence was another concern. Patel was sure it would be a mere formality, and the real power would remain in the hands of Indian ministers. He convinced Nehru that it was not wise to resist the dominion status.

Gandhi was left out of the final negotiations. It was Patel and Nehru who communicated with Lord Mountbatten. For the final discussion of Menon's scheme, later renamed the Mountbatten Plan, Nehru went to Shimla. He was in constant telephonic contact with Patel. He accepted the Mountbatten Plan with Patel's complete support. The responsibility of convincing Gandhi fell on Patel. Gandhi was adamant and wouldn't budge from his position. However, he promised not to oppose the Congress's decision.

In early June, Mountbatten announced 15 August as the tentative date for the transfer of power. A Partition Committee was formed under the chairmanship of Viceroy Mountbatten. Patel and Rajendra Prasad represented Congress in the committee that would be responsible for the partition of the assets. The All-India Congress Committee passed the resolution. Patel poured his heart out, expressing grief and hope for the newly divided India and best wishes for Pakistan. After provincial legislatures had ratified the decision to partition Bengal and Punjab, a separate department for integrating princely states came into existence and was assigned to Patel.

As the paramountcy of the British Crown was coming to its end, a new order was needed to unite all the ruling families. As per geographical realities, the princely states had to join either India or Pakistan and not harbour any dreams of independent existence. Patel had started meeting the rulers or their dewans even before he assumed official responsibility for the department.

Many major states like Travancore, Hyderabad, Baroda, Bhopal, and some in Rajputana started charting their course with a fertile imagination. In the herculean task of convincing princes by persuasion and making them face the reality of independent India, Patel was ably supported by the secretary of the department V. P. Menon and Viceroy Mountbatten. Securing Mountbatten's services by offering him to be the first Governor General of the Indian Union was a joint decision by Patel and Nehru. They knew well the weight the viceroy would bring as a member of the British royal family and how it would be useful in dealing with the princes.

Patel appealed to the rulers for accession on three subjects: defence, communications, and foreign affairs. He reminded them of India's rich heritage and assured them that Congress was not their enemy. By 15 August 1947, most states had signed the Instrument of Accession with the Indian Union. Patel at the age of seventy-two, with his failing health, contributed enormously to this achievement through his firmness, stability of thought, and courtesy towards the rulers. He did not hold any grudge against the rulers who hesitated to join the union and tried their best to avoid signing the document. He did not conduct the exercise to establish his power. It was a call of duty, and he performed it with utmost sincerity.

Patel also played an important role along with Nehru in selecting the first cabinet of the Indian Union, in which he was the deputy prime minister. On the historic night of 14 August, Patel made no speech in the Constituent Assembly. He only took vows of service. It was a dream come true, made possible because of the sacrifices of thousands of people. Patel was indebted to the grace of God as he felt fortunate to be alive to see that day.

Newly independent India found herself engulfed in the worst kind of communal violence. Gandhi had buried himself in the efforts to douse the communal fire. As home minister, Patel was accused of being anti-Muslim. In some cases, even Gandhi sought clarifications. But he thought of Patel as a large hearted leader who would be accommodative of all Indians. Many of Patel's words at that time, if quoted out of the context and without considering the political situation, could be used to portray him as a communal Hindu leader. But such generalizations would be a gross simplification of the facts, as is evident from some of his correspondences present in this volume.

Though Hindu–Muslim unity was not an article of faith for Patel, he was not anti-Muslim or an ideologue of the Hindu Rashtra. He was driven principally by administrative concerns and had a no-nonsense approach. He would not go the extra mile to win the trust of the Muslims. He wanted Muslims of India to distance themselves from the politics of the League that had resulted in the partition of the country. He would not tolerate the sentiment of '*Hanske liya hai Pakistan, ladke lenge Hindustan*' ('We attained Pakistan with ease, we shall win

Hindustan by force'). He could be bitter and hurtful in his speeches, and yet he did not hesitate to order actions against Hindu rioters.

There are several incidences when Patel spared no efforts to secure the safe passage of the Muslims. One of his famous speeches at Amritsar ensured the safety of Muslims from enraged Sikhs targeting Muslims migrating from West Punjab. Patel never claimed to be the protector of the Hindus or someone who taught Muslims a lesson. He did not pay heed to nasty anti-Muslim rumours and encouraged his colleagues to do the same. Establishing safety and peace in the wake of unprecedented communal violence was of utmost concern for him.

His conduct as the minister for Information and Broadcasting was considered high-handed by many. He was, for example, not amused by the constant, criticism of the newly formed government by Congress critic Acharya Kripalani, who wrote for the weekly magazine *Vigil*. Mainstream newspapers would reproduce his articles verbatim; Patel instructed those papers not to spread Kripalani's pieces any further. He thought the country needed constructive suggestions and not just criticism.*

Despite their diverse personalities, Nehru and Patel's unique areas of political expertise complemented each other. India was fortunate to receive the former's vision and the latter's administration along with Gandhi's idealism to start her journey as an independent nation. Gandhi had no direct role in the decisions of the government. But he was still the guru of Nehru and Patel. They were still answerable to him when it came to moral issues. Giving Pakistan its remaining balance of ₹55 crore (Pakistan's share of the assets of undivided India) was one such problem on which Nehru and Patel were on the same page.

In January 1948, Gandhi went on the last indefinite fast of his public life in order to extinguish the fires of communal violence. However, the political atmosphere was rife with rumours. Critics claimed that Gandhi's fast was against Patel's alleged communal policies apart form holding back the due amount of Pakistan.

---

*Interview with veteran Gujarati writer-journalist Prakash N. Shah. In Urvish Kothari, *Prakash N. Shah*, Ahmedabad: Saarthak Prakashan, 2019, p. 42.

Gandhi's assassination after two weeks brought the most damning wave of criticism for Patel. As the home minister, he was held responsible for failing to protect Gandhi even after an unsuccessful attempt by the assassins a few days before the fateful day. Following Gandhi's principle of non-violence, two of his sons sought clemency for the Hindu right-wing assassin Nathuram Godse. But Patel firmly declined.

The shock and burden of Gandhi's assassination took a heavy toll on Patel's health. He had a severe heart attack in March 1948. When he gained consciousness, his first words were, 'I had to go with Bapu.'* Tears rolled down from the face of the man known for his steely resolve.

Patel banned the Rashtriya Swayamsewak Sangh after Gandhi's assassination, only lifting the ban after six months with several conditions. Patel is often accused of being too lenient with the organization. There are authentic quotes to prove that contention. But it is only a part of the whole truth. Gandhi and Patel both believed that Hindus were more likely to flee than fight to protect themselves and their family when attacked. They thought RSS drills might inculcate discipline and courage in the community. Neither was sympathetic to the anti-Muslim ideology propagated by the RSS and Hindu Mahasabha. Patel did not encourage or condone anticipatory or proactive violence in the name of protecting Hindus and criticized Hindu extremist newspapers without hesitation.

Patel was critical of the idea of a Hindu Rashtra and summarily dismissed it. He believed that when the country had begun her journey in a fresh direction, everyone should be given a new chance to move forward. He suggested members of the RSS join Congress in the same spirit. It might appear ironic that Nehru, not known for his sound judgment of people, thought of RSS as an organization with fascist tendencies, whereas Patel, known for his sharp judgment, thought of RSS as one of our own, warts and all. His correspondence with RSS chief M. S. Golwalkar reflected this sentiment.

And yet, he would neither tolerate systemic instigation against Muslims nor would he be eager to consider Muslims as second-class citizens.

---

*Gandhi, *Patel: A Life*, p. 472.

~

Patel and Nehru had entirely different personalities. Though both were barristers from London, the former maintained his son-of-the-soil attitude with an extraordinary grip on organization and administration. He was the trusted lieutenant of Gandhi but not wedded to any ideology. Nehru, fourteen years younger than Patel, had a different background and temperament. He was an impulsive leader who enjoyed mass popularity second to none. Gandhi chose him as his heir almost a decade before he became the prime minister of independent India.

Their capacity to work together was tested repeatedly after independence. It is vividly reflected in their correspondence, some of which is included in this volume. As the prime minister, Nehru thought he had final authority over his colleagues in the cabinet. Sardar had a different idea. He considered the prime minister first among equals, not the supreme. Certain incidences widened their rift to such an extent that both offered their resignations. Gandhi knew that India needed both Patel and Nehru. He attempted to cement their differences during his lifetime and even by his death.

Patel was with Gandhi in what turned out to be the last hour of the latter's life. What transpired between them remains unknown. But Gandhi's assassination changed things. Patel's address to the nation on this tragedy was a reflection of his temperament. Still absorbing the shock of losing a man who had changed his life forever, he told people not to indulge in retaliatory violence. He always believed that Gandhi had already given what he wanted and it was up to his followers to walk in his footsteps.

Gandhi's assassination permanently sealed the bond between Patel and Nehru. Occasionally, he would be disappointed or enraged by Nehru's decisions. But he continued working dutifully, providing a counterbalance to Nehru's socialist idealism, enthusiasm, and frustrations.

~

During the process of geographical and constitutional unification, India faced three major challenges: Junagadh, Hyderabad, and Kashmir.

Junagadh, a coastal princely state in Kathiawad with a predominantly Hindu population and a Muslim ruler, declared its allegiance to Pakistan. It was neither logical nor viable. But Nawab Muhammad Mahabat Khanji III and his dewan Shahnawaz Bhutto were not in the mood to join India. A provisional government was formed by the activists in Bombay under the leadership of Shamaldas Gandhi, a journalist and freedom fighter not related to Gandhi in any way. On Patel's insistence, the Indian government took over the three feudatories of Junagadh without resistance, ignoring Governor General Mountbatten's suggestion of not availing the army and using the Central Police Force. The 'army' of the provisional government marched into Junagadh, prompting the Nawab to flee to Pakistan. Nehru had committed to Pakistan for a referendum in Junagadh, but Patel was against any gestures of friendliness towards hostile Pakistan. To him, it would amount to a show of weakness. Nonetheless, the referendum was held in the presence of foreign correspondents, and it was hugely in favour of Junagadh's accession to India.

Jinnah seized the opportunity and asked for a referendum in Kashmir, where a Muslim majority population was ruled by Maharaja Hari Singh, a Hindu king who wanted a state independent of India and Pakistan. Patel had previously indicated that he was open to the possibility of Kashmir joining Pakistan. He changed his mind after Pakistan accepted Junagadh's accession—if Pakistan could include Junagadh, India could very well have Kashmir. A referendum in Hyderabad would not favour the Nizam either.

Jinnah wanted both Hyderabad and Kashmir. Pakistan's overtures in Junagadh made Patel more vigilant and insistent about the Kashmir issue. Hari Singh showed no inclination to accede. Nehru was equally invested in Kashmir. His friend Sheikh Abdullah and his party National Conference were at loggerheads with the Maharaja. One of the major issues between them was preserving the interest of Muslims in a state where Hindus held the most important positions. Nehru trusted and banked upon Abdullah to sway Muslim opinion in the valley in favour of India. Patel was eager to have Kashmir with the Maharaja Hari Singh signing the Instrument of Accession.

Keen to capitalize on the Kashmiri ruler's delay in making a decision, a force of armed tribesmen managed by Pakistan invaded Kashmir. They created havoc by looting homes, raping citizens, and destroying utilities. As the threat increased, Maharaja Hari Singh appealed to India for help. Patel wanted to send troops, but Nehru was hesitant as the accession document was yet to be signed. Sheikh Abdullah was in favour of India sending troops. Finally, Nehru decided to send help but not before accepting Mountbatten's conditions of securing a signature from the Maharaja and holding a referendum once things were settled. Patel too accepted Nehru's condition of granting a larger role to Sheikh Abdullah after Kashmir's integration to secure the trust of Muslims.

Maharaja Hari Singh had shifted to Jammu for his safety, where he signed the document. Patel sent troops overnight, and Srinagar was saved when the attackers were just a few kilometres away. After the dust settled, Nehru assumed the independent charge of Kashmir and handed the state over to the officer of his choice, bypassing Patel. This development created a new low point in the existing Patel–Sardar rift. Both wrote to Gandhi. The events took a tragic turn, and the fissure ended with Gandhi's assassination.

Mountbatten persuaded Nehru to take the issue of Kashmir to the United Nations which had been formed after the end of World War II to resolve issues of international security and peace. Nehru went ahead with the suggestion, ignoring Patel's strong objection. The clear case of aggression became a dispute between the two countries, as Patel had anticipated, and put India on the back foot with the creation of Pakistan-occupied Kashmir.

Hyderabad turned out to be the third state where the intervention of troops was necessitated. Mountbatten tried the road of negotiation, eager to bag the credit for solving the problem before his departure. Patel gave enough time to Mountbatten, but the Nizam of Hyderabad, Mir Osman Ali Khan, did not yield. Communal violence inflicted by a paramilitary volunteer force called the Razakars was getting worse. Months passed. Nehru was still not in favour of military action keeping in mind, apart from other things, India's reputation on the world stage. Patel was even more concerned about the unfinished task. After many moments of failed hope, 'Operation Polo', a multi-pronged attack was launched to defeat the Nizam's forces and the Razakars. It was completed successfully in less than five days, with many more casualties on Nizam's side. The Nizam was not harmed and was made a constitutional head after he declared loyalty to the Indian Union in September 1948, thereby completing the process of integration.

A flurry of significant actions and decisions marked the last years of Patel's life. Patel worked hard to shape the first years of independent India. Most departments sought his expertise and advice on matters related to policymaking. His differences with Nehru continued and he did express his feelings. But Patel never defied Nehru openly or schemed against him. After Gandhi's assassination, he resolved not to leave the government and dutifully serve the country under Nehru's leadership.

His dislike for the socialists was palpable. He supported the creation of the Indian National Trade Union Congress (INTUC) to counter their growing influence. Socialist leaders accused him of being pro-capitalist and anti-labour. Patel had no sympathy for strikes or strikers and was undeniably closer to the capitalists. But he did not allow the phenomena of crony capitalism to develop. He remained a Gandhian, following the principles of frugal living even after becoming deputy prime minister. Jayaprakash Narayan, a noted socialist leader, admitted almost two decades after Patel's death that they erred in judging Patel.

Patel, accompanied by N. V. Gadgil, had visited the ruins of Somnath Temple in Kathiawad after the accession of Junagadh. He enthusiastically accepted Gadgil's suggestion to renovate the temple. After a discussion with Gandhi, it was decided that a trust and not the government should take up the project. Patel agreed with Gandhi that the government of India did not belong to any religion.

Congress leadership did not have fond memories of civil servants during the freedom struggle. Many civil servants feared hostile reciprocation from the Congress leadership. Patel dispelled their doubts and assured them of their freedom and dignity. He also created a similar service, the Indian Police Service. Both ICS and IPS formed the 'steel frame' of the central administration above provincial boundaries. Many civil servants, including his secretary V. Shankar, H. M. Patel, V. P. Menon, and N. M. Buch, earned Patel's trust. A man of few words and complete clarity, Sardar chose his officers carefully and gave them the freedom to operate with full backing.

As a chairman of the Advisory Subcommittee on Minorities, Sardar convinced all minorities and Muslims to abolish separate electorates and quotas, emphatically arguing in favour of quotas for Scheduled Castes and Scheduled Tribes. The resolution was passed in the Constituent Assembly by fifty-eight to three votes. Patel opposed Sikh leader Master Tara Singh's demands for reservation and later ordered his arrest when Singh declared a show of strength at Delhi.

Patel's stand on fundamental rights raised questions and criticism. He was not in favour of rights without restrictions. Many accused him of retaining more power for the state. His approach towards the media was similar. Such attitudes revealed Patel's thought process as that of an administrator and not an agitator.

The process of merging small states into the Indian Union continued for a long time. During one such event at Jaipur, Patel's plane met with an accident and was forced to land. News of the disappearance of his plane caused great anxiety and he was showered with affection by his colleagues, MPs, and party members on his safe return to Delhi.

When the constitution came into effect on 26 January 1950, India became a geographically unified nation ruled by a single constitution prepared by leaders from all religions and parties. Dr Ambedkar, a vehement critic of Gandhi and Congress, finished the momentous task of writing the constitution as the chairman of the Drafting Committee. When he married Dr Savita, a Brahmin doctor who became his caretaker, Sardar sent a note of congratulation with a remark that 'if Bapu [Gandhi] were alive he would have given you his blessings'.*

The Indian republic was part of the British commonwealth where the king was a symbolic head. Nehru accepted this condition and was strongly supported by Patel. But they had opposing views on who should become the first president of independent India. C. Rajagopalachari was

---

**Sardar Patel's Correspondence 1945-50,* Vol. 6, Durga Das (ed.), Navjivan Publishing House, Ahmedabad, 1973, p. 206.

the Governor General and after the abolishment of the post, Nehru was keen that he continued as the president. Initially, Patel had no preference. But Nehru handled the situation with impatience and in a somewhat arrogant manner. He suggested Rajendra Prasad withdraw, falsely claiming that he had already discussed the matter with Patel. Prasad, unhappy and hurt, brought up the subject with Patel.

The episode ended with Rajendra Prasad's selection as the first president of independent India as the party members rejected Nehru's choice. Nehru took their stance as a rejection of his leadership and offered to resign, asking Patel to assume the post. Patel had no aspirations to become the prime minister. He was only concerned about Nehru's enthusiasm for idealism and emotional decision-making and wanted to keep those tendencies in check. He could not prevent Nehru from getting Pattabhi Sitaramayya elected as the Congress president and sidelining Purushottamdas Tandon, an old associate of Nehru who exhibited rightist opinions on communal issues. While he agreed with Nehru's reservations, Patel also made it clear that the party structure would not accommodate Tandon's whims, and if he displayed such behaviour, there would be consequences.

However, Nehru could not stop Patel from ensuring Tandon was elected against Acharya Kripalani in the 1950 elections for Congress president. The election became a shadow contest between Nehru and Patel. Nehru even threatened to take Tandon's victory as a no-confidence vote against him. After a long-drawn battle, Kripalani lost. He did not receive a single vote from 'Sardar's province' Gujarat. Nehru's tactless handling of the situation and accepting Rafi Ahmed Kidwai's political advice were two major reasons for his defeat. Nehru was hurt but did not resign. Patel never wanted him to.

When Nehru insisted on Rafi Ahmad Kidwai's inclusion and threatened not to be part of the Congress Working Committee if his wish was disregarded, Tandon and Sardar fiercely opposed it. On the occasion of Gandhi's eighty-first birthday in 1950, Patel expressed his loyalty to Nehru in no uncertain terms. He declared Nehru as 'our leader', exactly how Gandhi appointed him as his successor and considered Nehru as his devoted soldier.

Patel criticized China's act of aggression in Tibet. Although foreign policy was not his department, he could see China's sinister designs behind their veil of friendship. Patel's letter cautioning the government against China was a testimony of his foresight even when his health was deteriorating.

~

In the last months of his life, Patel was overpowered to a large extent by his ailing physical condition. Nehru and Prasad came to see him off when he was shifted to Bombay on 12 December. His long-time friend Ghanshyamdas Birla was also present. Sardar was taken to Birla House. He had a heart attack in the early hours of 15 December 1950 and passed away the same morning. Nehru, C. Rajagopalachari, and Rajendra Prasad attended his funeral at the Sonapur cremation ground. Nehru suggested Prasad remain in Delhi as he was the president. Prasad disregarded the advice and flew to Bombay to pay his last respects to his lifelong comrade and a guiding force in many ways.

Prasad and Rajagopalachari spoke at the funeral. Before leaving for Bombay, Nehru had officially informed the parliament about Patel's demise, describing him 'as a great captain of our forces in the freedom struggle' and 'a friend and colleague on whom one could invariably rely, as a tower of strength which revived wavering hearts'.*

Patel was survived by his daughter Maniben and son Dahyabhai. Both joined politics, fought elections, and became members of parliament, but only after Patel's demise. Maniben remained loyal to Congress till the division of Congress in 1969, whereas Dahyabhai left Congress in a few years accusing the party of systematically forgetting his father's contribution. He joined the Swatantra Party, a right-wing organization famously known for its patronage of kings and princes and stalwarts like C. Rajagopalachari.

~

Vallabhbhai Patel was an inseparable part of the Gandhi–Nehru–Sardar swaraj-troika that in many significant ways shaped the history of Indian independence and nation building. His achievements and

*Gandhi, *Patel: A Life*, p. 533.

limitations cannot be studied selectively or by detaching them from the time in which he lived and worked. It is true for any great leader, but even more so for Patel whose characteristics tempt people, including historians, to draw oversimplified conclusions in an age marked by complete polarization.

SECTION I

'I AM JUST A SOLDIER': THE FORMATIVE YEARS

RECOLLECTIONS

The Editor has assigned to me one of the most difficult jobs which I have had to perform during a life of heavy responsibilities of various types in different positions. Sitting in this city of weird mixture of the old and the new, it is difficult to switch one's mind back more than three scores of years and recall one's life when one was a child. As a child it always pays to be either the eldest or the youngest. As the eldest, a child is the centre of paternal hopes; as the youngest, he is the object of paternal affection. It is the privilege of the eldest to order about all his younger brothers and sisters. As the youngest one has to wear the brunt of accumulated orders; but at the same time, unless one is particularly unfortunate, one gets accumulated blessings as well as showers of affection. Having been born between these two extremes, I naturally had the usual independence, initiative, and resources of a middling. When the time came, I could exercise a will of my own. It was seldom that I had to take into account the responsibilities which devolve upon the eldest child or the debt of affection which bends the back of the youngest.

Town Life Retards Free Growth

My own view is that town life gives little scope for the display of all that is best in a child. It places restrictions and limitations which retard his free growth, cramp his style, and make his mind revolve in a narrow groove; on the other hand, in the open space of a village, one can see infinity. The growth of a child is on terms of complete equality with his fellow-children. He has his share of the 'black eye' like any others. He rolls on dusty streets after a gentle [or] severe push as well or as badly as any of his equals or seniors or juniors in age. He is pushed in the village pond with the same vigorous and unexpected [rap] on the knuckles as any other child. It was in this atmosphere of equal 'give-and-take' that I grew up with all that sturdiness and determination which grow out of a healthy atmosphere of dare-devilry and juvenile buoyancy and of impish pranks, mirth, and laughter.

The Captaincy of Mischief

As far as I can remember, I yielded to none in the captaincy of mischief or of sly attempts to hood-wink one's elders. I can recall however it was almost always in a good cause—of course, a good cause from my own point of view. I took to studies as seriously as I took to play cheerfully. I had no patience with an indifferent teacher and never spared a lazy one. As children we had our own methods of correcting our teachers and we fully exploited all the subtleties of manoeuvres, which only children can. I can vividly recall one particular incident. My teacher at school got annoyed because I persuaded the class to make fun of him for being late. He prescribed a task for me as punishment. I came to school the next day without my task being done, and the punishment increased doublefold for each day that went by until it was my task to write out the sums two hundred times.

I wrote on the slate just the figure 200 and took it to my teacher with an innocent air. The teacher asked me where the *padas* (in Gujarati that means both sums and buffaloes) were. I told him I could write only 200 when the padas (buffaloes) ran away. The teacher was all sound and fury. I was presented before the Headmaster, who, instead of punishing me, took the teacher to task for not knowing the correct method of prescribing tasks.

Those Blissful Days

They say, '[The] Child is Father of the Man'. I do not know how much of what I am I owe to those blissful days. I know this much, however, my constitution today is what I built up as a child and the many qualities or defects of character which I might exhibit today can probably be traced to the characteristics which I displayed when I was a child. This does not, however, mean that I kept my development in a straight line. This can hardly be the case in a life full of varieties and of different experiences. Many are life's incidents which act as a corrective and a lesson which once learnt mould a person's future in a way quite different from the past. I had my share of these incidents and experiences, but, in the main, I am what I was or tried to be seventy years ago.

Delightful Company

Even today in the midst of my onerous responsibilities and heavy pre-occupations, I delight in the company of children. That brings sometimes a ray of hope in the midst of surrounding gloom, a heavy laughter after the perusal of a saddening report, and a relaxation during anxious hours.

Work is undoubtedly worship but laughter is life. Anyone who takes life too seriously must prepare himself for a miserable existence. Anyone who greets joys and sorrows with equal facility can really get the best of life.

It has been my good fortune to have borne a temperament which adapts itself equally well to the most taxing and the light moments. It was only some years ago that I used to wrestle and sport with my grandson. Very often I indulge in less vigorous pranks with children who can afford to give me the benefit of their company. It is only so long as a man can retain the child in him that life can be free from those dark shadows which leave inevitable furrows on a man's forehead. There is nothing more disgusting than perpetual pensive brows or the wry face of a curmudgeon.

Old Age Is Second Childhood

They say, 'Old age is second childhood.' I wish it were. The poet has said:

> 'Grow old along with me,
> The best is yet to be
> The last of life for which the first was made.'

So far as my own life is concerned, it is an open book. There are few, however, who have known me as a child, are now living. The words of those few are concealed in the wraps of distance and isolation from the gaze of publicity; but, in so far as I am competent to speak for myself, I would much rather be a child of seventy years ago than myself in the year of grace 1949.

IMITATING THE BRITISH

...Bhai Mohanlal [Pandya] has said...that once upon a time I used to imitate the British and their way. That is quite right. It is also true that sports consumed whatever spare time I had. I thought it was the best policy to imitate foreigners in our unfortunate country. I had been taught to think that the people of our country were of poor character and unworthy and that it was only the foreigners ruling over us who were good and could improve our conditions. We could only be slaves. This type of poison was being instilled in our minds. I was anxious to go overseas to see the people of England who were able to rule us for so long while staying 7,000 miles away. I came from a middle-class family. My father lived a humble and pious life and died in the temple he worshipped. He had no means to enable me to fulfil my ambition. I was told that only if I could get 7 to 10 thousand rupees, I would be able to proceed to England. No one was likely to give me so much money. One of my friends suggested that there is a possibility of securing the required amount as a loan with interest from the ruler of Idar, a state in North Gujarat. Both of us went to Idar but came back after moving around in the town like madcaps. I realized finally that if I wanted to go to England, I had to earn the money myself. I, therefore, studied very earnestly for my law examination and resolved firmly to save sufficient money for a visit to England. But my elder brother came to see my correspondence with the company through which I arranged the travel. On reading the letters he told me, 'I am older than you. You will have an opportunity to go to England once I return. But I will not be able to go after you.' I gave my brother fifteen days. He left for England on the fifteenth day.

I had to suffer family problems after his departure to England. He returned after three years. I went after that. On my return, we decided that if we desire freedom, one must become a *sanyasi*-an ascetic. One must work selflessly. It was decided between us that one of us will serve the country and the other will look after the family. Subsequently, my brother left his flourishing practice and started working for the country. The responsibility of the household fell on my shoulders. He took up virtuous work whereas I carried on the sinful work. But I was consoling myself that I have a share in the good work he was doing. With my business running smoothly, the old idea that prestige can be earned only by aping the rulers got consolidated in mind.

I was entangled in such trappings. Our political scenario was very murky at that time. Many of those working on behalf of our people were full of hypocrisy. A friend from the club where I used to play cards kept on telling me that if you want to serve the people, you must leave Ahmedabad. I left my practice as a lawyer after a bitter experience.

Along with Mahatma Gandhi entered the truth in our political arena. During Kheda Satyagraha, he asked for a man who can leave his profession instantly to take up full work of the Satyagraha staying at Nadiad. I took it up. Working with him convinced me that India was on the wrong path till now and it can arise only by taking the path shown by him....

Modasa, Gujarat, 29 March 1921

THE STRUGGLE FOR FREEDOM: THE KHEDA SATYAGRAHA*

Today the coastal land is consecrated by the arrival of Mahatma Gandhi. The people of Borsad are considered to be the most mischievous in the entire district—especially the coastal people.

As Satyagraha has begun in the coastal area, we must abandon quarrelling, plundering, and deceit etcetera and take the path of justice. Your rage should be utilized in the fight for justice. Do not misuse your strength. Stop raising long-handled sickles [for violence]. Live like brothers. Be humble and courteous. Ask for our rights firmly. Abandon the fear of taluka revenue officers. Speak out your rightful things courageously. You are not inferior to a revenue officer. Sometimes a revenue officer may not have 25 *bighas* of land. We should not go to serve him at his place. If you want to pay respect to him, invite him to your place. Never fear his pressure or pomp. Be fearless. The

*The Kheda Satyagraha was a non-violent civil resistance movement organized by Mahatma Gandhi during which peasants from the Kheda district in Gujarat protested against the high rates of taxation imposed on them at a time when the area was ravaged by floods.

main goal of our fight is to eliminate fear from folks and get rid of bad customs, disunity, and quarrels.

The government will test you the hard way. It will give you trouble. But there is no gain without pain. The best thing is to suffer the pain with understanding. I know you can take the right path if someone leads you to it. Our fight has got more elements of dharma. Considering the affection you have shown towards Mahatmaji, I am sure you will stick to the path shown by him.

What would the government do? Attachments, additional fines of *chauthai* (One quarter or 25 percent), and confiscation of land. But do not start rioting. I know you become violent when attachments are done. Do not raise your stick from now onwards. If they intend to confiscate land, the land of an entire village cannot be confiscated. Only you would plough your land. You know the potter puts one maund of load on his donkey. If it carries that load, he would add a half maund, and ultimately, he would make the donkey carry full two mounds. Similarly, the more load you carry, the government goes on to add more loads. Throw away the load you have been carrying till now and be fearless. Follow what is right. Then the government will say that the people are not worthless.

Lastly, I request you that do not break your pledge even if heaven and earth move. If you can do that, the name of the Kheda district will be the foremost in the history of Hind. The entire Hindustan is looking at you. Government has to deliver the justice demanded by the people. No government can oppose the united force of the people. This government calls itself just. How can it do the same?

The betterment of your future generations lies in fulfilling this pledge.

Raas Village, Gujarat, 18 April 1918

THE LONGER THE FIGHT, THE STIFFER THE TEST

A bitter war is on between the public and the blind administration. The government is determined to recover land revenue and is using all the resources at its command. It has appointed special officers and has even recruited clerks of courts throughout the district. It has auctioned many houses. It has imposed *chauthai* fines widely. It has auctioned standing crops. It has threatened imprisonment. But despite all this, the public has stood firm....

To give the agriculturists as much trouble as possible, even when another property could be auctioned, they took charge of milk-giving buffaloes and kept them in the sun. They separated them from their calves. This reduced the price of the buffalo by half. Even so, the agriculturists adhered to their pledge patiently and bore whatever hardship they were called upon to bear. Women found it difficult to be an eye-witness to the bad treatment that was meted out to their carefully looked-after cattle. Nevertheless, they showed courage.

The longer the fight lasts, the stiffer the test that the public has to pass. But without such hardships, they cannot have this unique experience. Many bureaucrats find they receive no welcome in any village. Persons who were obtaining whatever they wanted free of cost are unable now to get anything even on payment. Their attitude is beginning to change and it would seem as if they had a vague feeling that there was some truth in people's cases but they are helpless before the current policy of the Government. In such difficult circumstances if the Government oversteps the limits, is itself angered, and harasses us, we, for our part, should not act unreasonably, never be impolite or lose our temper but commiserate rather than be angry, and be always peaceful. Even the hardest heart can be conquered by love and the more the opponent is stiff the more should our affection go out to him. Only so shall we be able to win. That is the significance of Satyagraha.

1918

WHICH COUNTRY HAS ATTAINED FREEDOM EASILY?*

India's Aid in the War

...Hundreds of thousands of soldiers went from India to fight on the battlefields of Europe, Africa, and Asia. Today there is hardly any part of the world in which people are as poor as India, and yet we made a present of 1.5 billion rupees to England. Raw materials worth crores of rupees and other war-related materials were taken away. England was not too certain of India's loyalty and help during the War. But the people of England were surprised by the unexpected loyalty of India.... Our wise and able leaders were of the view that to give conditional help at a time of danger would not have been honourable. Our Muslim brethren crossed all the limits of loyalty. Ali Brothers, two eyes of the Muslim community, were imprisoned right from the beginning of the war till it ended. Several Muslim papers became the victim of the Press Act. Yet, thousands of Muslims fought against Turkey and lost their lives trusting the promises of the Prime Minister and other ministers of England.

The War ended at last. The empire won. But what did we get in return? We were given the Rowlatt Act which deprived us of freedom of action. India was surprised.... As a result, a section of our people in a fit of temporary insanity committed atrocities. We cannot defend these mad acts of our people. There is nothing wrong with Government acting tough and imposing sentences on those proven guilty. When innocent people are murdered, when Government buildings are burnt, Churches are burnt, and when women are attacked, it is only to be expected that the Government would react strongly and act without

*Post World War I, by the harsh terms of the Treaty of Sevrès (14 May 1920), Turkey lost its Islamic holy sites and places of pilgrimage, which were placed under direct or indirect British control, contrary to the British promise of respecting Muslim sentiments during the war. In response to this arose the Khilafat Movement, supporters of which protested against British policy choices in Turkey. This movement, combined with the anguish caused by the Rowlatt Acts (March 1919) and the Jallianwala Massacre (13 April 1919), provided Mahatma Gandhi with the impetus to call for an all-India mass movement to oust the British from India. This came to be called the Non-cooperation Movement, launched in the winter of 1920–21. Gandhi defined non-cooperation as the boycott of titles, civil services, police and army, and, finally non-payment of taxes.

moderation in taking effective and deterrent action.... But Government officers exceeded all bounds of reasonableness....

The Reward of Self-sacrifice

...The British Parliament is the last court of appeal for justice. There are people in this country who have greater faith in British justice than even in the existence of God. But these discussions in the British Parliament have opened the eyes of even such people. If a person who has been cherishing a stone for a long time, believing it to be a diamond, discovers one day when he goes to sell it in his time of difficulty that it is indeed nothing but a stone, can he blame the stone? Our condition today is what it is because of the blind faith we have had in British justice.... In the House of Lords, the Lords verily showed their nobility! They made little of the grave hardships and atrocities the people of Punjab endured. Murder of so many innocent men and women was to them nothing as compared with the honour of one callous Englishman: that officer they regarded as brave, and those innocent persons who were killed as rebels! ...Lord Sinha from the House of Lords advises us to forget the past. When Lord Sinha was appointed to the House of Lords, the entire India went gaga over it. We were admiring the sense of justice of the British. It proves how short-sighted we are in matters of politics....

General Dyer's intention was honest; he only made a slight miscalculation, he fired a few more rounds than was perhaps necessary and killed many men, women, and children. But, then, did he not save India? This was told in defense of Dyer in the House of Lords as well as the House of Commons.... I humbly want to ask those who tell us to forget that what are you trying to teach India after all? ...Should we try to learn enduring insults like this? ...The next generation has got some right over us. We are their trustees. If we leave the inheritance of insult for them, what is worthy of all our wealth money, and pomp?...

Condition of the Muslims

...Even the Viceroy admitted some of the conditions of the agreement could hurt the Muslims. By breaching the pious promises given to the Indian Muslims during the war by the [British] Prime Minister, and disrespecting the sentiments of the community, Allied powers abolished the power of the Caliph just out of selfishness. This injustice has torn the heart of the Muslim community.... The Hindus cannot remain objective when the Muslims are in such an unhappy state. They must share their sorrow if they wish for the friendship of the Muslims....

Non-cooperation

...Some leaders have issued a manifesto against non-cooperation. I have no reason to doubt the honesty behind their belief.... Mahatma Gandhiji refuted it effectively with facts in his speech at Madras. What else can I add to it? Some see a breach of religion in non-cooperation. I cannot claim to be as learned or to possess as deep knowledge of elements of religion, but I would ask them what happens to this argument when they advise people not to take part in non-cooperation, to keep away from it, and generally to non-cooperate with the non-cooperators? We would like to ask Sir Narayan Chandawarkar in all humility which *sloka* of the Gita prevents him from returning the title of 'Sir' when a man like Michael O'Dwyer can have a similar title in the Empire, a great poet Sir Rabindranath Tagore has already surrendered his title of 'Sir' and the person whom you regard as a prophet, worthy of the deepest respect has surrendered his medals.

The Risk of Doing Nothing

We hear non-cooperation involves risk. It involves the possibility of rioting. True, there is a risk. But which country in the world has attained freedom easily? Is there less risk in doing nothing, just keeping mum?

Isn't it anything but suicidal for people to sit idle, doing nothing in the present situation? If there is no other option left than a risky surgery to save a life, a good doctor would take the risk and advise it. The Muslim community is zealous by nature. Has anybody thought of the bloodshed Hindustan would have suffered if the community was not led on the path of non-cooperation? There is no doubt the Government could have suppressed the violence. But it could not have stopped it completely. The way thousands of Muslims are migrating out of the country right now, we can easily gauge how much their religious sentiment is hurt. The Government and the opponents of non-cooperation should just think of the consequences of not giving an outlet to the Muslim religious sentiment. The opponents of non-cooperation would serve the Government and the people better by using their minds and energy in training the people to keep away from violence, instead of agitating them against non-cooperation. Has anyone for the fear of possible risks given up great experiments which might greatly benefit the people? If the British, Empire builders that they are, had been afraid of the risk they ran, could they have survived so long? The journey on railways and ships involves the risk of an accident. But would anyone advise against it for that reason? It is the duty of the wise to take proper precautions.... If non-cooperation is dangerous, an alternative way should be suggested. Is the injustice of Khilafat and Punjab less insulting than that of the partition of Bengal? Why are those who set the country afire then not feeling anything now? Is manhood abolished from Hindustan?

The Reforms Are Useless

...The reforms are as defeating as the bloodshed for us. The current regime is like a machine that crushes people after extracting their richness and brightness. What difference will it make if some foreign parts of it are replaced with Indian ones? How are we likely to benefit from the appointment of an Indian as a Governor? Are there not among the British Governors also, men of noble character and great ability? Although a murderous assault was made on Lord Hardinge, he did not hurt anyone in Chandani Chowk of Delhi. Even so merely by throwing a few drops of Ganga water into the sewage, can one hope to purify it? ...What indeed do we stand to gain by entering the trap of reforms, so long as the entire structure is not changed, the Government of India is not run for the people of India, and the interests of foreigners are given priority...the rights of justice, liberty and equality are not given.... What guarantee is there that what happened in Punjab will not recur?...

We have paid a heavy price for the reforms. For years we have been demanding a reduction in expenditure incurred due to jobs of higher positions. But the expenditure on Administrative, Military, and other servants has been increased by 25 crores per year before implementing the reforms. Hence, we are deprived of the power to criticize the increase in expenditure. Expensive departments like public welfare [health] and education have been allotted to us instead. The people do not want such reforms. They want to save their selves from hunger, and insult and want to be nurtured in the atmosphere of freedom. Can you provide any of these through the reforms?...

The Police and the People

The police should be there for the protection of the people. But we can see how much the people are protected by the police. There are complaints of robbery from many villages in Gujarat. We cannot blame the police for not being able to protect them. Police constables are mainly found in the illiterate class. They cannot lead their life honestly just by the salary they get. As a result, they become partners in robbery or lead life by oppressing people in other manners. It cannot be unknown to the Government. Also, considering our political situation, it is high time that we must learn to defend ourselves. A group of volunteers should be created and trained in every village. This Conference should resolve to establish such a group of volunteers....

Responsibility of the Educated Class

The educated class has got great responsibility. They cannot abandon their responsibilities just by saying that the people are ignorant and not ready. Literacy is not required much for cultivating, training, and diverting people on the right path.... This cannot be achieved by going to Municipality, Local Board, or Assembly in their spare time. The educated class can see holes in the immorality of the government easily and naturally, they expose them and hence are disliked by the state. But their duty does not end there. The rise of the people depends on their courage, character, and their ability to make sacrifices.

Summary

We have got many parties. We use our energy and intellect in negating one another, cannot tolerate differences of opinion, and cannot see honesty in them. We intensify the quarrel by accusing one another. Poor innocent people get confused by this and cannot see the right path. If we want to secure justice and freedom, we should learn to see and correct our faults and learn to maintain tolerance, self-belief, and patience. In short, instead of looking at the shortcomings of those from whom we want to secure justice, we should try to imitate their huge qualities and their character. I pray to God to grant us that sense and help us....

Ahmedabad, 17 August 1920

BE COURAGEOUS

The students have been asking the leaders about the path they should take ever since the Calcutta Congress passed the resolution of non-cooperation. I am very happy and find it a good sign for the country that students are giving thought to such issues of public interest with national sentiment.... The students of Government schools and colleges have been advised to boycott their studies. Hence, all those students with national pride and self-respect should follow the resolution....

It is out of the question to worry about your condition once you boycott the study. Fifty-Six lakh illiterate mendicants of this country do not starve. Why do you worry? You will not remain illiterate. All you have to abandon is a fascination for the degrees. I see that many have a fascination to become lawyers as they imagine lawyers earn too much. But this fancy is not true in fact. People can become rich in business. You will see many *seths* who are non-matric and yet they are millionaires. The real thing is that you can only teach your teacher the first lesson of education when you leave school or college. Some think that we are in B.A. and it would be good if we join the movement after completing our B.A. Such resolve only comes from a weak mind. There will be the temptation of looking for advertisements, offering candidature in those advertisements, and searching for a job after completing a B.A. Thus it will be like coming back to square one. Even if Gujarat College becomes empty tomorrow, there will not be an exhibition of cattle on the campus. We can use the building under people's supervision. Hence, the students of Gujarat should be courageous enough to work effectively in this matter. The betterment of the country depends on your courage more than anything else. You can help a great deal in making the country free....

Ahmedabad, 28 September 1920

BREAK THE CHAINS OF SLAVERY

Sacrifice can be offered in several ways. Gandhiji raised the flag of non-violent cooperation after sincere thought and considering the situation of the nation fully. If the opponents do not find any stage of it appropriate, are they for the path of a bomb, sword, or cannon? Even a child can say that this country is not strong enough to use arms. The Bengalis experimented with the bombs after getting their experience from the West. It is not wrong if the youth's blood is boiling for immediate sacrifice. But we have seen that the use of brute force ends in more suffering for us. It does not elevate us but pushes us down. It might take years before we can succeed against the English by using arms. Even after years, I doubt whether we might get prepared like them.... The question is what must we do then? Keep rotting in slavery just as we were doing till now? The people are not ready for that. They want freedom. Non-violent non-cooperation is meant for that particular purpose. It requires sacrifices. But they are of a different kind. The English can offer sacrifice. It is their virtue that cannot be ignored. No great sacrifice has been asked from the people as of now. The only demand is to break the chains of slavery that have tied them up for years. We can be free from everything else if we can be free from the chains. The movement of the bonfire of foreign clothes is meant for that reason. There would be hardly anyone not knowing about the impact of the movement. When the movement was not even started and it was just resolved to burn foreign cloth, Lancashire became restless and now a deputation is preparing for a visit to India. Let them come. We should remain firm in our movement and must boycott foreign clothing with pure intentions. If the 33 Crore people of the country just follow this, there would be no delay in *swarajya* [self-rule]. The early or late arrival of *swarajya* depends on the restraint and sacrifices of the people. If we reach that day of complete unity, do you think the community of merely one Lakh foreigners would stay here? They are clever people. They will get the hint that they cannot afford to keep Hind slaves any longer.

Ahmedabad, 18 September 1921

REAL LEADERSHIP LIES IN SERVICE

The Congress sessions have never been held in circumstances similar to those of the current year. Instead of feeling sad by the absence of our beloved and revered workers, our joy is boundless today. I would not use the word 'leaders' for them, as we have learned during the year that real leadership lies in the service. We believe many great and learned Muslims, as well as Hindus, are having their well-earned rest in Government prisons. It is because they have served us and have suffered for us. They are having the pleasure [of imprisonment] which we are eagerly longing for—the pleasure withheld by the government claiming to be founded on law and order but, as it gets more and more clear day by day, is based on sheer force.

We hoped that we would be together for celebrating the festival of *swaraj*. Hence we prepared accordingly. But the celebration of the auspicious occasion has not become possible. The merciful God has sent suffering to test us and make us worthy of such a precious gift [of *swaraj*]. We have considered the events of imprisonment, physical violence, forceful frisking, and breaking the locks of our offices and branches [by the government] as signs of approaching *swaraj* and have continued with our decoration, musical programs, and other entertainment programs without making any changes or reduction in it, assuming it might provide a soothing effect to the wounds of the Muslim brothers as well as for the Punjabis….

Ahmedabad, December 1921

MAHATMA GANDHI HAS LEFT ENORMOUS WEALTH FOR US

Mahatma Gandhi, the guardian of the poor, has gone to jail. That should not be the reason for despair. He has left enormous wealth for us. It is up to us to use it wisely.

He tried hard to get *swaraj* before December [1921]. But the people at large did not pay the price he asked for. Those with the titles remained stuck to it. People still want to get justice from the [English] courts. The students could not abandon their fascination for degrees. Assemblies were full and those who left it have still got a fascination for it deep down. Liquor sellers do not want to part with their occupation. The merchants of foreign clothes want to stick to their business. People are not ready to boycott foreign cloth summarily. They feel pride in wearing colourful foreign clothes for the marriage ceremony. Women want to adorn their selves with thin sarees. Few are satisfied only with the white cap. Mill owners want to extract more profit by using foreign cotton and if the mill cloth is in demand due to the *swadeshi* movement, they take full advantage of it by raising its price. The rich want to increase their capital. No one wants to part with an easy life. Everyone expects *swaraj* by shouting about the victory of Gandhi Mahatma and offering him some money. Gandhiji has stressed time and again that *swaraj* can not be attained in such a manner.

Yet, the awareness caused by whatever response people offered is miraculous. Everyone agrees that the work of a century has been achieved in a year. Why should we become despondent then?…

Some people ask, 'What would the associates do after Gandhiji's departure [from the scene]? They do not have that kind of character or strength to lead his ship.' This is a fact. His associates are full of defects. There is a vast difference between him and his associates. His associates have endless shortcomings. It is because of their shortcomings that Gandhiji has to go to jail. His associates lack gentleness in speech, restraint, and tolerance. With all these limitations, it is good that they are fully aware of them.

A mason does not claim to have the knowledge of an engineer. Yet, he finds no difficulty in following the plan [made by the engineer] and builds the house. Similarly, if Gandhiji's associates understood the plan for the *swaraj* building designed by him, they will not be confused about continuing the work accordingly.

Their difficulties are immense. There is no one to hide their limitations. Yet, people's love for Gandhiji, their feeling of hurt due to Gandhiji's imprisonment, and the awakened spirit for *swaraj* are the biggest capital of his associates….

26 March 1922

THE CAPACITY TO SUFFER AND TO SACRIFICE

Brave Akalis of Punjab, who were pillars of the [British] Empire, have started the *yajna* [sacred offering] of non-violence and self-sacrifice. Decorated with the wounds of enemies' swords while serving the Empire at different battlegrounds and medals obtained for the service of the empire, the mighty Akalis with kirpan [a short knife with a curved blade] bore the blows of the police lathi-charge ordered by the same government silently. After realizing that the force of arms can work only on the cowards, the government preferred to depend on filling the prisons.

The Punjab government has to avail of new prisons. More than five thousand Akalis have gone to prison. A batch of one hundred Akalis get arrested daily and at the same time, recruitment for volunteers willing to go to jail is going on simultaneously. Akalis wear nothing but Khadi. The Akali women have shown great enthusiasm and courage in this *dharmayuddha* [battle of duty]. A hospital has been opened to treat the Akalis injured in the police beating. Akali women are nursing them. They have also taken up the work of preparing and serving food for hundreds of Akalis in recruitment camps and serving sick persons. Military-like training and organization can be seen in this work. Akali women also wear only Khadi…. Akalis have got the opportunity to conduct this great *yajna*, the fortune Bardoli could not get, while Gandhiji is in the prison. They have silenced those who were mocking non-violence and declaring the death of non-cooperation.

Gujarat cannot have less faith in non-violent non-cooperation than Akalis. Gujarat is its birthplace. *Ahimsa Paramo dharmah* [non-violence is the ultimate region] is the basis of Jainism. Gujarat is the main center of the Jains. So it is but natural for Gujarat to have great faith in non-violence. But has Gujarat the courage and bravery, the capacity to suffer and to sacrifice, the unity and the training of the Akalis?

Have Gujaratis or Gujarati Jains the religious fervour in the way Akalis have it in them? How long can Gujarat save its prestige by saying 'Had there been no Chaurichaura, Bardoli would have shown it.'? How long can the fact be hidden from the world that the business of foreign cloth is mainly conducted by the Jain community? As Punjab is immersed in Khadi, Gandhiji's Gujarat cannot abandon the fascination for foreign cloth. For how long can it be hidden? Gujaratis said let us consume what we have already purchased. But even after eight months of Gandhiji's imprisonment, there is no sign of the disappearance of foreign cloth and entry of Khadi. What is the reason? Not a single shop of foreign cloth seems to have shut down. Why?

Gujarat's work is not done just by saying that it is firm in a boycott of the council and there are no differences of opinion on that. Any Gujarati knowing Gandhiji well would not wish to go to the council. There should be no surprise in it. But the responsibility of Gujarat does not end there.

O Gujaratis, the people who followed Gandhiji madly and hailed him in his presence! Awake. If you want to save the reputation of Gujarat, shed…your laziness. Else, it will be told in the future that Mahatma Gandhiji was recognized by the world but Gujarat could not recognize him…. Gujarat has trusted Mahatma Gandhi's program; Gujarat has got money, management power, and discretion. But it lacks volunteers. Every patriotic Gujarati should spare one son in the service of the country.

Gujarat Provincial Committee has for now asked for only 2,500 volunteers. The picketing at the shops selling foreign clothes in Gujarat will start from 1-12-'22. If 2,500 volunteers will not be found in Gujarat for this purpose, the patriotism of Gujarat will be gauged automatically…

19 November 1922

RULES FOR SWADESHI TROOPS

1. The appointed volunteers must work under and act according to the local chief's instructions.
2. A volunteer must stand at a maximum possible distance from the shop. He should try to convince people not to purchase foreign

cloth. He may not come within ten yards of it if the shopkeeper objects to it.

3. He should take care that he does not cause any sort of obstruction to the traffic, in the act of dissuading people from purchasing foreign cloth. In case of gathering a crowd, he should request people to disperse; and if people do not disperse, the volunteer should inform the local office.
4. He should try to get sympathy from the houses around the cloth shop and try to sit or stand on a raised platform outside their home, trying to convince people from there only. This would avoid the possibility of creating any crowd on the road.
5. It is advisable to address the intending purchasers at the two ends of the bazaar rather than in front of the shop.
6. A volunteer should not talk to the customer leaving the shop after purchasing the cloth. He should not try to convince or preach to such a customer.
7. He should talk humbly and plead to the intending purchaser. He should not use harsh or hateful language.
8. He should take extra care of not touching anyone while trying to convince.
9. A volunteer should offer himself for arrest immediately when he is sought to be arrested.
10. He should give his name whenever it is demanded of him by the police. He should not enter into an argument with the officer seeking his name, and he should inform the local office about it.
11. A volunteer should maintain complete calm even when others riot. Even if he is beaten, he should suffer peacefully. He should not get excited or angry to any level of provocation or instigation.

November 1922

I AM JUST A SOLDIER

I am not a leader. I am just a soldier. I am a son of a farmer and I do not believe that swaraj can be achieved by arguments. We cannot compete with the government in [cunning]. It has not imprisoned those creating obstructions in the assembly. But it has sent Mahatmaji, who boycotted the assembly, to jail. The government is tired of non-violence, rejection of relaxations, and [our] power to suffer. If we participate in the movement for Legislature, people will get more inactive and the Congress will lose the confidence of the masses. The movement for Legislature will prove destructive for Congress. After Congress's call for non-cooperation, the farmers have come to join, the labourers entered the fray and the women started participating, as they think they can work and sacrifice in this area. The government knew the kind of people it was dealing with before the reforms [took place]. Honourable Mr. [Vitthalbhai] Patel went to England, especially for that purpose. The government knew the power of those people. Hence it prepared the reforms accordingly. But swaraj cannot be obtained by such weak movements of assembly even if they are conducted for a hundred years.

25 December 1922

SACRIFICE FOR THE SAKE OF THE PLAN*

O people of Gujarat! Does the invisible sound of the religious battle being fought on the battlefield of Nagpur strike your ears?

Remember, the flag you hoisted in presence of Mahatma Gandhiji at the Congress session held on the bank of Sabarmati River is being insulted at Nagpur. Looking at our lethargy and lack of faith, the rulers have turned reckless and shameless. They seem to have determined to undermine the symbol accepted by India.

This battle is not just about Nagpur. The [Congress] Working Committee has resolved to turn Nagpur into a religious battlefield of the entire India. Soldiers of different provinces of Hindustan offered sacrifices in this *maha-yajna* [great endeavour] during the last Gandhi-Parva. Gujarat also contributed respectably. Heartless servants of the arrogant power treated those soldiers as ordinary wanderers

---

*The Flag Satyagraha began with the district magistrate prohibiting the flying of the national flag on the municipality building in Jabalpur. The ban was extended to display of the National Flag on public road and especially on the road of Civil Lines. After police atrocities on the procession carrying the flag at Jabalpur and Nagpur, the Congress Working Committee decided to start satyagraha at Nagpur.

and added insult to injury. Do you feel that pain? Do you feel that insult is yours?

There cannot be a more pure and better opportunity for offering sacrifice. Every country has sacrificed thousands and millions of lives for the sake of its flag.

We do not know of any people who got their flag without sacrifices. The battle to make the flag permanent is going on. The government has also prepared to fight vigorously. That explains the importance of the fight.

When the very existence of non-cooperation is doubted, non-cooperation is ridiculed; a real chance to exhibit a pure form of non-cooperation is not worth losing. This struggle is just about self-protection. We do not aim to insult anyone personally or [to harm] anyone's property or to insult their flag. We do not have the slightest interest in harassing those foreigners who are wandering here and there and are out to stuff their stomachs by suppressing others.

Testing times for Gujarat have arrived. We have not faced an occasion that demands heavy sacrifices till now. But on this precious occasion, I hope Gujarat, reeling under the pain of Gandhiji's absence, will grab the God-send opportunity and show its mettle. The recruitment work is on. Join the troops, sign the pledge and be prepared to go to Nagpur as and when the order comes.

June 1923

EVERY BATTLE NEEDS SOLDIERS AND FUNDS

As Congress Working Committee has ordered me to stay in Central Provinces till the struggle for the national flag is going on at Nagpur, I am leaving Gujarat for Nagpur today. Only God knows for how long I shall have to stay away from Gujarat. I never imagined in my dreams that I would get a chance to serve another province [except Gujarat]. I am not worried about Gujarat. There are more loyal soldiers of Gandhiji in Gujarat than myself. I do not doubt that they will carry the burden of Gujarat. But what perplexes me enormously is what I would be able to achieve in the Central Provinces.

The struggle of Nagpur is not merely for the Central Provinces but for the whole country. Every province has greeted this struggle by sending their [non-violent] soldiers. If we cannot take the struggle forward in a proper manner, the honour of the country will be lost. Every battle needs soldiers and funds. The government has no dearth of handsomely paid officers and lowly paid soldiers. How can it be short of funds after all when it is fighting at others' expense? We shall not be short of soldiers. Each province is willing to send many soldiers. We do not need to pay them. But it costs lakhs of Rupees to bring those soldiers from their province to Nagpur. The railway fare to bring a Madras soldier to Nagpur costs Rs.60. Some of the provinces lack funds. Such a heavy struggle cannot be fought without funds.

If we want to put thousands of soldiers to the yajna at Nagpur, at least Rs five lakhs are required for the railway fare. If a Marwari decides, he can contribute such an amount alone. I came in contact with many Marwaris when I traveled to Hindustan with Shri Jamnalalji [Bajaj] for Congress work. I could see enormous respect for the Marwari community for Jamnalalji. He served the community well.... I am sure if we could inform the community, we would get this amount easily. I have sent Bhai Manilal Kothari to convey this message to the Marwaris.

But my hope is on Gujaratis. When there was darkness and disappointment all around, Jamanlalji created a stir by his renunciation and sacrifice single-handedly notwithstanding all difficulties, and drew the attention of the entire country. Gujarat contributed by offering its sons as a sacrificial offering. If we allow this struggle to dilute at this stage due to a lack of funds, I think we might lose our reputation. Gujaratis can shower money in the office of the Provincial Committee if they wish. Those who cannot join as soldiers should welcome this opportunity. I hope Gujaratis living anywhere would send their contribution to the secretary of the Gujarat Provincial Committee upon reading this appeal.

Ahmedabad, 20 July 1923

BE READY TO SUFFER MORE AND MORE TILL WE REACH OUR FINAL GOAL

I take this opportunity of making a final statement to dispel all doubts, to set at rest all the controversies that have been raised by the misleading, mischievous, and inaccurate reports circulated by interested persons regarding the happenings of the 18th August which resulted in the successful termination of our struggle. It is well known to all that this struggle had to be commenced when under the guise of regulating processions on public roads the District Magistrate of Nagpur prohibited processions with the national flag beyond the District Court buildings in civil lines by issuing an order on 1st of May, 1923. This order was regarded, and as later events have conclusively shown rightly regarded, as a challenge and an insult to the national flag and denial of our elementary right to possess and exhibit the flag and to carry it in a peacefully and orderly procession on public roads. For about a month even a single person, man or woman, attempting to carry a flag into the prohibited area was arrested. The flags of the arrested persons were confiscated. When such open prostitution of law unheard of in any civilized country that was being perpetrated in the sacred name of law order was publicly exposed, the Government of Central Provinces had to revise its notion about the legal definition of the term procession. A group of any two persons carrying a national flag continued however to be regarded as a procession right up to the end of the struggle. Another District Magistrate went to the length of publicly advising the people not to interest themselves in the national flag affair as their forefathers had no national flag, and latterly respectable persons coming to Nagpur were arrested on railway stations as vagrants or as persons not able to give satisfactory account if they happened to have a flag with them.

The campaign thus was directed not to claim an unrestricted use of public roads or for insulting the Union Jack, or for annoying any section of the people, but for the vindication of the honour of the national flag and against an attempt of setting up Highlands in the heart of India under the cover of police regulation. After a prolonged struggle of three months and a half national flag procession of a hundred volunteers entered through a prohibited area and passed through a prohibited portion of the Civil Lines without interruption amidst a surprisingly large demonstration of force all over the route through which the procession passed on the afternoon of 18th August, and this enabled me to publicly announce the victorious termination of the struggle that evening....

We have made no compromise or agreement with the Government nor have given any undertakings. The interview [with the Governor of the Central Provinces] took place on the 13th of August. It only afforded us an opportunity of placing each other's point of view.

Reports have been circulated that an application to the District Superintendent of Police to hold a procession was put in.... If I wanted to apply for permission, the struggle could have ended long ago.... I knew that a merely verbal request from me to the District Magistrate would have been enough. Ordinarily, there would be no objection to an application for such permission. Congress has not prohibited such action. But at the stage of struggle, I felt I could not do so without compromising the prestige of the Congress when an application was expected to be obtained at the point of the bayonet. It was the crux of the whole question. All other points were more or fewer matters of detail. It was easy enough for anyone to see that the struggle at that stage was crystallised and was concentrated mainly on one issue, viz. the determination to put down with all the resources of the Government what they called open defiance of lawful authority on one side and an equal determination of the people to maintain their right with all the sufferings and sacrifices that it may involve to offer civil disobedience against arbitrary and unjustifiable use of authority on the other side. In the intimation given to the District Superintendent of Police of my proposed plan of action against his order on the 18th, there was nothing by which it could be interpreted as an application. On the contrary, the copy of the program indicated that it was intended to test the newly issued order. In any case, I do not doubt that I would have failed in my duty if I had not given intimation of such an unusual change in the program in all its aspects especially when such a change was made for the first time since the commencement, and which is not for me to explain, amply justifies the need or such intimation.

If, however, that intimation or the details in the program regarding the conduct of the procession were considered convenient enough for retiring from an inconvenient battle, I should be happy to think that without sacrificing anything I also relieved to some extent the embarrassment of the Government and made it possible for them to retire with honour. But I repeat that no application has been put in nor has any permission or license been obtained....

It is not my desire to express any opinion whether the Council proceedings have helped or hindered me, as it is likely to be misunderstood. It is enough to say that the police order was issued after the Council Resolution and no effect was given to any of them till the end of the struggle; but as soon as the struggle ended all the under-trial prisoners were discharged. Let there be no delusion that a Government that claims to know its business best and recognizes nothing but the force, either moral or physical, can ever understand gratuitous advice, even if such advice assumes the dignified name of a Council Resolution. All such attempts afford opportunities for unfair and even mean attacks on those who are not there to defend themselves. Such resolutions can only serve the purpose of their convenient use at a suitable time for a suitable purpose if the matter is disposed of independently of them.

The Government was in honour bound to release all the prisoners in jail after the procession was allowed to pass and I thank the Government of the Central Provinces for acting honourably. I regret to find that seven out of a thousand prisoners released here have yet been detained for some offenses against jail discipline. I trust however that they will also be released soon. Even the little delay that has taken place is I do not doubt due to circumstances beyond the Government's control. I am glad that my brother who followed me in conducting the struggle almost up to the end, agrees with me entirely in this particular case, about the futility of those resolutions, though I must say, on different grounds. It is well known to all that we stand poles apart in our political convictions. But we both go back from Nagpur more or less confirmed in our political convictions.

I welcome you all who have returned from your self-imposed seclusion back again in our midst, where you will find ample opportunities for much higher sacrifice in greater struggle awaiting you. With your return amongst us today I stand on stronger grounds to reaffirm with greater emphasis what I had said on the last occasion that the Nagpur Flag Satyagraha struggle has ended in the vindication of the honour of our National Flag, the restoration of our right to take peaceful and orderly processions on public roads and in the complete triumph of truth, non-violence, and suffering.

But there is nothing to boast of in our achievement. Victory does not lie in what we have achieved, nor even in what we have suffered but, in our readiness, to suffer more and more till we achieve our final goal. Believe me when I say that the credit of our struggle is not due to me in the least degree but to all of you who have suffered and many others who were ready to suffer for the cause and to the indefatigable energy and the admirable sense of discipline which the Nagpur Congress Committee has shown throughout the conduct of the struggle.

I cannot close this statement without placing before the public as well as the Government one important fact which has come to my knowledge whilst I was trying to trace the source of all the mischievous reports that were circulated in the press about the happenings of the 18th. I came across a curious piece of evidence, which probably also accounts for the famous four letters appearing in the Times of India in the last week of June, after the arrest of Seth Jamnalal Bajaj and his co-workers, as also for the general attitude of that journal towards this movement throughout. The report of the correspondent of the Times of India of the same date appearing in the issue of the 20th of August under the heading 'Government authority recognised' happens to be a verbatim copy of the Commissioner's message appearing in the Statesman. Reading the two together it is difficult to make out whether the correspondent of the Times of India is the Commissioner of Nagpur or the Commissioner of Nagpur is the correspondent of the Times of India. It is possible that the inadvertence of the Statesman unlike its Bombay contemporary in publishing it as the message from the Commissioner of Nagpur instead of 'from its correspondent' has exposed him. For some time I did not believe that the statement was issued by him. On inquiry, I found that he had done so. I have been assured however that the Commissioner of Nagpur was not authorised to issue the statement that has been wired by him to the Statesman. Besides I have also found that the Government of the Central Provinces is unable to control the journalistic activities of the Commissioner. On a former occasion also he had brought the government into trouble by his activities in this direction in connection with this very movement, despite the order not to meddle with the affairs of the Government. In such a manner he goes his own way. Whilst I readily acknowledged the genuine desire of the Government for an honourable end of the struggle and whilst I do not doubt that his action is regretted, I feel bound to say that the Government cannot escape the responsibility of his action in the end.

We have to thank God that at a time when personal prejudices, party politics, and communal strife subordinated mutual tolerance, wider political vision, and higher common interest, and when forces of doubt and despair were getting the upper hand, He blessed us with this humble opportunity of demonstrating the undercurrents of solidarity, strength and the soundness of heart of the nation and despite all misunderstanding of friends and misrepresentations by foes, this neat, clean and courageous display of moral warfare will in future be remembered by the nation with pride, and will inspire greater faith in the superiority of weapons of truth, non-violence and suffering, which alone, as Mahatma Gandhi has said, are suited to the conditions and the culture of the nation. Vande Mataram.

3 September 1923

GREATNESS LIES IN GETTING BEATEN FOR THE SAKE OF DUTY*

...We must decide whether we should pay the fine. I want your opinion. If you do not want to pay the fine, you should know the reason behind it. If you are not willing to pay the fine for the petty reason of saving

*The Borsad Satyagraha began to protest a punitive tax imposed by the government on the villages of the taluka accusing them of sheltering outlaws. The tax was required to maintain an additional police force.

Rupees two and a half, there is no point in starting the fight. If you believe that we are not companions of the outlaws and even an almighty Government does not have the right to say this to us, only then we can begin the fight. Let the Government attach our goods worth Rs. Ten instead of Rs. Two. It is better to be robbed by outlaws than to pay Rs. Two and a half to the Government, which labels us as an accomplice of the outlaws. 'We are honest, respectable people. We shall not write the confession letter that we are an accomplice of the outlaws, just to save ourselves from the harassment of the outlaws. If you want to extract money from us, do it the way the outlaws do.' Take up the fight only if you have this understanding. This is the path of Mahatmaji. He has taught us to abandon falsehood, theft, immorality, and wickedness and to take the path of truth fearlessly. Let me remind you of one more thing. The people from the Government side as well as your enemies will try to mislead and instigate you during the fight. But you would not become violent. There is no space for a long-handled scythe or a stick in Mahatmaji's fight. Our back is enough. Let the Government thrash on our backs. If you abuse or attack the Government, it has many ways [to fight back]. It cannot arrest an outlaw but it will arrest you immediately for sure. There is no greatness in abusing or beating someone. Greatness lies in getting beaten for the sake of duty….

If you agree to these two points, let me ask all those who do not want to pay the tax to raise their hands. (All representatives raise their hands). Wisdom has no place against power. A soft ruler imposes the hardest punishments. Those who think they cannot fight against the Government and want to pay the tax, raise their hands. (No one opposed it).

A volunteer force

We have proof of the prestige of the additional police. The President of the Reception Committee has termed them as 'Grandfathers of Babar, the outlaw'…. We must deploy at least one volunteer in each village. I'm sure the village people will provide them with food. The people serving sweets to thousands of *bawa (fake ascetics)* will not hesitate in feeding the volunteers. Gandhiji's volunteer will not ask for anything more than salt and *Rotalo* (thick cake made by patting dough with hand, cooked on earthen utensil).... Our only prayer to God is that to protect us when we take the path of truth. Those who feel duty-bound to help the poor should give their names to Darbar Gopaldas. He will camp at Borsad till the fight continues. The leaders will always be present in the camp. The volunteers from the villages will inform them about the atrocities of the police.

I appeal to all the brothers present here that if you have helped the outlaws in any way till now, please resolve that it is wrong and the one who does it causes harassment to the entire community. The wrong must be abandoned to walk on the path of truth. The Baraiyas, Patanwadias, etc should not consume alcohol and convince others not to do it. I have been informed that the Government intends to shift the entire community from the Taluka. It is very bad if it happens. It is disgrace for the Taluka. The outlaws must be eliminated. But banishing the entire community for the crime of one should not happen in these times. You should reform and convince the wrong-doers that you cannot tolerate their harassment; that we can feed you if you just sit at home doing nothing, but abandon evil activities.

Borsad, 2 December 1923

OUR FIGHT IS NOT EVIL

...In a short span of one month, you offered heavy sacrifices and showed enormous courage, unity and enthusiasm. You could achieve your goal only when you did all these. It is not due to the skill of Darbarsaheb [Gopaldas], Pandyaji [Mohanlal], or mine. Today we have gained this victory because we walked along the road laid down for us by our *guru*, the great saint of the world who is in jail. We have merely paid back the interest of what we owe to him. We have to keep our heads low as long as we do not pay the debt. We have forgotten him. Else there would be no question of outlaws. Let us remember what we have forgotten, search for our weaknesses, and remove them.

Wind up amicably

...I gather you are celebrating the victory. It is fine. You celebrate but I advise you to also invite those who came for confiscation. Our fight is not evil. When the enemy rests his weapons, we should love them. Also, invite the police to participate in your celebration….

Land revenue

…This year there has been inadequate rainfall in the taluka. There is a difference of opinion between ourselves and the Government regarding the yield. The Government's estimate is made to collect as much land revenue as possible. Ours is made with a view to not paying it if possible. Therefore, there is a difference in our estimates. But if we do not pay this year, we shall have to pay it next year. We have only just concluded one struggle and it is not wise for us to start another so soon afterward, unless, of course, it is unavoidable. For the moment we would be well advised to concentrate our efforts on consolidating the gains of our successful struggle. Therefore, I advise you to pay your land revenue assessment following the Collector's orders. It is easy to accept advice that you approve of, but swaraj will be possible only if you are prepared to accept advice that you do not like….

Create pious atmosphere

First of all, thieves and dacoits cannot live among us. That does not mean we have to throw them out violently. There should be such a religious, pious atmosphere in our village that people doing such work shudder…. They should be led to the path of normal life. My appeal to the merchants is that you have borne the maximum brunt of the outlaws and if their activity continues, the situation will not change. You should take interest in such works that can prevent the loot. You should do business honestly and check the reason for anger in people. The police of government will not be able to protect you. It will come to take note of it only after the crime…. If you will not fear God and indulge in extracting money from the poor you will have to face the result….

Do not I know there are still many outlaws among you? They are not scared by the guns, but they are afraid of your unity…. If I were to meet an outlaw, this is all I would say to him, 'Living is futile for you. You may die by the bullet, you may be hanged, you will die just stumbling on your way, but you are going to die anyway. After all these sins, you should surrender at the police station or a Government bungalow and atone so that your sin gets a push backward.... There is bravery in hanging after confessing the crime. Hiding is cowardice.' If they meet you sometime, convey my message to them or arrange our meeting and I shall tell them....

The Congress work

...If the people of Borsad have understood the importance of the Satyagraha struggle, they should get themselves enrolled in Congress. Just like everyone above 16 years was liable for the government's fine, everyone above 18 years should register their name in Congress as a *swarajwadi* [believing in swaraj] and become eligible for swaraj. The annual fee is merely four annas and the amount of fee will be used locally in respective villages.... Secondly, you should not go to the police station for a complaint. If needed you can go to the Satyagraha Camp.... Those who have understood the essence of satyagraha would not need the court or the lawyers. If at all there is a dispute, get a panch [committee of five people] for securing justice. If they cannot resolve the matter, go to Satyagraha Camp.... When we have abandoned the government, why do we need its courts? People take the oath to say the truth there and still utter lie after lie. Why should we ditch our religion by going to such courts?...

Is the love true or momentary?

...You have shown love when we lead you in the fight against the Government. But your response in the fight with your limitations will determine whether your love for us was true or not. If you remain united, observe non-violence, and give up liquor, you will not need to fight with the Government. The Government is *maya* [illusion], it is a castle in the air, a bubble of water. It gets burst as soon as you identify it. But there are layers [of ignorance] on our eyes. So we can't identify it. That is the reason I tell you to use the brothers who are going to stay here.

Stop harassment

One last thing. Just as you were terrorized by harassment of the Government, your harassment invokes similar feelings in others. They find it hard. So do not misuse the power. I have come to know that twenty people in Asodar were ostracized from the village because they cooperated with the Government. This is wrong. It is oppression. Do not misuse the arrangement of village and caste. Those with weaknesses will grow better through our kindness. If we want them to be good, we should be better. If we will not be good, they will go to the Government. All are not equally powered. We should instill it in them.... If we become unjust, we cannot seek justice from others. Forgive those who have erred. Love them. If you do all these, we can start a Gujarat-wide big fight when the next land revenue is due. I pray to God to give you that strength.

Borsad, 12 January 1924

YOUR BATTLE IS BASED ON THE TRUTH*

...We have exhausted all other remedies. Now it would be in vain to expect that anyone will listen to us. We are left with only one option and it could be the last option for any people. That is might versus might. The Government has the might of power, arms, and brute force. You have got might of the truth. This is the fight between the two. If you are fully convinced that your side is true, the opposite side is unjust and if you feel deep within your heart that it is your duty to oppose the injustice, all the government power will be futile against it. They are takers. You are givers. If you do not give voluntarily, it is not going to happen. It is up to you to pay or not to pay. But if you decide not to accept the new assessment [of increased land revenue], not to pay a paisa, and let the government do whatever it can—attach or confiscate the land—the government will not be able to do it. It is not possible for any government. Even most oppressive regimes cannot survive when the people unite.... It is up to you. Do not decide based on my or anybody else's support. Do it only if you can fight on your own, you have the guts and willingness to sacrifice.

*Launched in February 1928, the Bardoli Satyagraha was a response to the unmitigated taxation of land by the colonial government. At a time when labourers and farmers were in dire financial straits, authorities attempted to raise taxes by 22 per cent. This satyagraha earned patel the nick name 'Sardar' and catapulted him to national prominence

...Higher the risks, the bigger the results. The work is equally tough and important. If you will bend on the application of the slightest pressure, it will be harmful not only for you but for the entire of India. Hence, decide with God as your witness so that later on nobody can point a finger towards you....

This is not about money. The real issue is here truth and self-respect. This government never listens to the farmers and you have to fight against it.... It is your dharma (duty) to oppose such a situation. You should confront in such a manner that whenever you have to answer to God, you can do it easily. Do fight but control your temperament, stay true firmly and observe restraint. The attachment officers will come, they will harass you and provide ample reasons to instigate you, will use foul language, and will attack your weaknesses. But you shall not deter. Observe non-violence. Tell them calmly, with restraint but firmly that they can do whatever they want to.... They can forcefully take things but we shall not give anything voluntarily. This is the basic thing. If you can do this, I do not doubt that you will get the desired result. Because your battle is based on the truth.

12 February 1928

SPEECH AT WANKANER

...If our sisters, mothers, and women do not come forward, we shall not be able to move ahead. Tomorrow there will be confiscations.... If we do not keep the women abreast of the ongoing fight...what will they do? During Kheda Satyagraha, I have seen the shock of women when the cattle were taken away. Cultivate your women for the fight....

...I have not seen a single confiscation officer who would take home the confiscated vessels himself. The government officials are lame. The Patel, the village headman, the labourer, and the revenue clerk should not help the government and tell that their prestige is not different from the village's prestige. What would they do with their leadership once their village's prestige is gone.... We should create such an atmosphere in the taluka that it smells of swaraj and not slavery....

...Throw your personal as well as village quarrels into the well for the time being. If you wish, you can fight them out later.... You are in charge of Gujarat's prestige today. Take care of it.... Some are afraid of confiscation of their lands. What is confiscation after all? Will they take the land to Surat? England? Whatever they do with the land, it is only on paper, in government documents. If you are united, you must ensure that no one else tills your land....

The fight has begun. Think of the villages as military encampments. Details from villages must reach taluka headquarters and the orders from there must reach and must be implemented in the villages. Our preparedness is the key to our victory. The government has a revenue clerk or a headsman in a village. We have got an entire village on our side.

12 February 1928

I WANT TO INOCULATE YOU WITH FEARLESSNESS

I see that these 15 days have taught you to cast off fear in your hearts. You are however not yet completely free from it. Two annas in the rupee are still there. Shake it off. Why need you fear? If anything, Government has cause to fear. No civilized Government can govern without the consent of the governed. At present moment they govern because your eyes are blindfolded, you are deluded into the belief that they are keeping you in peace and prosperity. It is not a reign of peace but a reign of fear. You have lost the capacity of righteous indignation against wrong. The absence of it is cowardice. ...It is your quiescence that has been your undoing. I want to inoculate you with fearlessness. I want to galvanize you into life. I miss in your eyes the flash of indignation against wrong.

1928

THE GNAT NEED NOT FEAR THE ELEPHANT

Government has been like a wild elephant run amok. It thinks that it can trample anything and everything under its feet. Even so thinks the mad elephant [riding itself on having trampled in the pat even lions and tigers to death, and scorning the little gnat defying him. I am teaching the little gnat today to let the elephant go on in his mad career, and then get into his trunk at the opportune moment. The gnat need not fear the elephant. The elephant can never trample it to death, but the gnat can certainly prove formidable to the elephant.

What is a little potsherd before a big pot? But it need not fear the pot, for a sherd can break the pot to pieces, but the pot cannot break the sherd….

Orgam, March 1928

BE PREPARED TO DIE FOR SELF-RESPECT

Initially, some of the people told me it was better to rise earlier in the morning and work for two more hours rather than entering such a quarrel and taking a risk. What would such people do by remaining alive in this world? They are better reborn as ox rather than living a life of an ox. I want the people of Gujarat to be spirited. No one should be able to say that a Gujarati with a weak and wicked business mentality can do nothing. Gujaratis can be brave like any other people. The only thing is he should learn to die for dignity. I tell you Gujaratis, you may be weak physically, but your willpower must be strong like that of a lion or a tiger. Be prepared to die for self-respect….

Sarbhon, March 1928

OUR FIGHT IS AGAINST THE BIGWIGS

I heard that the newly appointed Christian confiscation officer [in charge of property seizure on behalf of colonial government] is not getting the grocery from the village. I advise against it. The officer is not our enemy. The poor fellow has come as an obedient servant. He must not have the daring to disobey the order and leave the service…. To keep someone deprived of necessities like milk, vegetable, or from services of the washerman, the barber is not satyagraha…. It is cruelty. He should not be assisted in any confiscation-related work. The help of a cart, labourers, or *panch* [five persons required for endorsing the list of confiscated things] should be refused. He should be told clearly that we have nothing against him personally whether you are a Christian or a Hindu or a Muslim. All government servants are equal for us…. Our fight is against the bigwigs, not with such poor servants. Our power lies in suffering gracefully. It is a weakness of the government that prompts her to take the help of the police and try to oppress the people by using the revenue department.... Fighting against a starving army is not a *dharmayuddha* [battle of principles]. I advise Kadod to change the rules if they have already made any such rules against the officers.

Kadod, April 1928

MAINTAIN YOUR CALM

The Government has lost its cool this time. Let the iron turn hot. The hammer must remain cold. If it gets hot, it would burn its handle. You maintain your calm. Which hot iron does not cool down ultimately? No government can maintain its heat on the people. It must cool down. The people should be prepared enough....

April 1928

I DO NOT WANT TO REST

You urge me to take a rest, but I do not want to rest. I have to be with you day and night as long as I am free. You might not know but I am fully aware of the ghosts following you. They can seize your control and push you to madness. I must protect you [from such ghosts]. To remain awake all the time is the duty of a person who has claimed to be the guard of the taluka.... I must remain awake and keep you constantly awake too.

1928

ALL OF US ARE DISCIPLES OF THE SAME GURU

There are numerous people in unknown corners of the land following the principles of truth and *ahimsa* in a better manner than any one of us. But publicity is not their lot. We have the misfortune to be in the limelight instead. It is presumptuous for me to talk ahimsa. It is as though a man sitting at the foot of the Himalayas were to talk of reaching Mount Everest. I can only claim however that though I am no better than that man, I may be better than he who talks of reaching Mount Everest whilst he is quietly sitting at Cape Comorin. If the little that I have learned at Gandhiji's feet and placed before you can infuse in you a new hope and a new aspiration, I do not know what a tremendous achievement we would make if I was fully saturated with the principles of truth and *ahimsa*. I accidentally happen to be in the position of your Sardar but I would have been able to achieve nothing without my loyal comrades. Truly speaking any one of us may be a Sardar and anyone a soldier. Let us remember that all of us are the disciples of the same *guru*. All the praise and congratulations are due to him.

August 1928

WHAT WILL HAPPEN WHEN GANDHIJI IS GONE?

The citizens of Ahmedabad in giving me this address have described me as the chief disciple of Gandhiji. I only wish that I deserved that description; I know, however, that I am not worthy of it. I do not know how often I shall have to be reborn to achieve that distinction. Truly you have been so carried away by your affection for me, and have used such exaggerated expressions about me that I can scarcely accept them. …Far from being his chief disciple, I doubt if I am fit even to rank among one of his many disciples. If I had that fitness, I would have accomplished today what you hope I shall accomplish in the future. I am confident that there exist today in India many disciples of his who have never even seen him but who have completely mastered his teachings. People often say, what will happen when Gandhiji has gone? I have no fear of that account. He will have accomplished by then whatever he has sought to accomplish. What remains will be for you and for me to achieve. Only if we do so, he will have no regret. He has given us whatever he had to give, and it is up to us to do our duty.

I do not deserve the honour that you are giving me because of Bardoli. The condition of the peasants of India is akin to that of a bedridden patient suffering from an incurable disease, waiting only, as it were, to depart from this world and is suddenly restored to life by taking some miracle medicine given to him by a *Sanyasi*. I am merely the instrument through whose hands the Sanyasi administered the medicine to the patient. If anyone deserves honour, it is the giver of that medicine. Some honour is also due to the patient who carried out the strict injunctions of the Sanyasi, for, without the self-control that he exercised, the medicine could not have achieved its effect. If anyone else deserves to be honoured, it is my colleagues who showed astonishing discipline, and who had complete confidence in me. It was not I who trained such colleagues. If we have such men whom the whole of Gujarat is so justly proud, the credit goes again to Gandhiji. Thus, if the praise written in your address is duly distributed, all I would be left with is the plain paper.

Ahmedabad, August 1928

SECTION II

THE PARTY STRATEGIST

DISCIPLINARY ACTION

There seems to be in certain quarters some misunderstanding in regard to the Working Committee's resolution on disciplinary action.

The first part of the resolution lays down, firstly, that all Congressmen are expected to carry out the Congress programme and policies and secondly, that those Congressmen who are also office-bearers and members of the executives are in honour bound to carry out the programmes and policies.

The second part of the resolution refers to disciplinary action, which under the resolution may be taken only against office-bearers and members of the executives.

This disciplinary action is not to be taken if an office-bearer or member of the Executive merely cannot owing to conscientious objections, support the Congress programme and policies.

Disciplinary action is to be taken only when an office-bearer or member of the Executive goes further and carries on propaganda or acts against the programme and policies.

The question of disciplinary action, therefore, does not arise where an office-bearer or member of the executive, finding himself in disagreement for instance with the decisions of the Working Committee in regard to elections to the Legislatures, simply refrains from assisting in the election campaign, but it must arise when he goes beyond this.

11 August 1934

ADOPTING THE CONGRESS NAME

Pandit Malaviya holds that the new party [Nationalist Party] has better claim to use the designation of the Congress as part of its name than the Congress Parliamentary Board and further, that the association of Congressmen, who accept the Congress creed but differ with the Working Committee or even the Congress itself, on any particular point have the right to describe the party as the 'Congress Nationalist Party', as had been established by the precedent of the Congress

Khilafat Swarajya Party formed in 1923 by late Sjt. C.R. Das and late Pandit Motilal Nehru.

I must respectfully disagree with Malaviyaji.

The name, which the founders of the latter party popularised to use was the Swarajya Party. In my opinion it is not proper to use the Congress name without the Congress authority. If every differing group of members within the organisation, while publicly fighting with the organisation, attaches its name to its own party public mind cannot but be confused.

The new party may be called the Nationalist Party of the Congressmen, if its composition supports, and is strictly confined to Congressmen. But without the authority of the Congress being duly received, it cannot with propriety be called the 'Congress Nationalist Party' especially when it is formed deliberately to propagate a policy in direct contradiction to the official policy of the Congress.

The adoption of the Congress name cannot but confuse the popular mind; and I would respectfully urge Malaviyaji to reconsider the position and adopt another name to his Party which he had a perfect right to form for the education of the Congressmen and others.

26 August 1934

I AM NOT AFRAID OF MY OPPONENTS

You know that during the early days of the Khilafat movement in 1921, the Indian National Congress had decided to boycott the assemblies. The students had been asked to leave schools and colleges, those in employment were asked to resign, the lawyers were asked to stop practising law and the members of the assemblies had been asked to resign their seats. Nobody should be under the impression that we had taken that decision because of some wrong notions. This was the correct decision and it has shown excellent results....

When we boycotted the assemblies some others joined them and they helped the Government to crush our struggle. They helped in issue of orders which led to a wave of hatred against them throughout the country. These people say that we did wrong by deciding to boycott the assemblies.... During a short period of ten to fifteen years we have achieved much. The Government has come to realise that the people have got the right type of weapon to fight the authorities. That is why the Government found a new way to deflect us from our true course. It has promulgated a new constitution. This law brought forward with the object of putting the Indians in their right place has been enacted with the specific purpose i.e., to crush our national aspirations…. The Government is convinced that the country is unified and does not need any weapon other than non-cooperation. The Government are now trying to destroy that unity.

The Government first divided us and then it tried to see that three crores of people get the right of voting. The elections are being held for the purpose of our being able to show the world whether we vote for slavery or emancipation. This is the first time that we have got this franchise. If the Government can show through some stratagem that the people are not with the Indian National Congress it would have achieved its purpose. If we are unable to get in touch with those three crores who are going to vote, no amount of contacting the people at large would be of any help. This is a clever move on the part of the Government. It is possible that when we go to the assemblies we find that we have no powers and that all sorts of hurdles are being placed in our path. But if we do not use this franchise properly, the Government would announce to the world at large that the people are with it. If these three crores of voters refuse to cooperate, however it would be a different thing. People would go to cast their votes and we should see to it that they vote for independence and not for the continuation of slavery. Every vote cast against the Congress would be a vote against the struggle for independence.

The resolution to try to capture the assemblies had been passed at the Lucknow Session of the Indian National Congress with near unanimity. The only thing on which there was difference of opinion was whether we should accept offices of ministers or not. This question has created more worries in the South than in the North because one party [Justice Party] is in power there for the past 15 years. That party has angered you to such an extent that you want to wreak vengeance and want to harass it. But, our ideal is much higher and nobler than that. …We have decided to join the assemblies with a much nobler objective. Forget that party, therefore, and do not bother about it. After all, they are our brother Indians. We can afford to be liberal towards them. They are ashamed on their past behaviour…. Use your vote properly and do your duty in the right manner. If you do that, you need not worry about those people.

We should, for the present, concentrate all our strength on getting more and more seats in the coming elections. I like to consider the immediate steps that need to be taken. A pragmatic man will think of his duty today and would not consider what is to be done tomorrow. If you worry about today, tomorrow will automatically take care of itself. That is why all your strength and influence must be used for the achievement of this immediate objective, i.e., the victory of the Congress in the elections. If you are able to do this, there would be sufficient time to consider whether we should form ministries or not.

Only two months are left for the elections to be held. We should create public opinion during this brief period so that people are discouraged from contesting elections against the Congress candidates. If some people are prepared to spend in the hope that they can defeat Congress candidates, let them do so. They can distribute their money if they so wish. I say that nobody would be elected because money has been spent. The ballot boxes have to be filled with ballot papers and not with coins or currency notes.

This is not an easy job. It would need money and patience. The Congress is an organisation of the poor and most of its workers have during the last decade and a half sacrificed everything that they had. Some people are very eager to go to the assemblies, but there are others who are unwilling and they have been forced to stand as candidates. You must give contributions for such persons. If we do not make arrangements to take the voters to the polling stations and if the election campaign is not properly handled, we would not be able to succeed, however great our desire for winning the elections might be. It is futile to expect that the voters would go on their own and cast their votes in your favour. The reason is that the voters have not yet been properly educated about their duties. We have yet to make the institutions in our country which will handle such things.

I am not afraid of my opponents. I am not afraid of this powerful Government either. But I am afraid of the weaknesses of the party. If we do not act as the occasion demands and we do not give preference to the needs of the nation and forget our personal ambitions, our organisation would get a bad name for all times to come and it would lose its prestige....

I have had some experiences as Chairman of the Congress Parliamentary Board. I have found some Congressmen who feel neglected if they are not chosen as candidates for the elections. Some of them feel that it is their hereditary right to be elected to represent the Congress in the assemblies. Others feel that if they are not given the Congress ticket they get the right to raise the banner of revolt against the party. Let me tell you that the Congress does not depend for its existence on the sweet will of the people but that its strength lies in the fact that all the workers of the party should follow the orders of the party and implement its resolutions with vigour. Those who do not have any sense of discipline have no right to go to the assemblies as the representatives of the Congress. Those who lack the spirit of sacrifice and those who do not prefer the collective interest of the people of India to their own personal interest have no right to adorn the assemblies either. If we cannot show a high order of sense of sacrifice we cannot do justice either to India or to its people who vote for us.

...We can postpone other things but if we are remiss on this occasion and do not do our duty, we would have to face great difficulties in our struggle when the elections take place five years hence. If other people enter the assemblies, the struggle for independence would not cease. But, we should remember that in that case our struggle will become harder. It is our duty to ensure the success of Congress candidates so that the hurdles placed in our path are removed.

Madras, 26 September 1936

THE CONGRESS PRESIDENT HAS NO DICTATORIAL POWERS

I see that nominations for the annual honour in the hands of delegates to the Congress include my name also. Pandit Jawaharlal Nehru has since issued a statement setting forth his views. I have read it with the care such a pronouncement deserves, and after consultations with friends I have come to the conclusion that I must withdraw from the contest. It seems to some of us that at this critical juncture in the history of the Congress or the nation which the Congress has represented for an unbroken period of 50 years, unanimous election is most desirable.

My withdrawal should not be taken to mean that I endorse all the views Pandit Jawaharlal stands for. Indeed Congressmen know that on some vital matters my views are in conflict with those held by Pandit Jawaharlal. For instance, I do not believe in inevitability of class war. Whilst I detest Imperialism and admit destructive inequality between the capitalist class and the famishing poor I do believe it is possible to purge capitalism of its hideousness.

...There is no difficulty in my subscribing to the doctrine that all land and all wealth belong to all. Being a farmer myself and having identified myself with the peasantry for years, I know where the shoe pinches, but I know that nothing can be done except through the power of the people. Fortunately we have learnt what non-violent non-co-operation can do. When people learn the art of withdrawing their co-operation from the forces of evil it will perish for want of nourishment.

However, as Pandit Jawaharlal stresses, and rightly too, our present purpose is to free India from foreign subjection and thus destroy imperialistic exploitation root and branch. When we have attained this it will be time to enforce our theories and plans. For the present there should not be divided counsel but perfect co-operation between all forces that are to be found in the vast national organisation of ours.

One thing, however, is the immediate issue—the parliamentary programme and its implications. There is again no difference of opinion about the objective. All of us want to destroy the imposed constitution. How to destroy it from within the legislatures is the question. It will depend upon the resources and resourcefulness of those men and women who enter the legislatures under the Congress banner....

The question of office holding is not a live issue today, but I can visualise an occasion when taking office may be desirable to achieve the common purpose. There may then be a sharp division of opinion between Pandit Jawaharlal and myself or rather among Congressmen.

We know Pandit Jawaharlal to be too loyal to the Congress to disregard the decision of the majority, assuming that the majority lays down a policy repugnant to him. I am no more wedded to the parliamentary programme than to acceptance of office. I only want to say that we may in the course of events be driven to such acceptance but it shall never be at the loss of self-respect or a compromise of our objective.

The Congress President has no dictatorial powers. He is the chairman of the well-built organisation. He regulates proceedings and carries out the decisions of the Congress as they may be arrived at from time to time. The Congress does not part with its ample powers by electing any individual, no matter who he is. I therefore ask the delegates to choose Pandit Jawaharlal as being the best person to represent the nation and regulate and guide in the right channel the different forces that are at work in the country.

28 November 1936

A LETTER TO SUBHAS BOSE

My Dear Subhas,

Immediately after your election there was a report in the Press that we had all resigned from the Working Committee and the A.P. representative inquired from me at Bardoli. I asked him to contradict the report at that time.

Since then I got a wire from Maulana Saheb [Maulana Azad] suggesting that we should all resign. I thought that our resignation immediately after your election would be misunderstood and may perhaps cause embarrassment to you. Rajenbabu [Rajendra Prasad] has now written to me that it would be helpful to you if we resigned at this stage and supports his suggestion by arguments which have appealed to me as reasonable.

According to our constitution the outgoing Working Committee frames the programme for the Subjects Committee. It would be unfair to you to continue in the Working Committee till the last moment as such a procedure would embarrass you in framing your own programme for the next year. It is due to you that you should be left free to frame your own programme.

We are all now prepared to resign as soon as you intimate to me that it would not create any difficulty for you. If it is your desire that we should wait a little while more, we shall abide by your wishes, but so far as we are concerned, we are ready to resign as soon as it suits your convenience.

Kindly intimate to me your wishes in the matter by wire.

Yours sincerely,
Vallabhbhai

7 February 1939

A LETTER TO JAWAHARLAL NEHRU

My Dear Jawahar,

I got your last letter at Bardoli in reply to my request to you to sign that joint statement or to issue an independent one. I made that suggestion to you at the instance of Bapu. I showed your reply to him and he asked me to write to you what I felt about it. He himself was displeased with that letter, but I did not think it worthwhile to trouble you anymore. The joint statement was also issued at his instance. In fact, I told him that this will be one more pretext to hurl abuses against me, but he insisted and I obeyed him. Maulana withdrew at the last moment.

I am glad indeed that we are defeated. No effective work is possible without a homogeneous Working Committee and I have always prayed for such an opportunity.

What I hate most is the method adopted to achieve that end by those who claim to be Leftist and still more by the President (Subhas Chandra Bose) who charged us with having entered into a conspiracy with the British Government and also having provisionally formed a federation Cabinet. Our enemies have also given credit for our honesty, but not our President (Subhas Chandra Bose). In any case we are no longer in doubt of what we have to do and I have written to Subhas

(President) that we are ready to go out at his convenience. Jivat [Kripalani] will show you a copy of that letter which I have sent him yesterday.

I do not know your mind, but I do hope that at least you will not blame us for what we propose to do.

I think it is my lot to be abused. Bengal press is furious and they blame me for Nariman and Khare episode, although all my colleagues were jointly responsible for these actions. In fact, in Dr. Khare's matter Subhas was present from the beginning to the end and it was he who had handled the whole thing.

Yours Sincerely,
Vallabhbhai Patel

Bombay, 8 February 1939

A LETTER TO ACHARYA NARENDRA DEVA

Dear Mr Narendra Deva,

On the 21st instant when we met here in connection with the Working Committee meeting, Babu Rajendra Prasad showed me your statement which you had issued in support of Subhas Babu's election in reply to a statement issued by us opposing him. I had not seen your statement before. In that statement you have criticised me alleging that in 1929 when Pt. Jawaharlal Nehru was elected as President of the Lahore Congress, I had contested the election against Gandhiji and when Gandhiji withdrew from the contest, he found some difficulty in persuading me to withdraw. All this story is wholly unfounded. This was all news to me and I was surprised. I do not know who gave you this information. Your statement was also shown to Jawaharlal and Gandhiji. They were both equally surprised and Gandhiji asked me to write to you about it. I am writing this just to inform you that there is no truth in the allegation that has been made by you against me. You can ask Jawaharlal or Gandhiji about it if you have any doubt.

I am given to understand that both you and Jaiprakash harbour some bitter feelings against me personally. I assure you, I am not conscious of having given any cause to either of you for entertaining any such feelings. No doubt, politically we differ strongly, but you are the last man to resent such differences. It is just possible that having no personal contact you may have been misinformed as you have been about the Lahore Presidential election contest and you have formed your opinion about me on unfounded reports which you may have believed to be true. I shall be thankful to you if you will point out to me any instance in which I have given you any cause for such personal dislike or prejudice.

Yours sincerely,
Vallabhbhai

Wardha, 25 February 1939

A LETTER TO B. G. KHER

My Dear Bala Saheb,

In the copies of letter I find that the one which has come from Pt. Jawaharlal is rather difficult for you to answer and you must give a careful reply. If the stand that he has taken in the letter that the communist party stands for violence is far from correct is to be rebutted, you will require good evidence for that. Evidently his letter is written with a view to raise public controversy. You will not be able to prove the charge of violence unless you have evidence other than confidential C.I.D. reports. We cannot quote such report as evidence against our own people; when we have ourselves in the past condemned such a process when it was so used against us. It is also equally true that without any good evidence that the party stands for violence you cannot oppose removal of ban against the party. If it is the considered view of your government that the party as such stands for violence then you must be prepared to justify your attitude by reliable evidence and then take a firm stand on it. But if you have no such evidence or the evidence is not sufficient it would not be wise to oppose the ban on mere ground of suspicion. It appears that in the provinces the communists are functioning without let or hindrance. What difference would it make if they are allowed to function openly? It is a point worth considering; whether it would not be better to let that organisation function openly instead of a nominal ban which is not at all effective and which puts you in an embarrassing position.

In any case please send me a copy of your reply and send it as early as possible I have read the other copies of letters from the President. They are also intended for propaganda and it is better that you should send your reply soon. You may also send a copy of the same to me.

Yours sincerely,
Vallabhbhai

10 April 1939

A LETTER TO SUBHAS CHANDRA BOSE

My Dear Subhas,

...I am glad you have been able to return home and hope that you will not endanger your health again by putting yourself prematurely under undue strain. As I am writing this to you, I cannot refrain myself from telling you that Sarat's [Sarat Chandra Bose's] letter to Bapu immediately after Tripuri [Congress Session] had terribly distressed me, but when I saw that you also shared the sentiments contained in his letter my grief knew no bounds.* I can only say that you have been so wholly misinformed that you have done me great injustice for which I was not prepared in the least. You did not even care to hear me before attributing such mean and despicable conduct to me. We may differ in our outlook on matters of public importance, but why should there be anything personal amongst comrades who have no other ambition in life except working for the freedom of motherland.

I shall not say anything here about the venomous and vulgar campaign that is being carried on against Bapu and myself in Tripuri in a section of the Bengal press particularly the *Hindustan Standard*.

Yours sincerely,
Vallabhbhai Patel

24 April 1939

*Sarat Chandra Bose accused the old members of Working Committee, including Patel, of carrying malicious and vindictive propaganda against Subhash Chadara Bose, the president, suggesting that his illness was fake. The other charge was that of obstruction during a Congress session. (*The Collected Works of Sardar Patel Vol. 8*, p. 79.)

A LETTER TO RAJENDRA PRASAD

My Dear Rajendra Babu,

I have received your circular letter of the 11 July. I agree with you that we cannot decide this question finally in the absence of Mahatmaji and Jawaharlal. Both of them will be returning back from their respective places in the first week of August and we can keep the Working Committee meeting at the time of their returning. I am, however, strongly of the opinion that a prompt and clear indication of our attitude is necessary to prevent the rot: In August when we meet we can take no action against him [Subhas Chandra Bose], unless we finish the preliminaries beforehand. I would therefore suggest that a notice asking Subhas Babu to explain about his conduct in organising a country-wide agitation and a revolt against the decisions of the A.I.C.C. which he as the President of the Bengal Provincial Congress Committee is bound to respect and execute. So far as the Bengal Provincial Executive is concerned, it would be better to give notice to it as well. They had also disregarded your advice and committed a flagrant breach of discipline. Let them send their explanation and we shall consider the question of action to be taken in the next meeting. Any weakness on our part at this stage is bound to spread indiscipline and weaken our organisation. You must have seen Subhas Babu's statement on the prohibition policy of the Bombay Government. He has done worse than what our enemies could do. He is now issuing another statement in reply to Mahatmaji's statement....

Yours sincerely,
Vallabhbhai

12 July 1939

GANDHIJI DOES NOT WISH THAT WE FOLLOW HIM BLINDLY

You must have read Bapu's article in which he says that Sardar is sure to return but I have gone nowhere. I have given my opinion in the Working Committee as a representative of Gujarat and outside as my diagnosis about our country.

I have told Gandhiji that if he orders me to follow him, I have so much faith in him that I will run with closed eyes. But he says you follow this path not because I ask you to tread on the path, but if you are convinced that this path is good. If I can walk with him, I will be most happy but how can I say that I understand clearly what I am not able to comprehend, neither I nor anybody should cheat him....

When we met in Malikanda [Bengal], I had said that in present circumstances, it is not possible to practise non-violence perfectly. Our energy is limited. There is a difference of opinion between us and Gandhiji regarding the measure of strength of the country. It is not a question of a single individual. An individual can climb very high but here is the question of carrying the whole institution, whole country with us.

I do not think that we can administer without using necessary violence against the persons who commit atrocities on the society.

There is no place for arguments now neither there is time for discussion on principles. All of you must think whether people desire violence when there is internal disorder and external invasion.

We have seen with our own eyes that violence is non-effective at the end. They prepared Maginot Line as big as Himalaya and believed that not even pin can penetrate it. But it was pierced by violence.

Bapu appealed to the Britishers but only he can do it, I and you cannot. Even today he has many friends in England. Even Viceroy, as a friend, invites him for a friendly discussion. He would not call us. Many Englishmen have been hurt by Bapu's appeal. When there is such an exhibition of the futility of violence yet Englishmen would not think otherwise. We could not say that they are weak. Our non-violence is non-violence of the weak. Today we cannot go forward. We are unable to shoulder the burden of the security and defence of the country by remaining non-violent. That is the meaning of the resolution of the Working Committee. It does not mean that Congress has given up the principle of non-violence. It simply means we cannot go forward on that path. Since last two years Bapu writes that there is an atmosphere of violence in the Congress and the country. There is filth, and rot. If we think we will be able to find mutual faith which was there formerly is evaporating.

Bapu demanded that he must have the full liberty and scope of performing his experiments. That means he has left us. We told him that if we are not able to walk fast with him, we should not be a burden on him.

Today we have to decide that if we are getting independence and unrestricted power, shall we be in a position to rule without [an] army? If we get power shall we disband the army? If we say so, they won't transfer power to us. Mostly Muslims are against it. Those Muslims who are outside the Congress are in love with violence. If we postpone taking nonviolence to a bigger arena for a short time does not mean that there will be any change in the pledge of non-violence taken by the Congress volunteers. Yet I don't want to argue with nor do I want to lessen your faith in non-violence. Outsiders were calling me a blind follower. I was saying that if that was so, I would have been proud of it, but I am not such a person. Today I say that if he leads, we will follow him but he says to us to keep our eyes open and follow our conscience.

We have left everything, and have plunged, and have kept on swimming and reached here. So, now why should we separate from you? But this is unprecedented situation. It is impossible that its echoes won't be heard in the country. In the past two or three weeks ten to twelve countries were vanquished.

Working Committee has passed an eight-line resolution. It does not criticize the Government, people or anybody. The language is not at all ambiguous. It means that if India is independent and England also is independent, we will help them.

If you think what Bapu says is proper, you pass a resolution accepting Bapu's proposal and put his proposal to practice. But don't betray him afterwards. Nobody should think that this is a question of loyalty towards Bapu. If you think that you will be able to practise non-violence which he expects from you, then pass a resolution to that effect. But Gandhiji does not wish that we should follow him blindly. We have to tell him clearly about our capacity. To tell that Congress possesses that thing which it actually does not possess, will not work, it is harmful. How can I teach non-violence to a coward? If I put light thing before him, he is able to understand but if I put heavy thing before him, he is scared. So, if we make him walk on the path of a commoner, he will be able to walk and go forward.

It is good that uptill now we made experiments in non-violence. But people are cowards and they are not able to walk further, from the place where they are slanting. What could be done about that? This is not the time to allow them to stand where they are. The time has come when we have to make a choice.

Those of you who are engaged in implementing constructive programme, and desire to cling to non-violence under any circumstances have a higher responsibility on their head. If you think that Congress is trekking on a wrong path, then under any circumstances you have to take over the burden. I will certainly hand over to you.

19 March 1940

LETTER TO MAULANA AZAD

My Dear Maulana Sahib,

…I had received a letter from Dr. Rajendra Prasad suggesting some sort of a settlement proposed by Dr. Syama Prasad Mookerjee. He must have written to you also about it. I have opposed the proposals very strongly and written to Dr. Rajendra Prasad that the Congress cannot afford to enter into any settlement with the Hindu Mahasabha, which has no chance of winning any seat anywhere in the whole country. It would compromise our position without any compensating advantage. I do not know what advice you have given to him.…

Yours Sincerely
Vallabhbhai Patel

Poona, 15 October 1945

LETTER TO MAULANA AZAD

My Dear Maulana Sahib,

…I have already sent a cheque for Rs. 50,000, but I am afraid we are wasting good money for nothing and Congress reputation will in the end suffer badly. I am enclosing herewith a Press cutting from which you will see what type of candidates are being put up by the Ahrar party in the Punjab for whom they want our help. From this cutting you will see that immediately the League candidates' nominations were declared invalid, the Ahrar candidates, who remained on the scene and whose nominations were declared valid, joined the Muslim League. It is very sad that such candidates are chosen to oppose the League. In any case it is very unwise that we should be mixed up with such a shady transaction. I would still request you to reconsider the whole position and withhold the help. May I again remind you that my information is that the Ahrars will get no place except one or two in the Punjab?

I am afraid we have mishandled the whole Punjab situation. We have to fight the Akalis as there has been no settlement as was expected and we will not get more than 5 or 6 seats after a good deal of expense which could be easily avoided.

Please excuse me for bringing these facts to your notice, but I have done so as I have been considerably oppressed by a feeling of failure in duty at a critical juncture in one of the most important provinces in these elections. I do not wish to blame anybody but I do feel that if we continue to handle affairs in the same fashion, we will suffer a serious defeat in spite of such huge expenditure and a good deal of time and energy being spent over it....

Yours Sincerely
Vallabhbhai Patel

Poona, 15 October 1945

LETTER TO JAWAHARLAL NEHRU

My Dear Jawaharlal,

...The selection of candidates for the election is a bad business. I have been flooded with applications, appeals, complaints, protests and recommendations from various quarters. It is a sad thing to see this mad competition for going into the Councils. We must discourage this. Most of these complaints are absolutely false. No selection is possible which would satisfy all. There are complaints from all provinces. You say that you cannot help feeling disturbed at some of the choices made or proposed in the Punjab, Bengal and Sind. I do not know whether you refer to the selections for the Central Assembly or for the provinces. So far as the Central Assembly is concerned no selections were made from Bengal till the date of your letter to me.... The Bengal selections have all been made by Maulana [Azad] himself. I have no knowledge about these selections. About Sind, there is only one seat in the Central Assembly, and the man selected has been returned unopposed. His was a unanimous recommendation.... About the provincial nominations I have not yet received any proposal....

Yours Sincerely
Vallabhbhai Patel

Poona, 4 November 1945

LETTER TO MAULANA AZAD

My Dear Maulana Sahib,

...You will please excuse me for my writing to you in English, but as I have very little time to write myself in Hindustani I am dictating this letter to economise time.

You may continue to write in Urdu without any hesitation.

When we met last in Bombay I had spoken to Dr. Gopichand, and perhaps to you also, that a budget of the required expenditure for the purposes of these elections in your province should be framed as early as possible and also the portion that the Centre is expected to contribute as well as the amount expected to be raised in the province and that this should be communicated to me as early as possible. I have got it now from you as also from Dr. Gopichand. But I see from Dr. Gopichand's letter that he has shifted the whole burden on me. You will agree that it is not fair. And if all the provinces were to throw the burden in its entirety on the Centre, it would be very difficult to meet such a demand. Reasonable efforts should therefore be made locally and the Centre would undoubtedly help whatever help is needed....

There may be a number of candidates who will be returned unopposed and they should be able to contribute to the local fund for election purposes. They should be asked to do so. Lahore is a fairly rich city and there are other cities also which can contribute. We will settle this matter when Dr. Gopichand comes to Bombay after the Central Assembly elections are over, in the meanwhile I will send you a substantial amount for immediate help as soon as I reach Bombay. It must be understood between us that no seats should be lost for want of money....

Yours Sincerely
Vallabhbhai Patel

Poona, 18 November 1945

LETTER TO V. V. GIRI

My dear Giri,

...All through this unfortunate controversy, I have advised consistently that the election of the leader rests with the party. We can only give advice and it is for the party to accept or reject it. If democracy chooses to go wrong, it has a right to do so. In this case, it has grievously erred in not coming to a decision long ago. I had written to all the leaders of the province to meet together and come to some unanimous decision. They failed to do so, because of cliques and parties, as also due to personal prejudices amongst themselves and there was no evidence of any wider vision for the common good of the province, much less of the country. I can understand their objection to Rajaji's leadership, but I cannot understand their failure to come to a decision in due time and thus expose the Congress organisation to the kind of attacks and criticism to which it has been subjected in [British] Parliament, the proceedings of which must have been seen by you all. This is the first instance in Congress history where responsible Congressmen have failed to respond to a reasonable appeal from the leaders. It is not Rajaji's leadership that was objected to, but what we disliked was the motives which influenced all to combine in that opposition....

Yours Sincerely
Vallabhbhai Patel

New Delhi, 20 April 1946

LETTER TO V. V. GIRI

My dear Giri,

...I know Shri N. M. Joshi since many years. He has done very good service to the cause of labour and the country in his own way. But I do not think the Congress can take the risk of taking him in the Constituent Assembly. You know he is an open advocate of Pakistan, which is a matter of vital principle with the Congress. He has always advocated acceptance of all the claims of the Muslim League without any question. He is able to accommodate himself with the Communists or perhaps he is a Communist, and therefore he had to leave the Servants of India Society. Amongst the Communists also there are many able men but a golden knife cannot be used for committing suicide.

Yours Sincerely
Vallabhbhai Patel

New Delhi, 7 July 1946

LETTER TO HAREKRISHNA MAHTAB

My Dear Mahtab

...You have referred to two matters in your letter.... The second one is in connection with the Hirakund Dam of the Mahanadi Valley project. About this I had seen your letter to Gandhiji and I had advised Shri Sarat Bose 1 to send Mr. Khosla, the engineer in charge of this scheme, to go and explain the whole project personally to him. I understand he is doing so. As soon as he has finished doing so, you will come to know of it and I shall attend to the matter.

In such big projects, a considerable amount of hardship is bound to entail on account of the displacement of villages involved in the scheme. The poor villagers do not easily understand the benefit of such schemes; they are concerned primarily with their own immediate inconveniences caused on account of their being dishoused and they are naturally unwilling to leave their own ancestral huts, however poor they may be. It is up to the Provincial Government concerned to make it easy for them to go elsewhere, where better accommodation can be provided for with good compensation and other facilities. Educative propaganda will have to be started on a wider scale.

Perhaps you are aware that in the Tata hydro-electric scheme of Bombay, when it was first undertaken, a similar situation arose, where in Mulsipeta a satyagraha was started by the peasants whose lands and houses were affected. Several people were sent to jail and this agitation was led by local Congress leaders.

The Congress has advanced much more since those days and it would be easy for us, now being in power, to control and guide the agitation in proper channels. Two of your members are, according to your letter, carrying on agitation against the dam. It should be open to you to take disciplinary action against them. They have no business to agitate outside. They are members of your party and they can only discuss such matters in the party. They are free to discuss this also in the Congress organisation. But the decisions of the party and the [Provincial] Congress Committee must be binding on them; and if they do not accept such decisions, they must resign their Assembly seats and go out. You have not given the names of these people—otherwise, I would have written to them....

Yours Sincerely
Vallabhbhai Patel

New Delhi, 11 September 1946

LETTER TO FAAZKIAN NEBAL SINGH

Dear Friend,

...Regarding the Bihar Congress refusing acceptance of the resignation of Sjt. John in favour of Prof. Abdul Bari. You have also threatened to go on hunger-strike for the exclusion of Prof. Bari from the Bihar Cabinet. I am not an expert in fasting and I do not understand its philosophy. But I think a few days' fast will improve your mental and physical balance and it would do you a lot of good. So apart from your grievance against the Bihar Congress, it would certainly be wise to go on fast for a few days.

Yours Sincerely
Vallabhbhai Patel

30 March 1947

LETTER TO RAJENDRA PRASAD

My Dear Rajenbabu

...Apart from considerations of merit and the requirements of the Congress at this critical juncture, my purpose in asking you to stand was to save ourselves from the embarrassment in which we are bound to find ourselves in the face of competing claims from our colleagues.* I cannot press you further. If your decision stands, then I am afraid we shall have to face the music.

But I feel that once you have decided to stand out, the best policy is not to take any part, direct or indirect, in favour of any candidate. They are all colleagues of ours. They must be all preparing their own ground for a contest. To ask any one of them to withdraw is likely to be misconstrued as preference for this or that man. I am sure you will appreciate that, when all of them are our colleagues, this sort of impression of discrimination would not be good.

Nor do I think that for such a great position of honour as that of the President of the Indian National Congress we should import any provincial or regional considerations. It should be left to the electorate to decide who among the competing candidates should have that distinction. It would be short-sighted either to assume or to encourage the idea that it would resolve itself into a struggle between the North and the South. As far as 1 know, we have never approached this most momentous problem from the point of provincial or regional considerations, and I do not see why we should anticipate that it would necessarily result in such approach or it would lead to a conflict between North and South.

You are probably not aware that another candidate has entered the list, i.e. Kripalani. I understand that he has written to Jawaharlal apologising for his conduct in criticising Government and taking an anti-Government stand before the AICC. I cannot vouchsafe for it, but that is what I have heard. I also hear that he has stood at the suggestion of Kidwai who has been working behind the scenes.

*Patel makes this statement in relation to the presidential election of the Congress in which Rajendra Prasad proposed to withdraw his candidature citing his ill-health and to give others a chance. (*Sardar Patel's Correspondence*, Vol. 6, pp. 424–25.)

Lastly, even though you may be writing private letters to the various contestants, it is inevitable that these private letters would be made public and would be exploited. A position would be created when ultimately you would have to speak in public to explain your stand. I would advise you to do nothing which would compel you to take that step.

In all these circumstances, my sincere advice to you would be to keep entirely aloof, if once you decide that you should not yourself stand. That is, in my opinion, the best and the wisest policy, but of course it is for you to decide ultimately what you should do....

Yours Sincerely
Vallabhbhai Patel

2 October 1948

LETTER TO BASANT KUMAR DAS

Dear Friend

[...] I am deeply touched by the sentiments which you have expressed. The honour of being the first President of the Indian Republic* should be reserved for broader shoulders than my own. Everybody must be content with serving the country from a position which is assigned to him and where he can give of his best. I am quite content with mine. I hope, in these circumstances, you will give up the idea of nominating me.

With kind regards,

Yours Sincerely
Vallabhbhai Patel

New Delhi, 27 December 1949

*Das wrote to him seeking his permission to propose Patel's name as the first President of the Republic. (*Sardar Patel's Correspondence*, Vol. 8, pp. 226–27.)

LETTER TO RAFI AHMED KIDWAI

My dear Rafi,

... I do not know what gives you an idea that the leaders have completely lost their touch with public opinion. Refusing to be panicky or getting hysteric about a setback here or a setback there, a criticism here or a criticism there, is no index of our loss of contract. Everybody has his own ideas of what public opinion is, and if somebody else's run counter to them, then it is broadcast that the latter is out of touch with public opinion. When we assess the elections we have lost, we should assess them against the elections we have won. What about the UP by-elections last year, or the Bihar elections this year, or the elections in Surat and Ahmedabad? I know we must face facts; but then we must face them in their true perspective. Otherwise, we are apt to lose our sense of proportion.

... I certainly did not mind—rather, I welcomed—your writing to me frankly, I hope you will equally appreciate my frank reply. I am awaiting with interest your other letter on the present situation.

Yours Sincerely
Vallabhbhai Patel

New Delhi, 19 June 1949

LETTER TO RAFI AHMED KIDWAI

My dear Rafi,

Thank you for your letter of 11 January 1950, the tone and contents of which have not come as any surprise to me. With all the part that you have played in UP politics, there could hardly have been a different approach to my statement from that which you have taken. I must say, however, that you have read more into that statement than the plain English of it warranted. I never knew that I was capable of writing anything which could conceal its so-called 'real meaning' so well. I must also congratulate you on your powers of seeing through the words so well—in fact, of putting into the statement of others meanings and intentions which are never intended or expressed.

The same applies to your interpretation of the Working Committee resolution. However, I would ask you to read both the resolution and the statement once again; though you may still discover some inconsistencies in view of your predilections and prejudices, perhaps this study might assist you in revising some of your ideas about my statement. You will see that in the forefront of my statement I have placed the desirability of settling the matters amicably by mutual adjustments. Should these adjustments fail and group mentality is still existing, I do not see how, if work is to be carried on and not held up by failure to reach decisions, there is any escape from majority decisions.

You have displayed faith in Dr. Pattabhi's study of the functioning of the provincial organisation. In that case, you can better leave matters to him; that might give you some spiritual consolation.

I am certainly anxious that dissensions within the Congress should disappear. As I have stated in my statement, it is for the dissentients themselves to decide whether they are misfits in the Congress or not. If they are, there is only one honourable way open to them, namely, to quit. I have no doubt that this would be more beneficial both to the organisation and the country than the existence of these undermining influences inside the party. We have learnt to our cost during the last so many months how deeply and adversely these dissensions have affected the prestige of the organisation and how the continued existence of these undermining influences has been contributory to the flourishing of indiscipline and to the resultant confusion and chaos that have prevailed both in the organisation and in the country. It is not yet too late if the Congress President and the Congress Working Committee can still act; otherwise even the most confirmed optimist must begin to lose faith.

Yours Sincerely
Vallabhbhai Patel

Calcutta, 14 January 1950

LETTER TO JAWAHARLAL NEHRU

My dear Jawaharlal,

…

2. I have seen your draft statement and have no comments as regards its contents.* But I would like to make one more effort to persuade you to limit it only to the question of withdrawal of your candidature. It is good you have not expressed any open preference for one candidate or the other, but in view of the talks you have had informally with members of the Working Committee and other talks that are going on people are bound to interpret or to be told to interpret it against Tandonji [Purushottam Das Tandon]. In the first place, I have already suggested that it would not be fair to condemn him without a hearing. Secondly, the proper time for testing him will come when at the Nasik session the old principles and ideals are restated. He is a conscientious man, and if he feels he is out of tune with those principles and ideals he will not hesitate to say so; but if he adheres to them he will have to abide by them and act accordingly. To say anything indirectly against him at this stage will thus not only be unfair to him and his long and distinguished Congress record but will also be, if I may say so, placing the cart before the horse.

3. I know how much you feel for these ideals and principles. We all feel the same way, but the question is of timing and appropriateness; it is also one of achieving our object in a tactful and smooth manner. It will not avail us nor in any way help the objective to create any bitterness or controversy about it. Passion and prejudice merely cloud the issue. Whether we like it or not, personalities will come into play and will become the subject of talk and controversy. The ideals and principles will then fade into the background. We shall see party politics at their worst. Some of our own colleagues unfortunately are past masters in it. I earnestly feel we should avoid all this. I would,

*Though the statement is not available to us, Nehru did mention it in a letter to Patel on 9 August 1950. The subject of it was withdrawal of his candidature and his differences with the other candidate, Purushottamdas Tandon on communal issues. (*The Collected Works of Sardar Patel Vol. 15*, pp. 189–91.)

therefore, suggest with all earnestness at my command that you raise these issues at the Congress and not now. Otherwise, it is quite possible that the issues may get involved in personalities. To me it seems the best, the most appropriate and a clear democratic way of achieving the objective we have at heart.

4. I hope you will agree with me, and if you do I suggest that you issue only the first two paras of the draft.

Yours sincerely,
Vallabhbhai Patel

New Delhi, 10 August 1950

LETTER TO JAWAHARLAL NEHRU

My dear Jawaharlal,

...As regards your correspondence with Tandonji, your letter of 8 August, a copy of which you sent me, makes no mention of any intention to resign if he were elected. It is confined to the necessity of explaining your opinion in some form or the other. In fact, in your last letter to Tandonji dated 13 August, of which the latter sent me a copy, you said you would like to talk to him about the various matters or write to him. In the meantime you had issued your statement to the Press, and the correspondence which passed between us about Tandonji and the talks which I had with Rajaji left me with the impression which Rajaji shared that you would wait for the Nasik Congress and would not take any decisive step till then. It was for this reason that your letter of the 25th came to me as so much of a shock. Between my last letter to you dated the 12th and your letter of the 25th, I have never been consulted by you on this issue,* and there was,

*The issue was candidature of Purushottamdas Tandon as Congress president. Nehru was against him largely due to his communal bent and especially his participation in a refugee conference where hateful speeches were made. Patel thought it would not be fair to condemn Tandon without hearing him out. Patel believed that Tandon too felt the same way about ideals and principles but the question here was of timing and appropriateness. If Tandon did not feel in tune with the old principles and ideals at the coming Congress session at Nashik, he would say so. If he chose to adhere to them, he would have to abide by them and act accordingly. (*The Collected Works of Sardar Patel Vol. 10*, p. 191.)

therefore, no occasion for me to be enlightened about any change in your attitude or preference.

Regarding Tandonji, apart from my preference for him from among the candidates that are standing, the difference between your approach and mine is only this, that I am in favour of giving him a chance, and if he does not adjust himself to such decisions as the Nasik Congress might take naturally he has to go. There can be no question of your going out; on the other hand you condemn him right now and feel that his election itself would mean a defeat of your policy, etc. I hold that the latter is not in issue, since past decisions and policies of the Congress bind all presidential candidates, and the President is as much bound by it as any ordinary member of the Congress. This seems, strangely enough, somewhat similar to Kripalani's own view, as would be clear from the attached copy of his statement published a couple of days ago.

As regards candidates, you and I both agreed at Dehra Dun that Kripalani was out of the question. I strongly favoured Tandonji on personal grounds and disfavoured Shankarrao Deo. You disfavoured Tandonji and were prepared to accept Shankarrao on the principle of 'lesser evil.' I have throughout held that your condemnation of Tandonji was unfair and premature. I was not taken into confidence when recently your preference seems to have changed from Shankarrao to Kripalani. As I wrote to you yesterday, I refused to believe it at first; even now I am amazed as personally I regard Kripalani as having taken in the past, with reference to the points you hold against Tandonji, a more destructive and critical role against you than Tandonji has ever done. His speeches and writings in the Press will amply confirm it.

I really do not know what I can do at this late stage, practically on the eve of the election. I suggested an alternative name at Dehra Dun; we then agreed to Rajaji; Maulana and I agreed to Patil. Unfortunately, none of these was found possible. In this attitude of mental distress and doubt, I could think of only one way of relieving your mind. I am quite willing to issue a joint statement as in the draft [see enclosure] if it meets with your approval. Although I feel that any statement at this juncture is likely to be misconstrued by one side or the other, I am prepared to run the risk if it would in any way alleviate your apprehension.

Yours sincerely,
Vallabhbhai Patel

New Delhi, 27 August 1950

LETTER TO C. RAJAGOPALACHARI

My dear Rajaji

… I have already sent a reply to Jawaharlal's letter of last night. I do not know why he persistently keeps on saying that he kept me informed of his intention to resign. In fact, on this issue I always had the feeling that he avoided a full and frank discussion with me and took me into confidence the least.

I do not know if it would be wise to make any statement with persons determined to misconstrue anything we say. However, I thought by my offer of a joint statement I might be able to relieve Jawaharlal of his mental distress. I have, therefore, suggested to him the attached draft.

It is somewhat different, though not in substance, from your suggestion but having regard to the likelihood of misconstruction, I feel the less we say the better. The draft as it stands means quite clearly that we stand united on fundamentals and the successful candidate will either have to conform to them or get out. I think that should satisfy Jawaharlal that he can rely on me to stand by him at the Nasik Congress.

Since I wrote the above I have read his letter to you. It is difficult for me to express myself on it. However, I have acted up to your advice and hope he will even now be able to view the position dispassionately and objectively.

Yours sincerely,
Vallabhbhai Patel

New Delhi, 27 August 1950

LETTER TO JAWAHARLAL NEHRU

My dear Jawaharlal,

...I am so unhappy to find that I have completely failed to convince you otherwise and that your mental distress still continues. However, I am relieved to feel that you have agreed to give some more time during which, I earnestly hope, the tension will relax and we shall be able to do some calm and dispassionate thinking.

I am sorry it has not been possible for you to agree to the issue of a joint statement. I made the suggestion to relieve the oppression and tension of your mind and if it did not serve that purpose it was no use my persevering with it.

Let me, however, make one more appeal to you with all the earnestness and sincerity at my command. Please suspend your judgment on the organisation and the men who have been loyal and devoted to you all these years through thick and thin and test them on principles and not on personalities, attach so much importance to a symbol when what matters is the real thing—those principles and ideals for which the organisation stands and will stand.

I plead [with] you to reflect on these words and the consequences of the contemplated action carefully and calmly and not to come to any hasty or premature conclusions.

Yours sincerely,
Vallabhbhai Patel

New Delhi, 27 August 1950

SECTION III

SOCIAL ISSUES

THE DUTY OF THE HINDUS IS TO FULLY HELP THE MUSLIMS

Hindu–Muslim unity is a vulnerable sapling. It must be raised very carefully for a long time. Our minds are not as clean as they should be. We have a habit of distrusting each other in every matter. It is not going away. There will be efforts and ploys to break up this unity. The Hindus have got a great opportunity in a natural way to consolidate the [Hiṇdu-Muslim] unity permanently. The duty [dharma] of the Hindus is to fully help the Muslims in protecting their religion [dharma] and to trust the nobility of the Muslim community....

Bharuch, 31 May/1 June 1921

HINDU–MUSLIM UNITY

...I wish I could talk about the other major and widespread communal issue, the issue of Hindu–Muslim, with the same confidence. But owing to communal riots and the memory of brutal and cruel murders still alive, I fear I would not be able to infect you with the faith I have in Hindu–Muslim unity. Those having a larger public impact but could not control their pen and tongue are responsible for this bloodshed. We might be fated to see worse days. More people might get killed. But I am convinced that those who believe in the policy of revenge and vengeance will eventually see the foolishness or failure of their suicidal policy.

Till then the wise in both communities should know that communal riots or quarrels take place because of our inertness or indifference. As fresh blood starts running through the veins of the nation, most of the nuisance will disappear....

Bombay, 4 May 1929

DO NOT CRUSH YOUNG GIRLS

The worst sin committed by the farmers is they marry their children at a very young age. If I were in power, I would have a law passed that those who marry their girls of 12-13 years should be shot or hung.

How can you have water in your wells [ease of water supply] when the girls become mothers at 14–15 years and there are large numbers of child widows? I am telling you all these as a brother. Try to understand. You are killing your daughters. Reduce the expense of community feasts. Stop the killing of children in the name of honour. Do not marry a girl before she is 18. The English girls are unmarried at the age of 22–25 years and they run a clinic in our villages. They rule over men and women of an entire district. Do not crush young girls by imposing all burdens on them. She is a tender flower, a blossoming bud. Why kill her untimely? If you want to regain the earlier situation, rule of religion, *Ram rajya* [the rule of Lord Rama] and you have got the guts of your forefathers be brave and implement good things.

...There were child marriages in earlier times. But the girl was not sent to the in-laws for a long period of seven years. O Patidars! The Thakaradas and the Rajputs [considered socially backward] are following you.... I am ashamed that I have to tell you all this. But you must understand. May God give you enough intelligence, understanding, and power.

Chaloda, Taluka: Dholka, June 1927

WE ARE WALKING AT AN ANT'S PACE

How a village would look like in *swaraj*? It would be apparent just as we would enter the village. We have to cover our noses while entering the village these days. The farmer does not know where and how to dump dung heap. He does not know about excretion. He is doing it just like his bullock does. He wastes golden fertiliser and suffers in filth.

In an ideal village, the farmer would dig a pit and collect fertiliser there. He would also collect the urine of the cattle at the same place, cover it with a wooden slab and install a toilet on it. There will be no filth in the village whose farmers know this art. Not a single fly either. Why do the farmers live like hell when God has given abundant land, free air, and beautiful light?

The farmers would sprinkle water in their compound and their women shall plant roses there. They are using this space for the excretion purpose of their kids. It attracts flies and the same flies go to the room.

How beautiful the kids of farmers would be in such a village? Their eyes, nose, and face would be dirt-free. Their clothes would not be dirty. The red glow of blood would shine through their cheeks, just like a rose. But how would the wife of a farmer raise rose-like kids if she has not seen a rose? She has only dealt with the dung. She does not know how to raise a child. She keeps her kids quiet by using the opium tablet or beating them or making them asleep in the cradle and keeps on toiling. Can God be born in a farmer's house in such conditions?

The farmers would respect and love their womenfolk, and treat them as a partner in the ideal village. The farmers do not know how to behave with their women at present. They bring the women and push them away at will just like they do it with the cattle. They do not allow her to step out of the house. They do not allow her to come to such gatherings. A farmer is not brave. So, he does not trust his woman. Look at the English people. None of them come here leaving their women alone in poor conditions. If he leaves for his work on one horse, he takes his woman along on the other horse. He is brave. So, he does not fear that somebody will cast an evil eye on his woman. If the women are trusted and loved in such a way, the behaviour with them would be different, and the language used with them would be different. They would be dealt with love and affection. Brave children can be born and nurtured only in such conditions.

A drum, an ignorant, a shudra, cattle, and a woman / All of them deserve a thrashing

If you still believe in the above-mentioned couplet, that means we are and we will be slaves. Mind well, the woman will be a mother and deserves our respect, not stick. I do not want to harass you by leading your women on the path of extravagance, but I want to make them like goddesses and pious. They will enlighten your household. You will be ashamed by realising that they are more competent than you. You would not be able to abuse them. You would have to treat them with respect and decency.

The spinning wheel would be as common as sowing. A farmer who grows cotton but buys his clothes from elsewhere is not a farmer according to me.

…If only one village comes to me after shedding its infighting and jealousy and helps me in my experiment to establish the true swaraj of the farmer, we can have swaraj for the entire country easily. The farmers of Bardoli have gained fame, but are they taking it forward? We are walking at an ant's pace. It will not work. The world is moving ahead with full force. Indian farmers are trailing behind.

The real swaraj is will not come from the top. Farmers must get it. The building of swaraj has to be erected from the villages. Why should we look to the government for help if the farmers understand this? We have already shown in Bardoli what a farmer with this understanding is capable of. Getting swaraj is easy if you understand this. The farmers can shed off the state as easily as a snake takes off its slough. Why would a person like me come to the village if the swaraj were to come from the English?

Ena, Taluka: Palsana, 18 December 1928

NATURE DOES NOT RECOGNIZE ANY DIFFERENCE BASED ON CASTE OR RELIGION

…In this age of Western culture, those who are enamoured of the power of machines, have seen to it that those things which were produced in the village industries are produced in the mills and factories and have ruined our indigenous industry. This has led to a situation where the farmers are without any work after the agricultural operations are over…. This is the biggest sin committed by this Government. After the farmers, millions of craftsmen in the country lost their employment. Farmers should help Mahatma Gandhi re-establishing village industries so that those industries which are on the brink of extinction can be revived. It is the duty of each farmer to spin the yarn he needs for his clothes himself at home, in so far it is possible…instead of the farmer running to the cities to get necessities of life, he should learn to use the things which are available in the villages. Some help would thus be available to our villages which are on the verge of ruin. Blind aping of the west and consuming of tea, and cigarettes, which are completely unnecessary and harm the health, should be given up and these things should not be permitted to come to the villages. If the farmers have a true organisation they can be guided properly and their interests protected.

The farmers should stop holding funeral feasts because the money spent on these things is something which can easily be avoided… because of false prestige and ignorance, we hold feasts for the family members and others and express happiness. That should put us in the category of uncivilised people. Funeral feasts are harmful both for the giver and the person who is entertaining them. Both of them should be classed as fools…. If we have money and we want to do good to the deceased or want to immortalise him, that money should be invested in the education of the children or in sanitation which is a public service….

Similarly, at the time of marriage we should spend only that which we comfortably can…. Burdening young children with family responsibilities at such a tender age is akin to murdering them. It is because of these evils that the progeny of the farmer gets weaker and weaker. It is a matter of shame for us that the Government had to pass a bill to prohibit child marriages. This is cited as a reason for our being unfit for swarajya. This weakness of ours gives us a bad name throughout the world…. It is the duty of right-thinking farmers to remove their weaknesses and get rid of this evil habit. They would thus be saving their children from trouble.

…Heaps of dung outside the villages and heaps of refuse at any place in the villages are a matter of shame. We do not keep even our courtyards clean. Because of this filth, flies, horse flies, mosquitoes and other insects bother us all the time and spread all kinds of diseases amongst us. In all these matters we are more responsible than the Government. Defecating in the open spaces around the villages is against the norms of cultured behaviour; in addition, it leads to waste of such good manure…. Mahatma Gandhi and his companions used to remove that nightsoil, and I have been trying to teach these ignorant farmers as to how that human excreta can be turned into excellent manure. The farmers must get rid of their indolence and must learn how to keep their homes and the villages clean….

Many superstitions and hypocritical practices are rampant among the farmers and they are all there in the name of religion. We reject our Harijan brothers whose services are needed not only in agriculture but also in things nobody else can do and we hurt them, all in the name of religion. This is a sin. When a person we call an untouchable embraces another religion, he immediately becomes touchable. We see it happening every day. To remove this blemish from the Hindu religion Mahatma Gandhi has undergone many troubles.... It is the duty of every farmer not to consider anybody an untouchable. Those amongst them who want to hold the reins of government should never consider anybody inferior or untouchable....

There cannot be any caste or religious distinctions among the farmers. Farmers who till the land, whether small zamindars, farmers, or agricultural labourers are essentially farmers regardless of the caste and the religion to which they belong. All are in the same boat; they will sink or swim together. Nature does not recognise any differences based on caste or religion....

28 April 1935

WOMEN MUST GET THEIR RIGHTFUL PLACE

It is not proper to think that the problems of women will be solved after achieving swaraj. The reality is that the women have been unseated from their place. The real swaraj will only come after women get their rightful place.

Women must develop their self-confidence and get their rightful place. Such reforms have never been done or will not be possible by the laws.

We have the highest number of women in the legislature. But that is just a façade. It is like an actor donning the King's headgear. The assembly of Bombay has more women members than that of the British Parliament after their tradition of 400–500 years.

The credit for bringing awareness to Indian women in the last ten–fifteen years goes to Mahatma Gandhi.

...Seven to eight hundred women volunteers were working at Haripura without fear. They did not feel any inferiority there. We have to solve our problems by creating such scenes.

...The problem will be solved if thousands of Mridulas [Mridula Sarabhai] come out from us.

Ahmedabad, 15 June 1938

A GREAT MORAL REFORM

The day for which all of us and the whole of India were waiting has come at last. Those who witnessed Bombay yesterday saw the closure of wine shops and the scenes in Bombay streets must have been convinced that the Bombay of yesterday is dead at 12 o'clock at night and new Bombay has been born today. This day will be written in golden letters for Bombay in the history of India. The whole world is watching us. Many countries in the world are busy manufacturing weapons of annihilation and preparing to cut each other's throats. We, on the other hand, following our ancient culture, are cleansing Bombay by implementing tenets of Hinduism, Islam, and other religions. The city of Bombay is creating a new thing today. Some had doubts about whether the Government of Bombay will be able to implement prohibition in Bombay. But those who have seen the gigantic procession and meeting must have no doubts whatsoever in their mind. [Some] people think the prohibition will be short-lived. But I predict that any future government will not be able to break even a single brick of this edifice. We have not built a loose structure. For Congress, this policy is not a recent resolution. It has years of penance of Congress and Lokmanya [Tilak] behind it. Every year on this day the whole of India celebrates Lokmanya's birth anniversary. ... Lokmanya had said that 'even if God descends on earth and asks me to drink wine, I will refuse.' Lokmanya had started the agitation for prohibition thirty years ago. ...Prohibition was an important part of Lokmanya's declaration of achieving swaraj as our birthright.

Still, some skeptics amongst us have opposed this great moral reform. It is our duty to remove the doubts of such people. Whatever such people are writing or speaking, we should not pay attention and we must change their hearts by showering love on them. What we have done today is the gigantic work of ethical and religious reform. When Congress Working Committee, keeping in mind the pledge of years, decided to introduce prohibition in all eight Congress-ruled provinces, it had thought of all aspects. Critics ask why only the Bombay Government was so quick in introducing prohibition. It ought to have followed the example of Madras. The answer is, Bombay is the most prestigious city in India. So, it must lead from the front. All Congress provinces will follow sooner or later. Nobody can disobey the order of Congress.

Bombay is said to be the city of the rich, where a handful of rich people claim to consume liquor drink without injuring their health, but thousands of poor labourers are falling prey to the evil habit of drinking. Their wives and children have a dark future. What is the prestige of the city in such circumstances? Today rich and poor people of Bombay have earned real wealth for the first time. The affluent class never had thought about how their children were being educated. Alien Government squandered the money collected through taxes elsewhere and collected the income from the sale of liquor. The hard-earned money of our toiling labourers, the poor, and even our scavengers and Harijans was being washed away in the drains of liquor shops and from that money, our children were getting an education. Since 1920 we had decided that we must remove this blot. But we had no power. We were not running the administration. It was run by a foreign power and it was against prohibition. Yet in the midst of many conflicts and hurdles, Congress carried on a prohibition campaign for nineteen years. ...Many young men and women picketed wine and toddy shops, got their heads broken, suffered lathi blows and severe beating, and went to jail. ...Those who say that we did not give adequate notice and hastily took up such a huge step are mistaken. Now there is no place for any discussion on this matter. The very fact that you have gathered here in such large numbers, the enthusiastic and jubilant crowds you have seen throughout the entire route of the procession and you saw the children young and old, rich and poor giving ovations to you, the love and enthusiasm that you witness here overflowing is a befitting reply to our skeptical critics....

The success of the next phase depends upon the active cooperation and goodwill of the people. ...Join the Committees which have been appointed in every street, lane locality, and pockets, and engage yourself in propaganda work and rest only when you achieve glorious success. In your neighbourhood amongst your friends if there is anybody young or old who is against this program request him, implore him with folded hands, fall at his feet and lead him on a proper path.

Those who were saying that the public is averse to this program have been disillusioned. I know that some people have been taxed but in return, they will get the blessings of God for this great ethical reform. Prohibition was introduced in Ahmedabad last year and is now in Bombay. Next year we intend to implement the prohibition in the entire province. For that, we require one and a half to two crores of rupees. I can easily understand that Bombay alone cannot spare such a big amount. For that, we shall have to bang on the doors of the Central Government and might have to fight with it....

This program is for the well-being of all citizens—Hindus, Muslims, Christians, Parsis, Harijans, Sikhs, and others. Today thousands of people of all classes, labourers, people of the middle class, and poor have assembled here to show us that they support the policy of the Congress heartily.

Lancashire used to take away our sixty crores of rupees through cloth, most of which we had saved by tremendous efforts. Now through liquor, our seventy to seventy-five crores of rupees are flowing in drains, and we must save that amount. ...I firmly believe that because of this policy no business or industry will be adversely affected, nor any economic structure will crumble. Nobody will be ruined. Seventy to seventy-five crores of rupees of the poor will be saved, which will be distributed in the society, the business will prosper and everybody will be happy.

Mumbai, 1 August 1939

A RURAL UNIVERSITY

One of the greatest problems which India faces today is to rehabilitate its rural areas. It is largely from that point of view that we have set ourselves to the task of achieving a rural University with a rural bias based on the principle of co-operation, self-help and self-sufficiency. The task is one before which much stouter hearts may quail, but thanks to the public spirit shown by the selfless band of workers, we are gradually progressing towards achieving success in this great experiment. In doing so, they have, under the inspiring leadership of Bhailal Patel, brought about a happy blending of the old and the new. The credit for pursuading Gandhiji to give his consent to this experiment seeking to establish that modern science and methods could, with ingenuity and skill, be made to serve rural interests goes principally to Bhailal. Under his persistence and earnestness, scepticism yielded to conviction and with Gandhiji's blessings, we took up the experiment in right earnest, What shape Bhailal and his band of assistants are giving to those ideals is now for the world to see. Gujarat has the unique distinction of having attempted to work Gandhiji's constructive ideas in a manner in which no other part of India has done. It is, therefore, fitting that these ideals should have found their exponents and enthusiasts there and who have turned a land infested by dacoits and robbers into the seat of a great experiment....

June 1948

A GREAT ACHIEVEMENT

The Government of Bombay today fulfils after ceaseless efforts its solemn undertaking to introduce Complete Prohibition. It is undoubtedly a great achievement. It is possible that some persons belonging to the educated class subject to the influence of Western Civilization and captured by its false glamour, may not realize the importance of this great social revolution or may oppose it without understanding true significance. But with the passing of time, that class also will not fail to realize the good results of this drive.

When they will experience that benefit, they will also give up their opposition and will begin to appreciate it. Looking at it from a short-term point of view, this will no doubt mean a considerable loss to the Government just now. Some unpopular measures might have to be taken to make up this deficit. But I have not the slightest doubt in my mind that numerous poor families will be prevented from going down the path of destruction; and, not only that, they will also experience its economic and moral benefits and will bless the Government for it.

I hope the people of Bombay will give their wholehearted co-operation to the Government of Bombay in this great endeavour of theirs.

1 April 1950

SECTION IV

THE ADMINISTRATOR

LETTER TO GHAZNAFAR ALI

My Dear Ghaznafar Ali,

...

2. As you are probably aware, the Hindustani policy of AIR is not a matter of recent origin; on the other hand, it has been in force for the last so many years, and in its formation and shaping, Mr. Bokhari, the late Director-General, has taken a notable part and made a valuable contribution. That there is such a language as Hindustani which is generally spoken and understood in Northern India is the unanimous view of two committees, on both of which the Muslim community and protagonists of Urdu were represented.... I regret it is impossible for me to accept the view that the giving of its due place to Hindustani in the AIR broadcasts would in any way prejudice the interests of Urdu or, for that matter, Hindi. It is also imperative, from the points of view of listeners and of general utility, that broadcasts from All India Radio should include a sufficient portion of items in this common language.

...

5. Therefore, the general effect of my proposals would still be that Urdu would secure a predominant position from Lahore and will have almost the monopoly of non-Pushto programme from Peshawar. On the other hand, Hindi will secure a dominating position only from Lucknow, while from Delhi both Urdu and Hindi will secure parity. This hardly bears out your insinuation that the proposals 'produce a total net result of making Hindi a principal cultural language of Northern India and dislodging Urdu altogether from its pre-eminent position.'

6. I am afraid, having regard to the points already mentioned in the draft Press Note and in view of the position explained above, I am unable to agree to your proposal that the Delhi station should be set apart mainly for Urdu.

Yours Sincerely
Vallabhbhai Patel

New Delhi, 26 January 1947

LETTER TO LORD MOUNTBATTEN

My Dear Lord Mountbatten,

As a consequence of partition, numerous administrative arrangements will be necessary on or about 15 August 1947 if we are to avoid confusion in or breakdown of administrative machinery. For instance, in lieu of those going away to Pakistan personnel will have to be in position for operating and running telegraph services, railway services, civil aviation services, etc. Similarly officers and staff will have to be in position for the supervision of despatch of stores, equipment etc. going to Pakistan, and taking custody of those retained for India or vice-versa. Again, in view of certain radio stations being transferred to Pakistan, the P&T and the Civil Aviation Departments may have to alter their present arrangements for communications; the Meteorological Department may need some change in the machinery for communicating weather information to the Civil Aviation Department and other departments. The Finance Department would have to arrange for verification of the cash and other balances of treasuries and of branches of the Imperial Bank performing treasury functions in Pakistan as on 14 August. These are only some obvious instances but there will be a large number of matters in which detailed action will have to be taken by various executive organisations such as the Income-tax, Customs and Central Excise Departments. In regard to some of these matters action will have been decided upon already; in regard to others, decisions cannot be taken finally until the Partition Council has itself come to a decision, and in such cases alternative schemes will have to be kept ready which can be put into operation as soon as a decision has been taken. It is clear thus that over a very wide field, certain administrative arrangements will have to be made as a result of the very act of separation and in order that the necessary preliminary action is taken in good time, it is essential that all the important positions in every department and attached and subordinate offices are held well before the 15th of August by officers who have decided to remain in India.

2. Moreover, it is obvious that those who have elected for Pakistan

will no longer be interested in safeguarding the interests of India, but will be more concerned in doing everything they can to promote the interests of Pakistan even by prejudicing those of India. We cannot look for any co-operation from them even in the day-to-day administration, let alone in matters of importance. The possibility cannot be ignored of the enthusiasm of some of these persons outrunning their discretion, and we must provide against the danger of sabotage, etc. in certain key departments, as for example telephones. These circumstances, in my view, make it essential that we take these persons off their regular administrative duties and replace them as soon as possible by those who have elected to serve India. The former can be placed, for the time being until they leave for Pakistan, on special duty, or can be given special joining time.

3. I suggest that this change should take place with immediate effect.

Yours Sincerely
Vallabhbhai Patel

New Delhi, 9 July 1947

LETTER TO LORD MOUNTBATTEN,

My Dear Lord Mountbatten,

...As regards proportionate pension for members of the Central and Provincial

Services, I think a distinction must be drawn between those who wish to retire prematurely of their own accord and those whose services are not required. In the latter case, it will be open to the Provincial Governments to allow them proportionate pension, but in the former case, I feel there must be uniformity and I would certainly advise Provincial Governments in the interests of uniformity and as a matter of principle not to allow proportionate pension.

I much regret I cannot persuade myself to agree to any further guarantees regarding existing pay scales and conditions of service. I feel that we have gone as far as we could and that if anybody wants any further guarantees it can only arise out of a distrust of our intentions and of a challenge to our good faith. I would not regard such a person as an asset to Government service and would much rather that he left it.

Yours Sincerely
Vallabhbhai Patel

New Delhi, 27 July 1947

LETTER TO DR P. C. GHOSH

My Dear Prafulla,

...I am rather surprised that you should have agreed to the arrangement about grant of proportionate pension without reference to us. In this matter, uniformity is essential, because what you give in one province you cannot reasonably withhold in another. It was after very careful consideration that we decided not to extend the principle of proportionate pension to those who are retiring voluntarily, beyond the Secretary of State's Services. Your agreement puts us in a rather embarrassing position. Nor do I see how it serves your purpose. According to our information, this option would be open to them only for six months after 15 August which makes it likely that you will have to face the same problem, which you are wishing to avoid, within the next six months. That hardly provides you with any permanent solution of the difficulty which you mention, and if that difficulty has to be faced, it had better be faced now as regards than later. The interim period merely provides them greater opportunities of mischief if they are so inclined, and it is most unlikely that they will have any heart in their work. They would, therefore, be a deadweight in the Administration and not at all helpful as you seem to think. You should, therefore, reconsider this matter.

Yours Sincerely
Vallabhbhai Patel

New Delhi, 30 July 1947

THE REFUGEE PROBLEM

I need hardly dwell at any great length on the magnitude, urgency and supreme importance of the problem of speedy evacuation and resettlement of refugees. For the moment, the first question is uppermost in our minds and I shall therefore take it up in the first instance.

As all of you are probably aware, compulsion of events have necessitated evacuation of millions of men, women and children from West Punjab to East Punjab and from East Punjab to Wes Punjab....

It is of the utmost importance that this process of evacuation should get all possible help and facility by all the means at our disposal, and I should like to remind you that in this matter time is of the essence. If we cannot evacuate within as short a time as possible, we shall be faced with consequences too terrible to contemplate. It is, therefore, with great concern and anxiety that we have been observing recently the mounting toll of hold-ups of trains which has greatly hampered the progress of evacuation. Even, otherwise, our refugees on the other side were being attacked by the various elements of the West Punjab. Attacks on refugee trains lead to retaliations which are much more dangerous and savage. Besides these mad and furious attacks by unruly mobs on our normal lines of communications is a direct challenge to the authority of our State as well as yours and no Government worth the name can tolerate this for a moment. It is, therefore, in the interests of our own refugees coming from West Punjab that we should take steps to ensure smooth and safe evacuation of those who want to go away from India. Moreover, it having been decided that these Muslims have no place in areas where they were residing, or those who are willing or anxious to go, the sooner they leave India, the better in the interests of all concerned. This would save us from many problems, particularly of food and law and order; and, therefore, it is essential that we should send them away as quickly as possible.

As far as I have been able to visualize this problem of ensuring safe passage for these refugees, it is not only a question of escort for the trains but also of supplementary ground action. Such ground action must take two forms. One is ensuring the responsibility of the villagers residing in the neighbouring villages from whom the disturbing elements must be attracting some sympathy for the success of their operations. Such a collective responsibility involves the collection of intelligence and imparting of information to responsible authorities about the assembly of *jathas* [a small group of people], patrolling of the tracks lying in particular areas, prompt reports of attacks and identity of attackers. It is obvious that, if the villagers fail in these important matters, the only way punishment can devolve on them is by resort to imposition and recovery of collective fines. But I must emphasize that for these fines to be effective, it is necessary that they should be imposed immediately and recovered promptly and the amounts must be substantial. More stringent measures, more or less similar to those taken during the war period, of compelling able-bodied villagers to take up the responsibility of personally guarding the lines should be taken. The other means of supplementing escorts would be by adequate ground action, particularly to comb out nests of these jathas and to cover up the tracks of these jathas once they have been engaged by the escorts. To my mind, one of the reasons why these *jathas* have been acting with impunity is the almost complete absence of the visitation of punishment, apart from casualties inflicted by escorts. It is clear that we must remedy this grave lacuna in our machinery to deal with this menace for without this we would be seriously crippling the action which we propose to take.

It has occurred to me that the best way to tackle this problem would be to organize highly mobile patrols in these areas. It would be the business of these patrols to post themselves with information from villages, etc., regarding the assembly of these *jathas* and to exercise particular vigilance when a refugee train is passing through their jurisdiction. For this purpose, it is essential that both the patrols and the escorts of trains should be equipped with wireless sets. These patrols would also follow the trains by road which generally skirts along the railway line at some distance. In the first place, the attackers would find it difficult to assemble for attacks; secondly, even if they succeed in assembling, they would be caught between two fires and it would be impossible for them to escape the punishment of their crimes.

The third point should, in my opinion, be the effective organization of intelligence in the areas in which these *jathas* operate. For this purpose, it is essential that the civil authorities co-operate and co-ordinate with the Military, and it will be necessary for us to establish contacts and sources in villages in the vicinity of railway lines. I myself feel that, if we could successfully accomplish these three methods of combating this very serious problem, we shall have ensured as perfect a safety for the refugee trains as possible and thereby we shall have facilitated the evacuation of millions of our men on the other side....

26 September 1947

THE SALARIES OF THE MINISTERS

I agree with the Hon'ble the Finance Minister that for reasons stated by him and in order to do away with what is, in effect, discrimination between Ministers who have other sources of income and those who have not, it is necessary to fix emoluments on an income-tax free basis. I feel, however, that the figure mentioned by the Hon'ble the Finance Minister is on the high side. Particularly having regard to the fact that the present rate of emoluments, even when they are subject to tax, are generally regarded as being higher than the country can afford. I would suggest for the consideration of my colleagues that the salary of the Ministers should be fixed at Rs. 2,000 per month free of all taxes (including exclusion from calculating rate) and a free furnished house inclusive of electricity and water charges. I agree that an allowance of Rs. 1,000 per month may be paid to the Prime Minister as entertainment allowance.

As regards official entertainments, the occasions are comparatively few and in each case where a Minister considers an official entertainment necessary, ad hoc sanction of the Finance Ministry should be obtained. For this purpose, a Government Hospitality grant may be obtained from the Legislature every year. It may not in practice be possible to confine ourselves within this grant, or it may be that in some years the grant may prove more than adequate. Nevertheless, it is only proper that the Legislature should vote this grant annually, at such tentative figure as may be possible to fix.

3. In regard to other allowances, at present the Ministers are entitled

to an equipment allowance of £250 on their assumption of office. This was necessary at a time when Ministers had to equip themselves with costly uniforms. Now, as far as I can see, the only initial expense of a substantial nature that a Minister may have to incur would be on equipping himself with a car if he has none. I suggest, therefore, that the equipment allowance should cease, but that a Minister should be allowed an advance for the purchase of a car. The advance would be recovered in suitable annual instalments, and the car, until the instalments are paid, would be mortgaged to Government.

4. As regards other allowances, I feel that in present-day conditions a saloon is definitely out of date and unsuitable. If a Minister travels by train, he should be entitled to reserve a first class compartment. If he travels by car, the question of reservation does not arise, but I would like to suggest for consideration of my colleagues whether, in view of frequent use of aeroplanes by Ministers, two or three aeroplanes should not be purchased and kept in reserve for use by the Ministers. Other Government servants can use these aeroplanes if they are not required by Ministers.

5. In regard to car journeys, the present rate of allowances should be maintained. At present Ministers, when they are out on tour, get a daily allowance of Rs. 30. It is for consideration whether this allowance should be maintained at this rather high figure.

6. I would be grateful for the views of my colleagues on these matters. I am, therefore, circulating these notes with a view to discussion at tomorrow's informal meeting of the Cabinet.

15 October 1947

LETTER TO K. C. NEOGY

My Dear Neogy,

Please see the attached application. It is a very pitiable and sad case. I dare say there are several others of this type. I think the best course would be for Government to accept responsibility at once for the families of Central Government servants in Pakistan who had opted for service in India but who have been killed during the disturbances or are untraced. Temporary relief to be afforded should bear some relation to the salary which a Government servant was drawing and a scheme should be devised for suitable allowances for the education, marriage etc. of their children. I do not think that Government can shirk its responsibility for the families of Government servants who stuck to their duty up to the last and lost their lives and left their families in destitute conditions merely because they obeyed our instructions to continue to serve in Pakistan until we made arrangements for their posting to India.

Yours Sincerely
Vallabhbhai Patel

New Delhi, 27 October 1947

LETTER TO K. C. REDDY

My dear K. C. Reddy,

I have received a representation that Christians should be given their due share of representation in the Constituent Assembly, Mysore State. Dr. John Matthai has supported this representation and has suggested that a reasonable number of Christian representatives may be sent to your Constituent Assembly on the same basis as in our Constituent Assembly. I feel that the request is reasonable. It is in our own interests that we should give ample proof of consideration and regard for the minorities. We should see that the minorities feel a sense of security and confidence in the majority. From all these points of view. I hope you will examine the position and see that the Indian Christian community in your State is adequately represented in your Constituent Assembly.

With kindest regards,

Yours Sincerely
Vallabhbhai Patel

30 November 1947

LETTER TO JAWAHARLAL NEHRU

My Dear Jawaharlal,

I have been receiving several invitations to drink and cocktail parties from embassies, consulates-general etc. as well as from certain officers and public bodies in Delhi. At all these parties generally alcoholic drinks are served.

...

2. I feel that having regard to our declared policy of prohibition, it would be quite incorrect on our part to patronize such parties. I should, therefore, like to suggest at the Cabinet meeting tomorrow that Ministers should make it a rule not to give such parties themselves, whether officially or socially, and to instruct their officers to follow suit. We should also inform the foreign embassies, consulates-general etc. that, in future it will not be possible for us to attend functions where alcoholic drinks are served. Such a general rule would save a great deal of embarrassment; otherwise, consistent with this attitude, individual polite refusal would be the only alternative.

3. I would like to add that already there is considerable pressure that prohibition should be introduced in Delhi. Short of that measure, I feel that this is the least we could do. I hope, therefore, you will agree to take up this matter at the Cabinet meeting tomorrow.

Yours Sincerely
Vallabhbhai Patel

3 December 1947

LETTER TO JAWAHARLAL NEHRU

My Dear Jawaharlal

...I feel, on the whole, that Sir C. P. has done a good job of work and that his abilities and talents should be utilised by us in the service of the country. I know how bitterly he has been opposed to us, but I do feel that we should be generous and forgiving in our adversary's defeat and that we should not let go waste his undoubted talents and capacity. Men like Sir C. P. Ramaswami Aiyar start with a great advantage in external fields as they carry a prestige and a position which comparatively unknown personalities have to build up, and their already established contacts provide a useful stepping stone for further efforts in that direction. I would, therefore, appeal to you with all the emphasis at my command to utilise his talents in some suitable capacity in foreign countries. Personally, I would myself prefer that he goes to the USA as ambassador. I am confident that, in that position, he will be able to serve this country very well. The USA holds the key to the international situation today. We ourselves have to depend on the USA probably more than on the UK. Without the USA's support in men, money and machinery, I am very doubtful, notwithstanding Asaf Ali's views to the contrary, whether we shall ever succeed in our industrial policy, and it is on that policy that so much of the future of this country depends. For some years, therefore, whether we like it or not, we have to depend on the USA for our progress. Irrespective of party or personal considerations, therefore, we should have in Washington a very able and competent man. I feel that we have such a man in Sir C. P. Ramaswami Aiyar and that if only we could rise above the past, we could utilise him. You know that he never spared Bapu. Indeed, he has condemned him and opposed him in more bitter terms than he has ever used either in your case or mine. But Bapu always used him whenever he could and never let personal considerations intervene. I do hope, therefore, it would be possible for you to consider my suggestion.

At the same time, I should not like to press my views against your inclinations, and if you feel that that would not be possible, I should still suggest that during his forthcoming visit to Australia Sir C. P. may be given some semi-official or official capacity which would enable him to speak with some authority and some prestige....

Yours Sincerely
Vallabhbhai Patel

Mussoorie, 6 May 1948

LETTER TO JAWAHARLAL NEHRU

My dear Jawaharlal

… 1 have known Ghanshyamdas through Bapu for more than 25 years. The relations between Bapu and him were those of father and son; he had a spiritual bond with him which Bapu fully recognised and Ghanshyamdas maintained to the full and to the very end. But never throughout our long connections has he taken any undue advantage of these ties or exploited them, lie is a man of honourable character and straightforward views in life. Despite the calumny indulged in by some malignantly disposed persons, I am quite prepared to say that his association with both of us has been above reproach and entirely unselfish. Had it been otherwise, both Bapu and myself would have been the last persons to have spared him. It is, therefore, impossible for me to be a party to the proposal which, in my opinion, involves violence of the worst kind to the feelings of both Ghanshyamdas and Bapu.

I have, therefore, no doubt that the right and proper course for us is to hold firmly and strongly to our innermost convictions and resist the pressure for depriving Ghanshyamdas of his house. But for my very close and intimate connections with him, I would certainly have spoken out publicly long ago. On account of that handicap, therefore, 1 can only communicate to you my views for consideration. I hope you will reconsider the matter and reach that conclusion, which I feel is inevitable, and which alone, I am convinced, would prevent the perpetration of a great injustice and a grievous wrong. Should you, however, feel that we must yield to public pressure, I would suggest that before we go any further we should be clear in our own mind as to what we propose to do with the house and premises, and whether it should be taken over by Government or by a non-official trust, etc. You must not lose sight of the fact that if the house is to be taken over, it should be maintained in its present condition and it would cost—whatever authority takes it over—five to six thousand rupees a month in maintenance, etc. We should also be careful in deciding upon the use to which we are going to put this house and how we can implement and carry out the object which we might set before us.

Further, I feel that if we take the house over, we should at least in all decency give Ghanshyamdas a suitable alternative site, for which he will gladly pay an adequate price, where he could build a house for himself in Delhi. It would, in my opinion, be adding insult to injury if we took from him this house and left him as it were on the streets. Through many years of valuable contacts with men, prominent in business and public life, he has established for himself a position of a host to so many prominent personalities. It would be a great blow to him and his prestige and standing in public life if we rendered him incapable of discharging these obligations. I would, therefore, suggest that if we take over the house we should give him full facilities to resettle on another suitable site, making full allowance for his public and private needs.

Yours Sincerely
Vallabhbhai Patel

13 May 1948

LETTER TO THE PREMIERS OF STATES

My dear Premier,

The Prime Minister wrote to you on 4 October 1948 on the eve of his departure for Europe. ...The importance of his visit to Europe at this juncture cannot be over-emphasised. Not only important matters of common concern to all the members of the British Commonwealth but also some special matters concerning the well-being and future of this country required an exchange of views with His Majesty's Government in the UK and other Dominions. Recently, our stand and the policy regarding Kashmir and Hyderabad have come in for review and criticism on the part of foreign statesmen and Press. Such review and criticism have, in the nature of things, been prejudiced and extremely one sided. Reasons for this are obvious. The freedom of India has been the cherished desire of only a small number of Britishers. There is still considerable evidence of bitterness and chagrin at the loss of influence, prestige and power on the part of British civil servants and other vested interests. ...I hope the Prime Minister's visit to European countries would introduce a sense of proportion and understanding amongst these critics.

2. The affairs of the United Nations continue to give rise to apprehension. The forum of the UNO has become a platform for the exchange of abuses and bitter and hostile criticism between the two blocks in which the world is being sought to be divided (somewhat reminiscent of the old Papal Bull which divided the colonies of the world between Spain and Portugal in the Middle Ages). Whether it is the question of disarmament or the atom bomb or the Berlin issue, this cleavage manifests itself in its worst form. India has been trying to play the role of the Good Samaritan and trying to evolve order out of chaos and agreement out of differences. It has succeeded in resolving the deadlock over the revival of the Atomic Commission and Sir B. N. Rau, who has been elected Chairman of the sub-committee of eleven to examine the problem of international control of atomic energy, has been straining his best to bring the contending points of view of the Anglo-American bloc and the Soviet as near each other as possible. India has also been elected a member of the Economic and Social Council by an overwhelming majority.

3. ...The indications are that despite Pakistan's attempts to keep interest alive in the issue of Hyderabad the Security Council would let it slide into oblivion. In any case, we have instructed our delegation to refuse to be drawn into a discussion on the merits of the issue, but to restrict itself to a contention that Hyderabad has no locus standi, and that actually the issue has been withdrawn and is no longer before the Security Council. Perhaps a clue to the latest move, which has been made by the Pakistan Foreign Minister to claim an interest in the Hyderabad question, is provided by the evidence which has come in our possession that a major portion of about Rs. 14 crores, which that State has spent on the mad venture of mobilising international opinion and clandestinely obtaining arms and ammunition, has gone to the high-ranking Pakistan officials including the Foreign and Finance Ministers of Pakistan and their Defence Secretary and Financial Adviser.

4. In East Asia, our main problem is still the developing Communist menace in Burma. Despite the heroic resistance and even offensive on the part of Government forces, the insurgents still command a

hold over a number of provinces. The economic life of the country has been thrown completely out of gear. The administration is on the verge of a breakdown and conditions of transport and communications arc chaotic. In Indonesia, the Republican Government is faced with hostilities on two fronts—the Communists and the Dutch. There are, however, signs that Government forces are gaining some ascendancy over Communists. The Dutch, who seem to have tried to make some capital out of the difficulties of the Government do not seem to be in any mood either to learn or unlearn. In Malaya, the Communist forces seem to have suffered a reverse, but the country is still not free from their menace. In China, the National Government has suffered a grievous blow in the loss of Tsinan the Capital of Shanton province and the gateway to Central China. The critical situation in that country shows no signs of abatement. Indeed, the only bastions of security and law and order are India and Japan which General MacArthur seems to be converting into an anti-Communist fortress in the East.

5. The French Settlements in India have latterly been in the limelight. The Government of India and the Government of France agreed that the future of French Settlements should be decided by a referendum and that the procedure for such referendum should be settled by the Municipal Council of the five Settlements to be newly elected. Last month municipal elections were held in Chandernagore, which resulted in the party favouring union with India securing a large majority of seats. Elections in the other four Settlements were fixed for 10 October. In the meantime, certain complaints were received regarding the procedure prescribed for the elections and certain manoeuvres giving weightage to the opposite party. The Government of India, therefore, requested a postponement of the elections in order to give them time to go into these complaints. The Government of France agreed to postpone the elections till 24 October. But as this was insufficient we have asked for a further postponement. The results of these elections are of some importance to us as they would provide a basis for our negotiations with the Portuguese Government regarding Portuguese possessions in India.

6. Regarding Kashmir, the UN Commission is still writing its report. Recent indications are that the intensity of the conflict will

increase in the coming weeks. We are also trying to build up our supplies for the winter months. Now that we are free from any large-scale commitments in Hyderabad, we can concentrate better on our Kashmir operations. It would, however, be futile to expect any very quick results. There are signs, however, that the Pakistan Government are feeling the drain on their resources which this running sore involves, and it is possible they may be more amenable to any proposals for settlement which the Commission might put forward, as is generally expected.

7. Many speculations are rife in the Press and on the platform in regard to our policy on Hyderabad. As I pointed out in a public statement some time ago, our first concern is to establish law and order and to create conditions in Hyderabad in which it would be possible to hold elections to the Constituent Assembly in peace and tranquillity. Our efforts to establish law and order are meeting with increasing success. The Razakars have been dealt with to a very large extent. The Communist menace in Nalgonda and Warangal districts is being systematically faced. The administration is being gradually brought to normalcy. Once reasonable normal conditions are restored, it will be possible to hold elections to the Constituent Assembly for which we are pushing ahead with the preparation of electoral rolls. You will doubtless realise that the pacification of such a large area and the administrative overhaul of the State are very big commitments, particularly in the present depleted conditions of available manpower. With the help and co-operation of the provinces of Bombay, CP, and Madras we have been able to secure a bare skeleton of staff, both civil and police, and with the help of that staff we have made small beginnings. I am afraid we shall have to make further calls on provincial resources, and I hope our request will meet with the same prompt response which was extended to us earlier.

8. There is, I am afraid, only a superficial change in our relations with Pakistan. You must have read the many friendly references to Pakistan made in the Prime Minister's speeches and broadcasts. The Pakistan Prime Minister's reply was typical of him and the new State. In asking for deeds rather than words, he was merely quoting scriptures, and he has tried to make out as if Pakistan was doing the best it could

to maintain friendly relations, and it [was] we who were setting all these well-intended efforts at naught. The Pakistan Government also seem to have fallen a victim to the familiar Nazi disease of seeing enemies all round themselves. The hysterical search for fifth columnists which seems to have been started in the typical Hitlerian fashion has the appearance of another excuse to drive out the comparatively few non-Muslims that are left there. In this Government is being supported in season and out of season by a warmongering Press. False and virulent anti-Indian propaganda, full of hate and venom, is being put across, particularly by the Urdu Press against Indian leaders and Central and provincial Governments. The Home Ministry have issued a Press note which gives some glaring examples of such propaganda. The Pakistan Government have endeavoured to counter these allegations, but a comparison of the two their case would hardly stand scrutiny both from the point of view of importance of newspapers and their contents. Mr. Liaquat Ali Khan has sent a couple of telegrams to the Prime Minister professing friendship and peaceful sentiments, but he has taken care to emphasize that the Kashmir issue must be settled to their satisfaction. It is obvious that we cannot purchase peace at the expense of Kashmir. But from the repeated references to a settlement of the Kashmir issue which he makes, it seems quite clear that Kashmir is rankling in their breasts. In the meantime, annoyances of all kinds continue, typical of which are the restrictions imposed on East Punjab Liaison staff in Lahore and the frequent incidents they create in the Patharia forest reserves on the borders of Assam and East Bengal.

9. During the last fortnight we have announced some of the important anti-inflationary measures which we intend to enforce in order to meet the worsening economic situation. One of the most important of those is the drastic curtailment of Government expenditure. This would undoubtedly involve the merciless pruning of many favourite items on the part of Ministers, both Central and provincial; it would also mean the suspension or postponement of some important schemes of development. We are convinced, however, that there is no other alternative way of balancing our budgets which is so essential to create confidence and a sense of economic security. It is obvious, however, that the efforts of Government should be

fully backed by public opinion and by business men, industrialists, investors and labour. In times of crisis, panic is the worst enemy. For some time past industry and investment have been particularly subject to influences of rumours and utterances of all kinds. In such an atmosphere, the need for balanced words and carefully thought out phrases on economic matters cannot be overstressed. What is essential is that from men in authority or in the know of Government's minds, there should not issue any inconsistent statement or a jarring note on the essentials of our economic policy and programme. We should all, Central and provincial Ministers alike, therefore, make a concerted attempt not to give the least cause for speculation or alarm, to cultivate the virtue of silence where we are not able to speak with authority on economic matters, and to say nothing which would be inconsistent with authorised pronouncements on the economic position and programme. I am sure you all realise that the economic position of the country is causing us the gravest concern. Any further accentuation only makes the position more perilous and whoever is the instrument of that accentuation, be he an official or non-official, an employer or a worker an industrialist or an investor, does a positive disservice to his Government and the country.

10. The labour situation is undoubtedly causing us anxiety. Repeated counsel to labour to produce more seems to go unheeded by a no means insignificant section of the workers. The Bombay dock strike is the latest example of labour intransigence. We have already emphasised that increased production and prosperity and economic stability would be possible only if Government, the employers and the workers all co-operate in an intensive production drive. It is obvious that any one of this tripartite combination can render the other two either inoperative or partially ineffective. We must, therefore, deal drastically with any wanton defiance of the laws of social prudence and economic equilibrium and with unsocial elements which foster and promote such defiance.

11. In this task of dealing with the present economic situation we naturally depend on the maximum co-operation from the provincial Governments. We have already seen in the Press reports of instances of their determination to help us. It might be of some help to you

to know that we have set up a Priorities Committee of the Cabinet which would scrutinise financial and development schemes and deal with other cognate questions in an effort to implement our policy at the Centre. A similar business-like body in the provinces would, I have no doubt, be of great advantage to you in reviewing your budgetary position and schemes of development etc. Another sphere in which provincial Governments can be of great help to us is in ensuring that the machinery of economic controls functions smoothly, efficiently and honestly. Corruption and instances of want of integrity or laxity must be put down with a strong hand and evaders of control regulations must be dealt with severely.

12. In the sphere of law and order, the Communist menace demands constant vigilance. It is clear that we cannot allow a situation to develop which would create in India conditions even remotely suggestive of Burma, Malaya, Indonesia and China. It would never be allowed to deteriorate beyond a police problem and even there the less of a problem the better. A careful check of intelligence and co-ordination between all relevant sources of information is a sine qua non of success in dealing with a subversive movement of this kind. We have also to keep a ceaseless watch lor leaders and active workers who have gone underground. And we have to beware of the Communist cells inside Government itself, the increasing evidence of which is causing us serious concern. We are proposing to set up a high-level committee of Secretariat officers which will constantly keep the problem under review, obtain decisions of Government on matters of policy and ensure that those decisions arc promptly and effectively enforced. You might find a similar body useful in the provincial sphere.

13. You must have read in the papers about the meetings of the South-East Asia Regional Branch of the World Health Organisation and about the inauguration of the State Employment Insurance Scheme. Both these events are likely to mark an important stage in the advancement of social security and I have no doubt that their activities will increasingly claim popular attention and appeal.

14. In the sphere of States, an important landmark has been reached by the completion of the process of integration which was started last December and which, by the removal of the Hyderabad

sore, has attained a measure of unity which India had never attained during the last so many centuries. By the process of mergers, the formation of unions, the accession of those unions in all subjects on the federal and concurrent lists, and by the elimination of all pretence to independence from the biggest of the States, the Indian polity is now in a position to be shaped according to a common pattern. The problems of consolidation and administrative reorganisation must now claim our attention. Without a satisfactory solution of these the gains which we have so far registered will become largely illusory. Apart from this, we have to beware against regionalism and provincialism of an undesirable type. To some extent local patriotism is both desirable and necessary, but we have to take care that we do not overstep the limits within which this virtue must be contained. Similarly, we should guard against harmful manifestations of class or communal consciousness. These are all disintegrating forces which if not controlled and checked are apt to destroy all the good work of integration and unification that has been achieved. I do hope you will see that that situation is never reached.

Yours Sincerely
Vallabhbhai Patel

New Delhi, 15 October 1948

LETTER TO N. GOPALSWAMI AYYANGAR

My dear Gopalswami,

I understand that the Pakistan Government have not given us a complete list of prisoners not willing to go to India, and that we have information that there are some non-Muslims in Pakistan jails who have not been shown by the Pakistan Government in the lists of prisoners to be transferred. This reflects very adversely on the reliability of the list which has been supplied to us by the Pakistan Government. As I told you earlier several times, I would not let Qureshi [be] handed over to Pakistan until we were quite sure that we had got all our transferable non-Muslims into India from West Pakistan. Once we let him go and we have sent away the last transferable Muslim prisoner, we shall have no bargaining power left, with the result that the remaining non-Muslim prisoners in West Punjab will just rot there. I am, therefore, definitely of the view that we should not allow Qureshi to go, until we are quite sure that the list is complete and that all the transferable prisoners are actually brought into Ferozepur and handed over to us.

Yours Sincerely
Vallabhbhai Patel

New Delhi, 18 October 1948

I HAVE NO AGGRESSIVE INTENTIONS AGAINST PAKISTAN

I have no aggressive intentions against Pakistan, and I believe that the two Dominions must settle this problem amicably and by mutual discussions. I always desire peace. If I did not, I could not have spent a life with Gandhiji. I do not hesitate in saying what I feel, whether it displeases Hindus, Muslims or anybody else. I admit that I do so in blunt language, but to learn the proper language, I shall have to spend my next birth also with Gandhiji. It is possible, there may be other methods by which this problem can be solved, but if Pakistan has any alternative solution, she must put it down, so that we can discuss it amicably together. Whatever I am saying is not merely in the interests of the refugees, but also for the good of Pakistan. It is for Pakistan now to take concrete steps to solve the problem, otherwise India cannot undertake the burden of these refugees and will be crushed under its weight.

17 December 1948

SPEECH AT MADRAS

...You want more wages for the Labour. Is it that we want to starve them? Are we foreigners? Are we businessmen? Some people say that we are agents of the capitalists. Since I joined Mahatma Gandhi one thing I learnt from him; and, that is, that a public man, if he is to have his proper place, should not have any property. And I can challenge any Socialist or any Communist to play this game with me! I am prepared! But my quarrel with them is that they gave up the second part of Mahatma's advice. They want to use violence. It is there that I have a quarrel with them. So long as they were playing that game underground or over-ground when we were under a foreign power, we made allowances for it and we are paying for it! For an evil, once tolerated, grows, and that is what we see in Hyderabad!

Why are these Communists creating trouble and disorders there? How did they grow? It was because the Hyderabad Government was foolish enough to allow them to grow for its own safety and security and we had no control then to suppress them and see what is happening today? In the three or four months time two hundred or more Congressmen, their own brothers, have been murdered! Is this a sign of freedom? And once they are driven out from that area, where are they to go? They will harass you! They will have the same game with you. What then are we to do? My appeal to them may be in vain because they do not listen to anyone. Immediately after my release, I told them that I was prepared to take them in the Congress provided they gave up their method of violence and gave up drawing inspiration from the foreign countries. Even now our offer is open. But that creed is their religion and terrorism is the only method they want to employ—for, they cannot defeat us at the polls and cannot separate us from the masses of India. Then it is our misfortune that we have to put our dear young men and women into prison or drive them underground; or, if you may say so, allow them to go underground. It is a misfortune.

The other is the R.S.S. I have made them an open offer. Change your plans, give up secrecy, respect the Constitution of India, show your loyalty to the Flag and make us believe that we can trust your words. Whether they are friends or foes, and even if they are our own dear children, we are not going to allow them to play with fire so that the house may be set on fire. It would be criminal to allow young men to indulge in acts of violence and destruction.

Then we have our Sikh friends. Some of them also began to threaten us. Now it is the only community in India which is allowed with the unanimous voice of the Constituent Assembly to keep arms. Why did we do it? Not for the purpose that they will threaten the Government with the use of force. So when anybody from that community tells us: 'We have not yielded to Aurangzeb and we are not going to yield here' we reply, 'The days of Aurangzeb passed long ago. These are the days of the people of India; and, therefore, everybody is equal and everybody has a full scope and full responsibility. Anybody who is going to play false and tries to threaten the Government, it will not fail the people. Now see how many forces are we handling simultaneously in the first or second year of our Freedom! We know we have your affection, your love and your confidence; but that is not enough!'

23 February 1949

THE CIVIL SERVICES

As regards the Services, [the I.C.S., the Indian Administrative Service, the Police Service, the Secretariat Service], I need hardly dilate on the necessity of maintaining their discipline and morale and keeping them contented; in no other circumstances can we draw from the Services loyal and efficient service except by trying to appreciate their difficulties and their work. We have often criticized the Services, which we have a right to do, but Services, after all, are composed of human beings and unless we put ourselves in their place, we are not likely to appreciate their full worth. It is our duty to see that the machine with which we have to work is kept in good humour and good temper. We are entitled to criticize it, but we are also to see what type of Service we have had. This is a Service which we inherited from the past Government and it had created it for a particular purpose. It has served that purpose very efficiently and admirably. That Service has a reputation of efficiency and strength. The honourable members of the House are aware that that Service was considerably depleted and a large part of its main strength was taken away immediately on the transfer of power. Those who used to rule this country by their strength, by their power, by their capacity; and, by the resources of the Empire behind it, have all left. The increasing activities of the Government of India in several departments together with the creation of new departments have also made larger calls on that Service. So we have the strength of the Services considerably depleted.

That Service was known or was styled as the Steel-frame. Whatever may be the meaning attributed to them, I believe, and you will also agree with me, that if we know how to take work from the Service, there is no reason why they should not give better work than they gave to the foreign masters....

Now there are complaints about corruption. I realize that there are cases of corruption, dishonesty and misbehaviour. We should all search our own conscience and ask ourselves--who amongst us has not erred, and then judge the extent and nature of these failings. We must allow for the ravages of war on men's morals and material resources. We must concede that in reality, what they get today, is—on account of the rise in the cost of living and the increased burden of taxation—only one-third to half of what they were getting before. I am sure that if we will allow for all these, we will find that, on the whole, despite their individual lapses and shortcomings, they have stood us and the country well in crises. In judging, therefore, the Civil Servants, or any grade of Service, the House should bear in mind the difficult circumstances and the exceptional stress and strain through which the Services have passed; and we must also appreciate the immensity and the heaviness of the burden that devolved them with their ranks terribly depleted, with their standards definitely lower on account of much quicker promotions and on account of all-round discontent with the conditions of living and employment.

Now, almost the first question which I took up when I assumed charge of this department was the securing of the liquidation of the Secretary of State's Services and their replacement by Indian or India-controlled Services. I convened a Conference of Prime Ministers of all the Provinces and held long discussions on this question in the last week of October 1946. And I am glad to see that the timely and advance action which we took not only helped us in hastening the change-over from European to Indian control but also to laying down the foundations of new Service. The House will recall the long discussions I had with Mr Arthur Henderson,* the then Under-Secretary

*Mr Arthur Henderson, undersecretary of state for India. It was with him that Sardar had carried on protracted negotiations for termination of these British Services for India.

of State for India. I am now confident that if we treat the new Services with the consideration and sympathy which the Permanent Services deserve, we shall go sufficiently far in promoting not only a unity of administration, but also a uniformity of administrative efficiency in all provincial units.

The House will notice that we have also a plan to extend the Services of this type to all the States who wish to join in this plan. And I have no reason to doubt that there will be any State in India which will keep out of this plan. If, as I hope, all of them accept this plan, for the first time, we shall have achieved the integration of the key services in India on a countrywide basis; and, I am sure, we shall have laid the sure foundations of an administrative structure which will be a great asset in fighting disruptive or fissiparous tendencies all over India....

The Ministry has also to deal with a large number of refugee employees and with also those who formerly served in Pakistan but have opted for service in India. The House will observe that within a comparatively short period of 18 months, almost the whole of this huge establishment has been catered for. I realize that many are not so well-off as they were before and that many questions of seniority, fixation of salaries, promotions, etc., are still agitating the minds of these employees. But our first task was resettlement so that these employees may not wander about for want of suitable jobs. I am sure, it is clear to the House, that in resettling these employees and in dealing with other incidental questions, we have to bear in mind that the administration cannot be at a standstill and its wheels have to be continually kept moving and that we must secure a balance between experience and ability of our existing employees and bear in mind the need for giving a fair deal to the 'refugee' employees without any appreciable loss of efficiency. If we bear this essential point in mind, I am sure, we shall be able to appreciate correctly the worth of the work done so far by this Department....

I shall now deal with the opposition relating to the maintenance of internal security and law and order. On this question, I have throughout been guided by twin principles, namely, that the country must be rendered safe against any threats of internal peace from whatever quarters it may come and that it should be the exclusive responsibility of the Police to deal with internal disorder leaving the Military free to deal with any threat of external aggression. I claim that in the implementation of these two principles we have had a very large measure of success; and that except for the disorder that engulfed the East Punjab, Delhi and some other small areas immediately after Independence, the country has steered clear through such threats of disorder as it was faced with. These threats have been both communal and communist. The communal threat has come principally from the R.S.S. and the Akali Dal. In so far as the R.S.S. might seek to bring about a regeneration of the Hindu Community by peaceful and legitimate means, there can be and need be no quarrel with its activities. It is only when it seeks to achieve this object by spreading poison and hatred against other communities who are entitled under the law to equal protection from the established Government and when it seeks to achieve its object by resort to unlawful or violent means then it pits itself against the forces of law and order. None is more conscious than myself of the zeal and energy which lie contained in the youth of this Organization. I have made more than one appeal to the members of this Organization to give up their wrong methods and to follow the constitutional means. The final reply to these appeals came in the form of the so-called Satyagraha movement of December last year. The House is fully aware of the subsequent history. I am glad that the Leader of the Organization accepted the suggestions made to him for the calling off of the Movement. It now rests in his hands to retrace the steps which he has taken and to place the movement on cultural and lawful lines which would bring its activities within permissible limits. It is only then that we can satisfy ourselves that there has been that change and revolution in the mentality of the sponsors and followers of the R.S.S. movement which would make it no longer a threat to communal peace and security of the country. I should also like to acknowledge the assistance and co-operation which the general public have extended to us in dealing with this movement and to say that never did I expect our action to meet approval with such understanding and support from the general public as at that time.

So far as the Akali Dal is concerned, I have made my position quite clear in the speech which I delivered at Ambala and to which I would again invite the attention of the honourable members. None can be more sympathetic to the claims of the Sikh community and none has done more to serve the cause of that community than myself. I have been their constant friend and I am glad to say that they have been very considerate to me. I still recall with pleasure and gratitude the response that they made to my appeal at Amritsar at a very crucial time in the evacuation of mass populations between East and West Punjab. I fully appreciate their apprehensions and the disquiet with which they have to approach their position which has been so badly dislocated by the partition and its aftermath. I have nothing but admiration for the manner in which they have accommodated themselves to the new facts of geography and political history and have settled down the various spheres of life seeking new openings everywhere. It was, therefore, most painful to me that a section of that community was misled into putting their faith in a futile and harmful extremist policy of which Master Tara Singh was the exponent. We dealt with him and that section of the community with patience and forbearance and it was only when they took to overt acts of defiance of the law and became a serious threat to peace and security of the capital city that we had to take action. None would be happier than myself to see Master Tara Singh released but as I said at Ambala, the key to that lies in the hands of his followers. If they will convince him by their action of the utter futility and wrongness of the methods they are pursuing, it will not take long for Master Tara Singh to be released.

Perhaps I may say a word about the Muslims of India. Except for sporadic activities of their old organizations, such as the Muslim League and the Muslim National Guards, which I think they would do well to forget and give up in the light of present conditions, they have on the whole kept the peace of the country and have settled down, somewhat disillusioned but more or less willingly to their new loyalties. I can assure them that, so long as they behave as loyal citizens of this country, they shall have every protection to their life, property and religion which this Government can extend to them. No better proof of this could have been given than by the steps we took to guarantee their safety in the City of Delhi itself. We willingly agreed to keep their houses vacant against the return of those who had fled to Pakistan, although a large number of homeless refugees were at our hands. The work of restoration of mosques, which has been virtually completed, and the one-way traffic of return refugees from Pakistan, are sufficient testimony to the peace and amicable relations which prevail in this country. High posts, both in the Army and Civil Service as well as in public life, continue to be shared by them. Thus, the cause for which Gandhiji fasted and for which he had to lay down his life, has been fulfilled. In return for all this, the State does not expect from the Muslims anything more than what it demands from other communities, namely, a complete and unquestioned loyalty to their State. I feel certain that the more the Muslim community settles down peacefully and loyally the greater would be the impression that it would create on the majority community and its position would be much more secure and safe and free from any apprehension.

As regards the Communists, I should like to assure the House that we do not seek to exterminate the ideology underlying Communism. Our quarrel with them is in regard to the methods which they employ, those anti-social and anti-national activities which they pursue with such ruthlessness and remorselessness. Their philosophy is to exploit every situation to create chaos and anarchy in the belief that, in such conditions, it would be possible for them to seize power. Alas! We have seen too well how their methods have been put into force with such violence in the neighbouring countries in the Far East. I have no doubt that the House will not in any way tolerate those methods in this country. We are wedded to constitutional progress and peaceful means. It is open to the Communists to use those means to change the social order or to change the Government but if they resort to other methods or means-violent, treacherous and mischievous, then Government must take up that challenge and suppress them with all the forces at their command. I am glad that the country has stood solidly behind the Government in dealing with this threat. Attempts to stage strikes have generally been unsuccessful. Where we have dealt with such threats with firmness and determination, we have generally succeeded in achieving our object with popular support. I have no doubt that, if we continue to follow the same, as I hope to, so long as I am here, we shall be able to deal with this threat to internal security successfully and efficiently. Their

I know that another question has been agitating the members of this House, namely, the question of Civil Liberties. Faced with the threats to which I have referred and those relating to the aftermath of partition, both Central and Provincial Governments had no alternative but to resort the extraordinary powers which they have taken under the various Public Safety Acts. These Acts are temporary in duration. Even so, they have been designed for an emergency and are being treated as such. They have been used very sparingly. The number of persons detained, considering the size of the country and magnitude of dangers that it is passing through, must be considered extraordinarily small.

We have advised the Provincial Governments that they should set up administrative tribunals to ensure that the actions of the Executive authority are properly scrutinized and confirmed. If these actions are scrutinized by a tribunal appointed as suggested by us, the danger of Civil Liberties being jeopardized unreasonably will be minimized. In the Centrally-administered areas also, we have recently taken that step; and, I hope, the House will be satisfied that, whatever action we have had to take was dictated by a painful necessity, and a moment these threats become a thing of the past, these extraordinary powers would also disappear.

As early as May 1947, I had impressed on the Provincial Governments the necessity of so organizing their Police Forces so as to render it unnecessary for them to call forth the Army in aid of the civil power. I am glad to inform the House that the Provincial Governments have generally accepted this advice and that they have made substantial additions to their Police Force at not inconsiderable cost to the provincial revenues. The result has been that the occasions for calling in the Army have been very few, and generally the new forces combined with the old ones have succeeded in maintaining intact the peace of the country.

17 March 1949

INDIAN COMMUNISTS

I have seen several young men here who masquerade as Communists. They are not Communists in its real sense and they do not deserve an epithet which they bear. The real Communism is of a different variety and the Communism that is practised in India is of a different nature. There is Communism in England but they do not commit murders or dacoities. They do not disrupt the communications. If one or two rails are removed, the safety of many lives is jeopardized. Can we allow such things to go on? You cannot expect Police to be present everywhere on the lines. Nor can we allow Communications to be disrupted. Let them try to win over people through a ballot. Bút if they persist in their ways, they will have no place at the polls also.

There are people who say that they should ban the Communist Party. They say it out of sheer disgust. But we will like to allow them a free field if only they will take to constitutional methods. If you find such people among you, it is your duty either to win them over or inform the Government for the safety of all. This is my special message to you.

13 May 1949

LETTER TO JAWAHARLAL NEHRU

My dear Jawaharlal

...The problem is difficult; on the one side, we have undoubtedly Hong Kong's imperialist history; on the other hand, we have to reckon with the growing Communist menace in China. If Hong Kong is to be a bastion against Communism, there is something to be said for reinforcing it, but if it is merely going to be an imperialist domain, then it is obvious we can have nothing to do with it. We have also to realise that India is the only country which can withstand Communist expansion in Asia. At the same time, it is obvious that we cannot do it alone; if we have to safeguard our frontiers against Communist infiltration and encroachments, we shall have to depend on outside sympathy and support. I should not, therefore, like to send a reply to Attlee which he might misconstrue or which might hurt his feelings.

Howsoever much, therefore, we may abhor the past imperialist history of Hong Kong, we have to bear in mind the practical considerations of today.

I entirely endorse your action in sending a company of troops to Gangtok in Sikkim. We have to strengthen our position in Sikkim as well as in Tibet, The farther we keep away the Communist forces, the better. Tibet has long been detached from China. I anticipate that, as soon as Communists have established themselves in the rest of China, they will try to destroy its autonomous existence. You have to consider carefully your policy towards Tibet in such circumstances and prepare from now for that eventuality.

I can quite understand your feelings in regard to the Constituent Assembly debates. I try to follow them through the papers as much as I can, but frankly speaking, most of it seems to me to be irrelevant and beside the point. Only if we could control some of these persistent speakers, our pace would be quicker....

Yours,
Vallabhbhai Patel

4 June 1949

LETTER TO C. RAJAGOPALACHARI

My dear Rajaji,

...

2. I had a long talk with Kishorlalji [Mashruwala] when he was here and conveyed to him almost identical views as your proposed to do in your note. I told him that no sensible man would think of abolishing the death penalty in India in the conditions which prevail today. We have been going through so many mercy petitions and we ourselves find, with the best will in the world, that in a majority of cases the death penalty should be sustained. If the death penalty is not to be abolished, then I could not think of a stronger case for the infliction of the death penalty than that of Godse. He has committed the worst crime imaginable and as you said in an earlier letter 'he stabbed the heart of India itself.' ...If in spite of all this he [Kishorelal]

feels that he should share his thoughts with the readers of the Harijan, you and I cannot help it.

3. I have also received your letter regarding Master Tara Singh's release. Nobody is more keen on his release than myself. Indeed it was most distasteful to me to place him behind the bars, but he asked for it and from what we know he is unrepentant and unchanged. I had hoped that after the principal Sikh demand was met he would be more sober. Giani Kartar Singh and two of Master Tara Singh's lieutenants saw him shortly after this decision was taken. They found him adamant and unmoved. Recently two other Sikh leaders went and saw him and I enclose a gist of their interview with him. The Sikh leaders themselves arc apprehensive lest after his release mailers might get worse. He is a fanatic and seems to suffer from some hallucinations about the coming of Sikh Raj and you will notice that he even goes to the extent of saying that those who cannot reconcile themselves to the demands of Sikhs in East Punjab, should clear out. At the same time, 1 realize that his detention cannot be permanent. I am watching the situation and you can rest assured that as soon as I am able to do so, I shall release him.

Yours Sincerely
Vallabhbhai Patel

Dehradun, 4 July 1949

THE QUESTION OF HINDI

My dear Munshi,

I have had some enquiries from Delhi regarding the question of Hindi.... I feel that it might be of some assistance if I gave you, and through you to the party, an indication of my views on the question....

...

5. To sum up, therefore, I would to the party for consideration the following propositions:

(a) Hindi in Devnagari script (both letters and numerals) should be recognized as the national or official language.

(b) Government must make every effort to ensure that Hindi attains its due position as official language as soon as practicable.

c) With a view to realizing (b) above, Government would take such administrative measures as may be necessary, progressively to replace English by Hindi at the end of ten years.

(d) During this period, both Hindi and English shall be recognized as official languages, but the extent to which each could be used to the exclusion of, or in conjunction with, the other should be determined by the President on the advice of a committee of the Legislature elected on proportional representation.

Yours Sincerely
Vallabhbhai Patel

Bombay, 19 August 1949

I AGREED TO PARTITION AS A LAST RESORT

Sir, I am distressed that a senior Member like Mr Ananthasayanam Ayyangar, a responsible Member of this House, who is the Deputy Speaker of the Assembly, considers and expresses the opinion that the members of the Service were carrying on a very difficult administration for the last two, three years, and, at the same time, harbours the feeling that they are enemies of our country. If that is so, it was his business and the business of those people who think on those lines to move first a resolution to dispense with them and run the administration in vacuum—for there is no substitute of which he has thought of, except the Congressmen or the Congress workers. I feel very sad that the very instruments from whom we have to take work, we have been continuously quarrelling with. If that is so, we are not doing a service to the country. We are doing it a great disservice. Now he made a point that this guarantee should not have been given. What was he doing all this while? To those people who think on those lines, I say, this was not done in secret. No arrangement that was made with the British Government was done in secrecy, nor done by an individual, but by the representatives by all the duly recognized representatives of the Nation. …Their status, their time-scale of pay, everything was to be settled before any question of transfer of power could be considered. Now I had long negotiations and it was then a joint Government at that time and these negotiations resulted in certain conclusions which were placed before the Cabinet. It was a joint Cabinet at the time and they were accepted by them. Then those conclusions were sent to Parliament; and they were accepted there. Many of the Europeans who were in the Service here have left now, but when the negotiations were going on, I told them to leave the case of Indians to us, and that we shall deal with them as we deemed just, that they will trust us and we will trust them; and, finally they agreed on certain conditions. Now I wish to point out that hardly anybody raised any objection to the arrangements that we were making at that time. But if they had suspected us, then there was at that time plenty of scope for them to come out and get better terms from outside agencies. Even now, if you are not willing to keep them, then find out your substitute and many of them—the best of them will go.

I wish to assure you that I have worked with them during this difficult period. I am speaking with a sense of heavy responsibility and I must confess that in point of patriotism, in point of loyalty, in point of sincerity and in point of ability you cannot have a substitute. They are as good as ourselves, and to speak in disparaging terms in this House, in public, and to criticize them in this manner, is doing disservice to yourselves and to the country. This is my considered opinion.

...I give you this inner history which nobody knows; I agreed to partition as a last resort-when we had reached a stage when we could have lost all. We had five or six members in the Government—the Muslim League members. They had already established themselves as members who had come to partition the country. At that stage, we agreed to Partition; we decided that Partition could be agreed upon on the terms that Punjab should be partitioned they wanted the whole of it, that Bengal should be partitioned-they wanted Calcutta and the whole of it. Mr Jinnah did not want a truncated Pakistan, but he had to swallow it. We said that these two Provinces should be partitioned. I made a further condition that in two months' time power should be transferred and an Act should be passed by Parliament in that time, and it be guaranteed that the British Government would not interfere with the question of the Indian States. We said: 'We will deal with that question; leave it to us; you take no sides. Let Paramountcy be dead; you do not directly or indirectly try to revive it in any manner. You do not interfere. We shall settle our problem. The Princes are ours and we shall deal with them.' On those conditions, we agreed to partition and on those conditions the Bill in [British] Parliament was passed in two months and agreed to by all the three parties.

Show me any instance in the history of the British Parliament when such a Bill was passed in two months. But this was done. It gave birth to this Parliament. You now say: 'Why did the leaders give these guarantees?' In order to allow you to have an opportunity to attack the leaders on this very point! What else? You are responsible members of the Parliament of a huge country. You say why did the leaders give these assurances? Think of the past. Why do you forget it? Have you read your own recent history?

What is the use of talking that the Service people were serving while we were in jail? I myself was arrested. I have been arrested several times. But that has never made any difference in my feeling towards people in the Services. I do not defend the black-sheep; they may be there. But are there not many honest people among them? But what is the language that you are using? I wish to record in this House that if, during the last two or three years, most of the members of the Services had not behaved patriotically and with loyalty, the Union would have collapsed.

Ask Dr. John Matthai. He is working for the last fortnight with them on the economic question. You may ask his opinion. You will find what he says about the Services. You ask the Premier of all the Provinces. Is there any premier in any Province who is prepared to work without the Services? He will immediately resign. He cannot manage. We had a small nucleus of a broken service. With that bit of Service, we have carried on a very difficult task. And if a responsible man speaks in this tone about these Services, he has to decide whether he has a substitute to propose and let him take the responsibility. This is not a Congress platform....

But I am prepared to admit that if the Indian Government is to be run today on the basis Gandhian philosophy without army, I am prepared to change the whole thing. You are today spending 160 to

170 crores of rupees per year on the Army. Are you going to change that set-up? Tomorrow the whole of India will be run over from one end to the other if you do not have strong Army.

The Police which was broken has been brought to its proper level and is functioning fairly efficiently. The Heads of Departments of the Police in every Province are covered under this guarantee. Are you going to change that? Are you going to put your Congress volunteers as Captains? What is it that you propose to do?

I am grieved to find that in a Parliament of this kind, Members, senior Members, speak in this strain. I would refer you to the Indian Independence Act which gave birth to the Parliament and you find that the guarantees have been included there. When the Indian Independence Act was to be passed in Parliament the draft was sent here. The leaders of the Nation were called for; the Cabinet was there; the Congress President was there, your President was there; and your leader today was there. Mahatma Gandhi was also present. Every section was scrutinized and the draft was approved. After that it was passed in Parliament. Now these guarantees were circulated before that to the Provinces. All Provinces agreed. It was also agreed to incorporate these into the Constituent Assembly's new Constitution. That is one part of the guarantee.

Have you read that history? Or, you do not care for the recent history after you began to make history! If you do that, then I tell you we have a dark future. Learn to stand upon your pledged word; and, also, as a man of experience, I tell you, do not quarrel with the instruments with which you want to work. It is a bad workman who quarrels with his instruments. Take work from them. Every man wants some sort of encouragement. Nobody wants to put in work when everyday he is criticized and ridiculed in public. Nobody will give the work like that. So, once and for all, decide whether you want this Service or not. If you have done with it and decide not to have this Service at all, even in spite of my pledged word, I will take the Services with me and go. The Nation has changed its mind.

The Services will earn their living. They are capable people. They were trained in a different setting. I know a senior member of the Service with about twenty-five years' service who went to England for higher education and training in the Civil Service and spent about fifty thousand rupees. He took a loan; he had no money. But there is a glamour for the Civil Service on the part of the Indian youth. He went there, he passed with distinction and came here. He served very ably, very loyally, the then Government and later the present Government. His business is to serve the Government that he is serving. He had a sense of patriotism. Often he came into difficulties with he then Government when he had to carry out orders against the Congress people putting them in jail and otherwise. But he could not go beyond a certain limit. Now all his balance today at the end of twenty-five years' service is ten thousand rupees, and his wife and children, when he dies, will get some Provident Fund.

These were the circumstances in which many of the Service people took their training, came here and served. Now we can say; very well, they did it with open eyes, let them suffer. Then you make up your mind to prepare for a substitute.

If you want an efficient all-India service, I advise you to allow the Service to open their mouths freely. If you are a Premier, it would be your duty to allow your Secretary or Chief Secretary, or other Services working under you, to express their opinion without fear or favour. But I see a tendency today that in several provinces the Services are told: 'No, you are Service. The Union will go-you men, you must carry out our orders.' will have not a united India if you have no good all-India Service which has the independence to speak out its mind, which has a sense of security that you will stand by your word; and that, after all, there is the Parliament, of which we can be proud, where their rights and privileges are secure. If you do not adopt this course, then do not follow the present Constitution. Substitute something else. Put in Congress Constitution or some other Constitution or put in R.S.S. Constitution—whatever you like but not this Constitution. This Constitution is meant to be worked by a ring of Service which will keep the country intact. There are many impediments in this Constitution which will hamper us, but in spite of that, we have, in our collective wisdom, came to a decision that we shall have this model wherein the ring of Service will be such that will keep the country under control.

As I told you, this agreement and these guarantees were circulated to the Provinces and to individual members of the Service. Their agreement has been taken and signed by the Provinces. They have agreed-both of them.

Can you go behind these things? Have morals no place in the new Parliament? Is that how we are going to begin our administration of our post-Freedom era? I have seen people who express their opinion about this Service as they used to talk in old fashion when 50 or 60 per cent of them were British element who dominated the Service and our Members of the Service had hardly any freedom to express their opinion and they were not independent. Today, my Secretary can write a note opposed to my views. I have given that freedom to all my Secretaries. I have told them: 'If you do not give your honest opinion for the fear that it will displease your minister, then please, you had better go. I will bring another secretary.' I will never be displeased over a frank expression of opinion. That is what the Britishers were doing with the Britishers. We are now sharing the responsibility. You have agreed to share the responsibility. Many of them with whom I have worked, I have no hesitation in saying that they are as patriotic, as loyal and as sincere as myself. Those who think that the leaders were mistaken in giving these guarantees, they do not know their mind. They do not know what would have happened. They do not even now know that we have difficult times ahead. We are talking here under security kept in very difficult circumstances. These people are the instruments. Remove them and I see nothing but a picture of chaos all over the country. I have difficulty because we have paucity of men. Provinces also suffer and they ask for more men. We have appointed a Special Commission to recruit about three hundred to four hundred men. They have just been selected. They are not selected from the I.C.S. cadre. They have no experience. But yet we want instruments. They will learn from these people.

Now what is it that you want to do? My advice to you is all members of the Parliament should support the Service except where any individual member of the Service may be misbehaving or erring in his duty or committing a dereliction of his duties. Then bring it to my notice. I will spare nobody, whoever he is. But if these Service people are giving you full value of their Services and more, then try to learn to appreciate them. Forget the past. We fought the Britishers for so many years. I was their bitterest enemy and they regarded me as such.

But I am very frank and they consider me to be their sincere friend. What did Gandhiji teach us? You are talking of Gandhian ideology and Gandhian philosophy and Gandhian way of administration. Very good! But you say: 'These men put me in jail. Let me take a revenge.' That is not a Gandhian way. It is going far away from that.

Therefore, for God's sake, let us understand where we are! Today, if you want to take anything from the Service, you can touch their heart, but do not take a lathi and say: 'Who is to give you guarantee? We are a Supreme Parliament.' Have you supremacy for this kind of thing to go behind your words? That supremacy will go down in a few days if you do that. That is my appeal and sincere appeal to you. Remember it and carry it to the Provinces and Congressmen also who are working outside. That is the way of administration. Otherwise, it will go down. When the country is stabilized and when it is strong enough, then if you want to make any change, it would not be difficult for the Service people to be persuaded. If the Princes could be persuaded to give up their kingdoms, how would it be otherwise with the Services who are our own people; whose children will also be serving with us and who have laboured all day and night for the country. They are men who prefer honour, dignity, prestige and deserve the affection of the people. Very few people would like to serve only to be considered as enemies of the country. So do not speak in those terms and I appeal to you to consider my word and give your judgment.

10 October 1949

A NATIONAL LANGUAGE IS NOT FORMED BY FANATICISM

My dear Diwakar,

Thank you for your letter of 5 December 1949 regarding the language policy of All India Radio and the I. & B. Ministry.

I am afraid our approach in regard to AIR has to be somewhat different from our approach to the question of national language. AIR's language policy, while taking note of the official language, must have due regard for the objective. The objective of AIR cannot be contained to the propagation or promotion of the national language.

It is much more comprehensive, viz. it has to make itself understood and appreciated by the common man. Any attempt on the part of AIR to mould public opinion, or to promote and improve public tastes, is bound to fail, if it does not express itself in a language which can be understood by the greatest possible number.

...As regards the nature and extent of the bias, that must obviously be more and more pronounced as Hindi becomes the generally accepted language of the whole of India. The fact that it is not so today is implicit in the recognition of English as the official language for the first fifteen years. You cannot assume, even now, that at the end of the period of fifteen yean, Hindi would automatically take the place of English. We have found what difficulties we have to face in getting Hindi recognised and accepted. What attitude of mind will be displayed at the end of fifteen years is an uncertain factor. Your language policy, therefore, cannot even proceed on the assumption that, fifteen years hence, Hindi would make such rapid strides as to become the generally acceptable language of the people, even though it might be the generally acceptable official national language. The difficulty proceeds as much from the fact that Hindi has to contend with the linguistic pride of the various linguistic areas as from the fact that the protagonists of Hindi itself have to realise that a national language is not formed by fanaticism, nor is it imposed by statute, but grows consciously and subconsciously by the efflux of time with the inevitability of gradual recognition.

If we, as I think we must, accept the criterion of general intelligibility, then obviously the standard of AIR language has to be different from the literary conception of orthodox Hindi. AIR is not, and should never be, a literary club. Once it is constituted into a club of that sort, it would become exclusive and cease to be a national institution. Whoever is at the head of AIR has, therefore, to be guided by a breadth of vision and of outlook which should transcend extremism in language, in literature, in the choice of words and in the selection of forms or idioms of expression....

As regards to Urdu, I am doubtful of either the propriety or the wisdom of relegating it entirely to the regional domain. In a sense, Urdu, like Hindi, cannot belong to one region. Those who speak and understand this language are not concentrated in one geographical area.... There are four crores of Muslims, most of whom speak this language. There are refugees from Punjab, a majority of whom definitely speak and understand this language better than any other Indian language. In the East Punjab, even this year 69% of those who appeared for the Vernacular Final Examination adopted Urdu as their language. In UP there is a large concentration of those who speak the Urdu language.... If you recognise this fact, as I think you must, I do not think it will be possible for us, at least for the time being, to treat Urdu merely as the language of a particular region and thereby to consider it as the main or the main subsidiary language of any particular AIR station. It is possible to include it as one of the main languages of AIR stations in Punjab and UP, but I feel that, if we have to make AIR effective as an instrument of publicity and promotion of ideals of a secular State and culture amongst a large majority of Muslims and refugees, we must, for the time being, assign a portion of our AIR programme from Delhi to Urdu....

Yours Sincerely
Vallabhbhai Patel

New Delhi, 14 December 1949

WE MUST HAVE INDUSTRIALIZATION

Many say that we should adopt Gandhiji's programme. But they hardly realize that the Government which has to maintain the Army must have industrial installations too. For that, we must have industrialization. Some say that we should not industrialize it but build our economy on rural life. I spent a lifetime with Gandhiji. I am not a fool to forget his teachings. I also But what is the position in which you find yourself? Villagers are foresaking the villages for cities. If we do not have industries what will happen? Will villages equip the Army? Will they supply all the transport, guns and ammunitions, petrol, steel, clothing and other things which a well-equipped Army must possess? Instead of looking at the problem one-sided, we have to do justice to both-towns and villages....

Some say that we should root out corruption. How are we to do it?

Can we remove it as we get rid of our headaches by swallowing quick-acting pills? You have to remember that even in removing corruption, we have to act according to law; and, in that task, if the help and support of the people are not forthcoming, then obviously we cannot punish those who are guilty or who have wronged the people of the country. Some say that the Police does not perform his duty properly and efficiently. Please consider whose Police it is and under whose orders it is functioning. It is no longer a foreign agency; it is our own. If we do not appreciate its virtues and perpetually harp on its defects, would that be an inducement to put forth its best?

4 January 1950

LETTER TO JAWAHARLAL NEHRU

My dear Jawaharlal,

I have carefully read the draft letter which you propose to send to Liaquat Ali Khan in reply to his regarding the 'No War' declaration.* My own reading of Liaquat's letter is that he is cleverly trying to commit us to a line of procedure both in regard to outstanding and future disputes which would give Pakistan, in view of its complete disregard of scruples, principles or moral behaviour, a perpetual advantage over us. While everything binds us, nothing seems to bind them. A perpetual war of nerves, a series of accomplished facts, continuous pressure backed by persistent vilifying campaign and absolute denial of even the most glaring facts which take place in its territory are all quite familiar to us. We have had sufficient experience of the implementation of agreements with Pakistan. We have also had a bitter taste of the protection which it affords to minorities. If anybody had any little faith in the good intentions of Pakistan, East Bengal should shatter it completely. To me, the whole matter seems

*Liaquat Ali Khan wrote to Nehru that Pakistan desired most sincerely to remove all causes of friction with India and welcomed a proposal to issue a joint declaration, essentially to renounce war as a method of settling the disputes. In a draft letter, Nehru suggested to work towards a solution always by negotiation and mediation, and if they fail, by arbitration. (*Sardar Patel's Correspondence Vol. 10*, Durga Das (ed.), Vol. 10, pp. 108–11.)

to be so unrealistic in the present circumstances that I wonder if we cannot put an end to this talk, at least for the time being. We seem to be offering a counsel of peace where the spirit and mentality of war exist, and where, to the best of our information, all preparations for war are being made....

8. To sum up, therefore, my view strongly is that we should not get involved into a discussion of individual items of dispute or of the machinery to be provided for settling those disputes. We should confine ourselves to the simple proposition which we have put forward, but over which there is a fundamental difference of approach between ourselves and Pakistan. If you feel that it is not possible to confine ourselves to this simple issue, then the best course would be to get out of the whole business by pointing out this fundamental difference in approach and indicating to Pakistan that this approach is suggestive of their having mental reservation on this simple issue. That being the case, and with the East Bengal situation facing us and the attendant campaign of vilification (of which their radio news of 10,000 persons killed in Calcutta is a glaring example), it is not an opportune time to pursue this matter at least for the time being, until relations between the two countries assume a character in which it would be possible for Pakistan to subscribe to the simple issue of outlawry of war without any mental reservations and it would be possible for us to put faith in such intentions. Any other approach at this time would not only land us in entanglements, from which we would find it difficult to extricate ourselves except by prejudicing whatever advantages we have gained, but also likely to be misunderstood and severely criticised by public opinion in India. I sometimes wonder, having regard to the present situation, whether we could really talk of peace with Pakistan when it is quite clear that it is thinking and preparing in terms of war and is doing everything possible to cast on us a burden which would break our back.

I am returning the copy of the draft letter sent by you.

Yours sincerely,
Vallabhbhai Patel

New Delhi, 25 February 1950

LETTER TO MORARAJI DESAI

My dear Morarji,

I have seen Bhat's telegram to Menon regarding liquor permits for rulers. I am really surprised that in such a comparatively small matter, you should take such an adamant attitude. There can be no question of principle involved since you had already departed from the prohibition policy in regard to salute rulers. The only question was that of doing it more gracefully and of extending it to smaller rulers, if and when they visited Bombay. Even these departures were to prevail for the time being and the whole question was to be reviewed during Menon's discussions with you in the first week of May. Was it too much to expect the Government of Bombay to accommodate the Central Government to such a small extent? Frankly speaking, I am unable to appreciate this attitude at all. A rigid and an unbending behaviour has its virtues but when carried to extremes is likely to result in unnecessary embarrassments. Grace and consideration bring in their own rewards. Even if you felt that our approach was wholly wrong, the heavens would not have fallen if you had held your hands for a fortnight or, if you liked to discuss it with me, for a month or so when I came down to Bombay. I hope you will still reconsider the matter and accept the proposals we made.

Yours Sincerely
Vallabhbhai Patel

New Delhi, 15 April 1950

LETTER TO RAMKRISHNA DALMIA

Dear Seth Dalmia,

I have seen your statement which you have published in The Times of India of yesterday, in which you have referred to the collections for Gandhi National Memorial Fund being motivated by an expectation that by making the contributions the donors would not be dragged into sphere of action of the Income Tax Investigation Commission and that either they might escape it or the case might be settled amicably.

You have said that you were one of the victims of this temptation and donated many lakhs to the Fund through industries controlled by your family members. I was both surprised and pained to read this. I do not think you came to Mussoorie when I invited industrialists for a meeting. The question of income tax evasion, etc. was not raised in the remotest manner possible. The question of exemption was raised and that was easy because it was a charitable object.

I am not aware of any donor who misled himself to such an extent as you seem to have done. Nor do I see any possible connection between contribution to such a sacred object and escape from punishment from the consequences of evasion of income-tax. After all, the contributions were from business firms and not individuals and I do not think any of the industrialists would sink so low as to try to profit, for their own selfish ends, from contributions made out of shareholders money.

Had the contributions been made in individual capacity, it might have been argued that direct or indirect benefits flowing from such contributions would flow to the individuals. If I might say so, it does no credit either to the intelligence or the good sense of any donor if he felt that by making contribution to the Fund in such a manner there was any chance of his escaping consequences of his own act. Such a connection was, apart from being entirely impossible, most unworthy and deserves severe censure and condemnation. If any donor has made a contribution under that belief or in that impression, I would regard it as tainted money and would certainly see that the amount so collected is returned. I would therefore, be grateful if you would kindly let me know what contributions you and your family members have made to this Fund, so that I can cleanse the Fund from any taint of the type which you have now communicated to it.

I cannot help feeling that, by making this statement, you have libelled that whole business community. I do not know how your colleagues in the field of business and industry will read or interpret your statement. I do feel, however, that it was most unfair to them that you should project your own shadow to such an extent as to cover so many business colleagues of yours, for whom you had no right to speak. If you intended, as seems to have recently become a habit with you to make a public confession of your failings this could have been done without maligning or questioning the motives of so many, in whom I am quite certain no thought of any escape from evasion on account of these contributions entered.

If you have any feeling of guilt or of repentance for having evaded taxes which were lawfully due to Government, the proper place for you to make a confession and make amends is not a press statement but the Income-Tax Investigation Commission. If you have to make a clean breast of your transactions anywhere, I suggest you go there, instead of dragging the Fund with such charitable and high significance into the mire.

Yours sincerely,
Sardar Vallabhbhai Patel

4 May 1950

LETTER TO JAWAHARLAL NEHRU

My dear Jawaharlal

...

2. I have carefully gone through the correspondence between the External Affairs Ministry and our Ambassador in Peking and through him the Chinese Government. I have tried to peruse this correspondence as favourably to our Ambassador and the Chinese Government as possible, but I regret to say that neither of them comes out well as a result of this study The Chinese Government have tried to delude us by professions of peaceful intentions. My own feeling is that at a crucial period they managed to instil into our Ambassador a false sense of confidence in their so-called desire to settle the Tibetan problem by peaceful means. There can be no doubt that during the period covered by this correspondence the Chinese must have been concentrating for an onslaught on Tibet. The final action of the Chinese, in my judgment, is little short of perfidy. The tragedy of it is that the Tibetans put faith in us; they chose to be guided by us; and we have been unable to get them out of the meshes of Chinese diplomacy or Chinese malevolence. From the latest position, it appears that we shall not be able to rescue the Dalai Lama. Our Ambassador has been at great

pains to find an explanation or justification for Chinese policy and actions. As the External Affairs Ministry remarked in one of their telegrams, there was a lack of firmness and unnecessary apology in one or two representations that he made to the Chinese Government on our behalf. It is impossible to imagine any sensible person believing in the so-called threat to China from Anglo-American machinations in Tibet. Therefore, if the Chinese put faith in this, they must have distrusted us so completely as to have taken us as tools or stooges of Anglo-American diplomacy or strategy. This feeling, if genuinely entertained by the Chinese in spite of your direct approaches to them, indicates that even though we regard ourselves as friends of China the Chinese do not regard us as their friends. With the Communist mentality of 'whoever is not with them being against them,' this is a significant pointer, of which we have to take due note. During the last several months, outside the Russian camp, we have practically been alone in championing the cause of Chinese entry into the UNO and in securing from the Americans assurances on the question of Formosa. We have done everything we could to assuage Chinese feelings, to allay its apprehensions and to defend its legitimate claims in our discussions and correspondence with America and Britain and in the UNO. In spite of this, China is not convinced about our disinterestedness; it continues to regard us with suspicion and the whole psychology is one, at least outwardly, of scepticism, perhaps mixed with a little hostility. I doubt if we can go any further than we have done already to convince China of our good intentions, friendliness and goodwill. In Peking we have an Ambassador who is eminently suitable for putting across the friendly point of view. Even he seems to have failed to convert the Chinese. Their last telegram to us is an act of gross discourtesy not only in the summary way it disposes of our protest against the entry of Chinese forces into Tibet but also in the wild insinuation that our attitude is determined by foreign influences. It looks as though it is not a friend speaking in that language but a potential enemy.

3. In the background of this, we have to consider what new situation now faces us as a result of the disappearance of Tibet, as we knew it, and the expansion of China almost up to our gates. Throughout history we have seldom been worried about our north-

east frontier. The Himalayas have been regarded as an impenetrable barrier against any threat from the north. We had a friendly Tibet which gave us no trouble. The Chinese were divided. They had their own domestic problems and never bothered us about our frontiers. In 1914, we entered into a convention with Tibet which was not endorsed by the Chinese. We seem to have regarded Tibetan autonomy as extending to independent treaty relationship. Presumably, all that we required was Chinese counter-signature. The Chinese interpretation of suzerainty seems to be different. We can, therefore, safely assume that very soon they will disown all the stipulations which Tibet has entered into with us in the past. That throws into the melting pot all frontier and commercial settlements with Tibet on which we have been functioning and acting during the last half a century. China is no longer divided. It is united and strong. All along the Himalayas in the north and north-east, we have on our side of the frontier a population ethnologically and culturally not different from Tibetans or Mongoloids. The undefined state of the frontier and the existence on our side of a population with its affinities to Tibetans or Chinese have all the elements of potential trouble between China and ourselves. Recent and bitter history also tells us that communism is no shield against imperialism and that the Communists are as good or as bad imperialists as any other. Chinese ambitions in this respect not only cover the Himalayan slopes on our side but also include important parts of Assam. They have their ambitions in Burma also. Burma has the added difficulty that it has no McMahon Line round which to build up even the semblance of an agreement. Chinese irredentism and Communist imperialism are different from the expansionism or imperialism of the Western Powers. The former has a cloak of ideology which makes it ten times more dangerous. In the guise of ideological expansion lie concealed racial, national or historical claims. The danger from the north and north-east, therefore, becomes both communist and imperialist. While our western and north-western threat to security is still as prominent as before, a new threat has developed from the north and north-east. Thus, for the first time, after centuries, India's defence has to concentrate itself on two fronts simultaneously. Our defence measures have so far been based on the calculations of a superiority over Pakistan. In our calculations we shall now have to reckon with Communist China in the north and in the north-east, a Communist China which has definite ambitions and aims and which does not, in any way, seem friendly disposed towards us.

4. Let us also consider the political conditions on this potentially troublesome frontier. Our northern or north-eastern approaches consist of Nepal, Bhutan, Sikkim, the Darjeeling [area] and tribal areas in Assam.... I am sure the Chinese and their source of inspiration, Soviet Russia, would not miss any opportunity of exploiting these weak spots partly in support of their ideology and partly in support of their ambitions. In my judgment, therefore, the situation is one in which we cannot afford either to be complacent or to be vacillating. We must have a clear idea of what we wish to achieve and also the methods by which we should achieve it. Any faltering or lack of decisiveness in formulating our objectives or in pursuing our policy to attain those objectives is bound to weaken us increase the threats which are so evident.

...

6. I suggest that we meet early to have a general discussion on these problems and decide on such steps as we might think to be immediately necessary and direct quick examination of other problems with a view to taking early measures to deal with them.

Yours,
Vallabhbhai Patel

New Delhi, 7 November 1950

LETTER TO JAWAHARLAL NEHRU

My dear Jawaharlal,

Your letter dated 21 November 1950 about the appointment of Wanchoo as the Chief Justice of Rajasthan has been with me for some time. I deliberately did not reply to you immediately, as, to be frank, I was both distressed and annoyed. In the first place, I felt intensely that you had chosen to place your views on record without even giving me an opportunity of explaining matters. Secondly, it was quite clear to me that in your note you have given expression to conclusions formed on appreciation of incomplete material. I assure you that it is no pleasure to me to contradict you on paper and would, therefore, have much preferred the opportunity of a personal discussion before you came to any conclusions. I also feel confident that, if you had ascertained the full facts either from me or from Menon, you would have felt and thought differently in regard to this case.

I fully share your view that the appointment of a High Court judge, being one of the highest that we can make, not only requires great care and consideration, but also consideration at the highest level. Nor am I in the least unmindful of the necessity of strict observance of decorum and courtesy towards the judges. It is for this reason that I have had it provided in the instructions that formal correspondence on this subject should invariably be between me and the Chief Justice of India and the Chief Minister concerned. I have always insisted upon rigid adherence to this procedure and this has been the invariable rule in the case of scores of appointments with which I have had to deal. During the exploratory stage, however, a personal or informal approach is often not only desirable but inevitable, and succeeds in saving both time and correspondence. I have also found from experience that it is more effective than formal correspondence. Menon, who has handled this work before as Secretary to the Governor-General (Public), had often to resort to an informal approach of this kind with tentative suggestions before putting up formally a regular proposal.

I knew that Wanchoo was one of the ablest judges of the Allahabad High Court. I had heard about him from different sources. I also knew that the Chief Justice of Allahabad would be unwilling to spare him. It was for this reason that, after my mind was made up in regard to getting a suitable Judge with administrative experience of the type of Wanchoo, Menon asked Shankar to approach the Chief Justice of Allahabad, because he is intimately known to him and puts up with him whenever he visits Delhi. Shankar had taken care to mark his letters to Malik 'Personal' and there was no room for any confusion of the kind referred to by you; nor was there any misunderstanding of the position on the part of the Chief Justice of Allahabad.

Throughout, both Menon and Shankar acted under my instructions and whatever took place was within my knowledge. The decision to bring in Wanchoo originated in my personal discussions with the Chief Justice of India after his visit to Rajasthan some time in December-January last.... Wanchoo's name was originally suggested to Menon by Bhola Nath Jha, Adviser to the Rajasthan Ministry, and accepted by Hiralal Shastri [Chief Minister of Rajasthan]. I accepted this suggestion. I myself had a talk with the Chief Justice of Allahabad about it when he passed through Dehra Dun on his return from Mussoorie last summer. It has, therefore, pained me much to read an imputation that my officers had done something behind my back. If, after having known me for so many years, any of my colleagues still feel that I can be led, misled or ignored by my officers, I can only blame myself for having impressed them so poorly.

You have referred to the correspondence between Shankar and Buch; both of them are Joint Secretaries in the States Ministry and naturally seek assistance and advice from each other. If Secretariat officers cannot be free and unfettered in their correspondence and discussions and express themselves on the merits of persons or proposals involved, it would seriously derogate from efficiency....

I am also sorry that you have referred to the final concurrence of the Chief Justice of India as a surrender. You know how determined and persistent the Chief Justice is. He is the last man to yield to pressure. In fact, I recall what you and Rajaji said about him when in January last he proved recalcitrant over the appointment of a Muslim judge in Madras. I do not know whether you noticed that in his subsequent note he expressed an opinion about Mr. Wanchoo which was quite different from the view which he had expressed earlier. Coming from the Bar, he had generally a low opinion of the Service judges and naturally hesitates in accepting them. I have found it difficult—sometimes impossible—to succeed in persuading him otherwise even when State Chief Justices have expressed definite preference for them. I was not at all surprised, therefore, to find him so reluctant in this case, but to say that he has 'surrendered' would be quite unfair to him.

In spite of all the efforts made at various levels, it has taken us 10 months to achieve it. That should convince you of the difficulties experienced and the obstacles surmounted. It is, therefore, very distressing to me to find that, after securing a Chief Justice for Rajasthan, about whose ability and competence there is no doubt at all, it has been necessary for me to put in such an elaborate defence of how this was achieved.

However, I do not wish to go further into details. This was one of the matters in my mind when I told you the other day that I wanted to have a long discussion with you as soon as I was fit enough. Receiving from you and writing in reply long letters is a new experience to me. Frankly speaking, I do not relish it. I shall, therefore, leave it at that, hoping that I would be soon well enough to have an early opportunity of that discussion.

Yours,
Vallabhbhai Patel

New Delhi, 1 December 1950

SECTION V

COMMUNAL ISSUES

PROCESSION ATTACKED

Reached here this morning. People of all groups heartily and enthusiastically welcomed me. My procession was passing from mosque. Some Muslims, when my car arrived, as per schedule plan rushed, and attacked procession with lathis, axes and knives. Nanabhai was in front of my motor car. He had smelt a rat, so he stood in front of mosque. Those people asked him to leave. He refused to leave till Sardar's car safely passed from there. Immediately his head was struck with lathi. He came near my car his head bleeding. Other four persons severely injured. One died. Condition of others very serious. Procession stopped. Nanabhai taken in the car and car driven towards hospital. Wound bandaged. Now condition good. Situation under control.

Vallabhbhai

Bhavnagar, 14 May 1939

I DESIRE UNITY AMONG ALL COMMUNITIES

You know the reasons for our assembling here. The unfortunate happening resulted in the death of Bachubhai. Among the injured including Nanabhai and others, Jadavjibhai's condition was serious from the very beginning. His wound was so deep that some portion of his brain had come out. Doctors tried hard but Jadavjibhai today left us while serving Bhavnagar.

We must do a memorial of the tragic incident. We must give a concrete shape to our feelings. Many a time the tide of feelings is high, just like *smashanvairagya*—the momentary detachment felt at the crematorium. But the importance of the incident is forgotten very soon. I see danger in it. If it is not solved cleverly and carefully and cleverly, it is risky.

Nothing wrong should be done by us in any circumstances. We must know our hearts fully well. If we do not settle our internal quarrels, identify and separate the miscreants and suppress them, they will overpower society.

I desire unity among all communities. But if we want to achieve real unity, the persons behind such heinous acts should be found out and we should not abandon the issue till they feel remorseful for their deeds. We should not look like fools and feeble. Some might advise us to forget what has happened, but it would be akin to accepting a day as a night and vice versa.

The people giving shelter to the killers or sympathising with them are equally dangerous. We must think about how long we can be friends with them. We must consider how long we want to keep our heads in a snake hole.

I am an enemy of cowardice. I would never be willing to support the cowards.

...It is in the interest of the state to eliminate such dangers forever. Even if the state may or may not perform its duty, we should be ready to perform our duty. We have to work wisely.

...We must brace for self-defense identifying the need of the hour. This is the time when criminals are moving freely around us. If we give them reasons to believe that we are cowards, the goons will roam without fear.

Bhavnagar is not the only place with lawlessness. The atmosphere all over Hindustan is similar. ...This is not the first such incident for me. It keeps happening around me. But God protects me.

The reason for attacking me was my encouragement to the progressive and democratic forces in British India as well as the native states. It was not an attack on an individual but it was an attack on the forces I have been supporting. The attacker is a fool. The plotters who pulled the strings should be found out.

...I am sure that every citizen will contribute and help in erecting a fitting memorial to the two departed young men.

Bhavnagar, 16 May 1939

LETTER TO RAJENDRA PRASAD

My Dear Rajendra Babu,

...Since the Hyderabad agitation commenced the Arya Samajists have made Sholapur as their base and have been sending all their *jathas* through that centre. The Bombay Government have been put to considerable strain on this account. Yesterday when their procession passed through a masjid, there was some small quarrel and immediately the Arya Samajists came with knives from their camps and killed two Muslims and wounded several. We cannot allow such gun-powder and fire continuously so close together and the Bombay Government have taken today strong action in Sholapur ordering the removing of all the Arya Samajists from Sholapur. It will create some trouble for us, but we cannot afford to be weak in the handling of such communal situation....

Yours sincerely,
Vallabhbhai

22 May 1939

LETTER TO RAJENDRA PRASAD

My Dear Rajendra Babu,

...The last answer of Mr Jinnah in reply to your letter puts the whole burden on him for further initiative. I think we are spoiling our case by making persistent approaches, but in this matter Maulana Saheb's advice must be the last word. I have a strong conviction that there can be no settlement of the communal question till Mr Jinnah feels that he cannot coerce the Congress.

Yours sincerely,
Vallabhbhai

16 October 1939

JINNAH'S UNFOUNDED ALLEGATIONS

Ordinarily I would not have concerned myself with Jinnah's appeal to the Muslims to celebrate the so-called 'day of deliverance'; but in this case, when he has concentrated his attack on what he terms 'The Congress High Command'* and has invited his community to a course

*The address referred to here was given by Jinnah on 2 December 1939 in Bombay. In it, he said 'I wish the Musalmans all over India to observe Friday the 22nd December as the

of conduct likely to stir up communal strife, I, as the Chairman of the Parliamentary Sub-Committee, would fail in my duty if I did not refute the unfounded allegations made by Jinnah in the appeal and the draft resolution.

The country is, by now, familiar with Jinnah's vague allegations which are growing every day in their extent and vagueness. But when the Muslim League, through the Pirpur Committee, first made definite charges against the Congress Ministries, I instructed them to enquire into each allegation and submit a report. These reports, which in all cases were published by the respective Provincial Governments, showed that the charges were entirely unfounded. When the Congress asked the British Government for a declaration of their war aims and their immediate application to India, Jinnah again returned to the charges of oppression in general terms against the Ministries. Dr. Rajendra Prasad, the President of the Congress, thereupon offered to submit the charges, if specified, to an independent Tribunal for inquiry, but Jinnah spurned the offer, stating that he had placed the charges before the Viceroy. But before the Viceroy could speak, we have his latest outburst in which his community and the world in general are invited to accept his unsupported assertions as proved facts.

I am constrained to characterise these allegations as wild, reckless and intended to endanger communal peace. When the Congress Ministries took office, as Chairman of the Parliamentary Sub-Committee, I instructed the Ministries scrupulously to respect the rights of the minorities. Grievances of a communal nature were carefully examined by the Ministries and in several cases re-examined by the members of the Parliamentary Sub Committee. Furthermore, every Premier [Chief Minister of Province], at my instance, had invited his Governor unhesitatingly to intervene in matters affecting the rights and interests of the minorities, whenever the Governor felt that the action of the Ministry was not correct.

When Jinnah recently made the charges, I again instructed every Premier to invite his Governor's attention to them as they also affected

---

'Day of Deliverance' and thanksgiving as a mark of relief that the Congress regime has at last ceased to function. …[I]t is the High Command of the Congress that is primarily responsible for the wrongs that have been done to the Musalmans and other minorities.'

him, and I was informed that the Governors considered the charges as unwarranted. The Governors, though invited to contradict, however, could not possibly do so at the time for reasons of constitutional propriety. But I have no doubt that they must have submitted their reports to the Viceroy. Had the Governors taken the view that there was any substance in those charges, they would have certainly drawn the attention of their Ministers to the same and I am absolutely confident that before no fair judge could Jinnah establish a single charge made against any Congress Ministry or against the 'Congress High Command.'

It is unfortunate that even now the Viceroy and the Governors, for reasons of their own, do not reply to these charges with which they are as much concerned as the Ministers. The Ministers accepted office at the request of the Governors and went out of office voluntarily for a nobler cause, and their record of work has been highly spoken of by all British statesmen, the Viceroy and the Governors. I, therefore, consider it unjust to them that their fair name should be allowed to be exposed to such unmerited calumny.

What motive Jinnah had in issuing this appeal when he and Jawaharlal Nehru are about to meet in order to explore the possibilities of a settlement, it is difficult to see. But if what Jinnah says is his confirmed view, many will be driven to the conclusion that he has no desire to see that the negotiations are brought to a successful end. It is humanly impossible to carry on any negotiations with self-respect unless this highly offensive statement is withdrawn. It is also inconsistent with the dignity of a great national organisation like the Congress to negotiate under the threat of such a country-wide communal demonstration.

11 December 1939

DIVIDE AND RULE

My dear Dr V. K. John,

...It is clear that the Christian community on the whole is in favour of joint electorate, and the younger members of the community are more in tune with the changing conditions in the country and the world. After all the change of faith is a matter of one's conscience, and it has nothing to do with the political or economic condition of the country. Separate electorate given to the Muslims has done irreparable damage to the cause of India: this was done deliberately as a policy of divide-and-rule, and we are paying dearly the price for this act of mischief. Let us hope that all communities will realise in course of time that it is more in the interest of the country and of the community as a whole to fall in line with the general national regeneration of the country as a whole.

Yours Sincerely
Vallabhbhai Patel

New Delhi, 16 December 1946

LETTER TO DR MOHAMMAD ALAM

Dear Friend,

...The Interim Government has been announced and we propose to take charge on 2 September. This is an event of unusual importance in the history of our country and we can all feel proud to have seen the day when an Indian National Government has been formed for the first time. Unfortunately the Muslim leadership of today has chosen to take a different course. We all feel ashamed of what has happened in Calcutta. No Indian can help feeling sorry about it. It has brought discredit to the country and has disgraced the League all over.

You must have heard about the dastardly attack on Sir Shafaat Ahmed, who chose to differ from the League, and his place with us. Where the League leadership will lead the Muslims by this method one cannot say. The Muslims may well say that they may be saved from their so-called saviours.

Yours Sincerely
Vallabhbhai Patel

New Delhi, 25 August 1946

LETTER TO K. C. NEOGY

My Dear Neogy,

...You must have noticed from the activities of Mr. Suhrawardy in Calcutta that he is considerably unnerved by the agitation of partition of Bengal which is sure to separate Calcutta from Eastern Bengal which is destined to be the League portion of Pakistan if it persists in its demand. I am afraid this cry of a sovereign independent Bengal is a trap in which even Kiran Shankar [Roy] may fall with Sarat Babu [Sarat Chandra Bose]. The only way to save the Hindus of Bengal is to insist on partition of Bengal and to listen to nothing else. That is the only way to bring the Muslim League in Bengal to its senses.

I am aware of the threat which Suhrawardy has given in his statement and which he may try to execute in the event of partition, but we shall take all possible precautions to prevent such a catastrophe. At present unfortunately the proposed announcement has been postponed for a fortnight and during that period the tension and war of nerves will continue but there is no help....

Yours Sincerely
Vallabhbhai Patel

New Delhi, 13 May 1947

I DO NOT THINK IT WILL BE POSSIBLE TO CONSIDER HINDUSTAN AS A HINDU STATE

Dear Brij Mohan,

I also feel happy that the announcement of 3 June at least settles things one way or the other. There is no further uncertainty.

I quite agree that Bengal leadership is very problematic, but that is a question largely for Bengalis to solve.

I do not think it will be possible to consider Hindustan as a Hindu State with Hinduism as the State religion. We must not forget that there are other minorities whose protection is our primary responsibility. The State must exist for all, irrespective of caste or creed.

Yours Sincerely
Vallabhbhai Patel

10 June 1947

INDIA IS ONE AND INDIVISIBLE

...The Congress had pledged to rid the country of foreign domination; and, after making considerable sacrifices and bearing prolonged sufferings, it has now succeeded. But the Congress has also strived for United India and a union of all communities. Unfortunately, it could not lay claim to success on that count. This was due to factors beyond its control. Their joy on August 15 would have been fuller and greater had not India been divided!

I would make no efforts to explain away the responsibility of the Congress to divide the country. We took these extreme steps after great deliberation. In spite of my previous strong opposition to partition, I agreed to it because I was convinced that in order to keep India united it must be divided now.

My experience in office during the past year showed that it was impossible to do anything constructive with the Muslim League in. The League Representatives during their continuance in office did nothing but to create deadlocks and their role was entirely an obstructionist one. Besides, I found that the Muslims, save for a few exceptions, engaged in all capacities in the Government, were with the Muslim League. Thus the rot that had set in could not be permitted to prolong any longer except at the risk of a disaster for the whole country. Indeed, at one stage, things had become so bad that with the killings at Calcutta riots spread all over and it became a perilous adventure for Hindus and Muslims to visit one another's localities. The economic life of the country was paralysed and there was little security of life or property.

The only way out of the sickening situation the Congress realized, lay in the elimination of the third party-the British Power. The British, on their part, declared that they would quit by June 1948. But the period was long. Also their Statement promising to hand over power to the authorities in the Provinces gave rise to a vigorous effort to dislodge the Ministries in Assam, the Punjab and the Frontier Province. The League succeeded in the Punjab. Even though they failed in the Frontier Province and Assam, the League movement caused great misery and bloodshed.

In order to settle the issue immediately and prevent the slaughter of innocent people, the Congress decided to agree to the division of the country and demanded the partition of the Punjab and Bengal. This was no surrender to the League threats or the policy of appeasement.

Today the partition of India is a settled fact and yet it is an unreal fact! I hope, however, that partition would remove the poison from the body politic of India....

India is one and indivisible. One cannot divide a sea or split the running waters of a river. The Muslims have their roots in India. Their sacred places and their cultural centres are located in India. I do not know what would they do in Pakistan and it would not be long when they would like to return.

Despite the division, it must be remembered, we have 80 per cent of the country with us which is a compact unit with great potentialities.

The main task before India today is to consolidate herself into a well-knit and united power....

The need of the hour is to increase the wealth of the country and this can only be done by putting in more and more work and thus increasing production. This necessitates preservation of peace in the country. For one year now, there has been disorder in the country. Now that Pakistan has been established, there should be no more fights between Hindus and Muslims. If, unfortunately, there would be a recurrence of strife, it would not be the cowardly killings of innocent people, but it would be between two armies of the two States....

India has nothing but goodwill towards all. But if her safety is endangered she must have strength to defend herself; and, for that, people must work hard.

Delhi, 11 August 1947

LETTER TO RAJENDRA PRASAD

My Dear Rajen Babu,

...

2. I am sending you herewith a copy of the Delhi Daily Situation Report for 4 September 1947 which will show what the factual position is in regard to attacks by one community or the other. You will notice that the attacks have been almost all one-sided and the aggressors have been Hindus or Sikhs. This seems sufficient to disprove the fears entertained by Hindus and reported to you....

3. There is a sufficiently large number of Muslims amongst the police force in Delhi, but it is difficult to displace them because they are permanent Government servants, and to discharge them without any charge would involve the payment of compensation. We suggested to the Pakistan Government that they might exchange with us the staff in the Chief Commissioners' provinces who might opt for Pakistan with the staff in Baluchistan who might opt for India, but the Pakistan Government were unwilling and therefore the matter had to rest there. Nevertheless, we have been able to restore the balance in the representation of various communities in the upper ranks of the police force. As regards the lower ranks, the position is difficult, but I am trying to have the Muslim element rendered as innocuous as possible.

4. Regarding arms licences, we have already given licences to two or three Hindu dealers for the sale of arms. We have also, during the last six or eight months, been giving arms liberally to non-Muslim applicants, but it would be impossible during the present disturbed conditions of Delhi to embark on any more liberal policy, as in the present atmosphere surcharged with distrust, suspicion and grievances against Muslims for the tragedies of West Punjab, we cannot be certain that this would not be used in aggression against Muslims, thereby resulting in the creation of a complete state of lawlessness.

5. As regards the postscript in your letter, the news regarding finding permanent accommodation for a further quota of 35,000 Meo refugees is incorrect.... I am doubtful, however, whether we need give the matter

such prominence as to issue a contradiction. Canards like this appear from time to time, and the best policy seems to be to ignore them.

Yours Sincerely
Vallabhbhai Patel

New Delhi, 5 September 1947

WAR OF THE JUNGLE

I remember how in this very city, Amritsar, I had discussions, a few years ago, for raising a fitting memorial to the martyrs of Jallianwala Bagh and how it was at Lahore, for the first time, that Hindus, Sikhs and Muslims took the pledge of Complete Independence! In the blood-bath of Jallianwala Bagh was mingled the blood of Hindus, Sikhs and Muslims. It bleeds my heart to think that things have now come to such a pass that no Muslim can go about in Amritsar and no Hindu or Sikh can ever think of living in Lahore. The erection of a memorial to Jallianwala Bagh martyrs has become a painful memory. It is indeed tragic that this hard-won Freedom has been followed by such unspeakable tragedies. This is a situation which has brought dishonour and disgrace to all of us and India. After the attainment of Independence we were looking forward to raise her stature in the eyes of the world. But alas, she has now to hold her head in shame!

The butchery of innocent and defenceless men, women and children do not behove brave men. It is the war of the jungle and the hallmark of inhumanity and barbarism. There would be occasions and opportunities to all of us to show our zest for fight. It is not a time to be foolhardy or desperate, but it is a time to reflect calmly on our course of action.

We have won our Freedom to make our country great and prosperous—not to destroy what little has been vouchsafed to us by our alien rulers. If we are not careful, we shall lose even our long-cherished Freedom which we have secured after such sufferings and struggles. We must remember that the lives of millions are at stake and they cannot be gambled with to satiate the spirit of vengeance or retaliation in us.

I am quite certain that India's interest lies in getting all her men and women from across the border and sending all Muslims out from East Punjab. We can then settle down to the tremendous tasks of repairing the damage done to us and to make this land by our labours the same fruitful garden as our refugees has left behind.

I deprecate the demand for Police and Military aid. Such a demand may befit the weak; but it does not suit the brave and able-bodied men of the Punjab. They should organize themselves on the right lines. The safety and defence of the frontiers are the concern of the Government. But at the same time people should also organize themselves. The Government will give them arms and equipment if they knew how to use them on right lines.

I have come to you with a specific appeal and that is to pledge the safety of Muslim refugees crossing the city. It is hardly creditable to us that we do not realize wherein our good lies. Muslim evacuees are going under agreed arrangements of exchange of population. They should really need no protection and they should be allowed to go in peace. Bitterness fed by the years of propaganda of hate has gone too deep to allow any Muslim to remain in East Punjab and any Hindu or Sikh to live in West Punjab. It is, therefore, in the interest of every one that this exchange should be effected peacefully and smoothly. Any obstacles or hindrances would only worsen the plight of our refugees who are already passing through fire and brimstone with great courage and endurance.

It behoves ill for a brave people to perpetrate deeds of brutality on defenceless men, women and children. This is not dictated by any code of chivalry or honour. If others cast chivalry and honour to the winds, it does not justify us in debasing ourselves. If we have to fight, we must fight clean. Such a fight must await appropriate time and conditions and you must be wary in choosing your ground. To fight against the refugees is no fight at all. No laws of humanity or war among honourable men permit the murder of people who have sought shelter and protection. Such misdeeds on the other side could be left to be tackled at a more opportune moment.

I appeal to you to act with prudence and foresight. You should allow free and unmolested passage to the Muslim refugees.

Let there be a truce for three months in which both sides can exchange their refugees. This sort of truce is permitted even by laws of war. Let us take the initiative in breaking this vicious circle of attacks and counter-attacks. They do good to nobody. They can only do a great deal of harm to us.

If you have no faith in Pakistan Government or in its people, you can hold your hands for a week and see what happens. If they do not observe the truce in right spirit, the world will know who the offenders of the law of humanity are. We shall have then every justification for holding them to account. Let the whole world see that we mean well and we mean business.

Amritsar, 30 September 1947

I WANT HINDUS AND MUSLIMS TO FORGET THE PAST

I have a special word of advice to say to Hindus and Muslims of Kathiawar. I recall how in the past Muslims of Kathiawar contributed to the League's 'Two-Nation Theory' propaganda and how they took part in League politics. But I have forgotten the past which is dead and gone if only they will treat it as such. But if they still feel an attachment to the 'Two-Nation Theory' and look to an outside power, they have no place in Kathiawar.

It was to put an end to this dual loyalty that we agreed to create Pakistan so that those who preferred to abide in that faith can find a place where they can pursue it. In India, there is no place for such persons. If they stay in India, it can only be as loyal citizens; otherwise they have to be treated as foreigners with all the attendant disabilities. They should live in India like brothers and in harmony with non-Muslims.

I call upon Hindus to follow Mahatma Gandhi in his creed of non-violence. Recent disturbances have disgraced India in the eyes of the world and it is for us to win back our lost reputation by correct behaviour and noble conduct. At the same time I deplore the tendency to get panicky. If we have to die, we must die like brave men. As human beings with a sense of human dignity, we cannot die crying.

I want Hindus and Muslims to forget the past and to live happily together. To make it possible, let Muslims in India search their conscience and ascertain if they are really loyal to this country. If they are not, let them go to the country which claims their allegiance.

Rajkot, 12 November 1947

THE DANGERS OF PREDOMINANTLY MUSLIM OR PREDOMINANTLY HINDU AREAS IN THE CITY

My Dear Neogy,

I have just now seen an office memorandum signed by [S. K.] Kirpalani intimating that it has been decided that houses in certain predominantly Muslim *mohallas* in Delhi, which have fallen vacant, should not be let to non-Muslim refugees, but given instead only to Muslims so that certain *mohallas* could form compact Muslim blocks in the city. As far as I know, there is no Cabinet decision on this matter. If any such decision was reached, it is obvious that it has wide repercussions from the internal security point of view and I feel that I, as Home Minister, should have been consulted before this decision was reached.

2. The dangers and evils of predominantly Muslim or predominantly Hindu areas in the city or outside have been clearly and unmistakably emphasised during the last disturbances. I thought we should be wise after this experience, but I regret to find that the decision which has been notified to all of us is going to perpetuate these dangers and instead of increasing mutual confidence and trust between the major communities it is going to create eyesores and miniature Pakistans and Hindustans in the whole city.

3. I should be grateful if you would kindly apprise me of the circumstances leading to this decision and would also withhold the implementation of those orders until the matter has been considered in all its aspects and a policy decision taken.

Yours Sincerely
Vallabhbhai Patel

New Delhi, 21 November 1947

LETTER TO JAWAHARLAL NEHRU

My Dear Jawaharlal,

...

2. It is because I sincerely felt and still feel that the creation of Muslim pockets would be directly contrary to that policy that I ventured to take this matter up with Neogy. Creation of Muslim pockets in the city would not restore conditions of security. Instead it would lead to constant friction and conflict between rival camps entrenched in their respective positions. I also feel that the mere fact that a certain number of wrong type of persons settled in some localities have given rise to some trouble should not be decisive. We could replace them by better elements. It is also difficult to believe that in a predominantly Muslim locality a few non-Muslims could create a situation which would compel Muslims to leave the locality. The answer in such cases is to replace the unruly elements and to make adequate security arrangements to ensure that this kind of mixed locality prospers rather than vanishes. I also feel that the notion that Muslims can feel or can be given a sense of security only in Muslim *mohallas* is a negation rather than corollary of the AICC resolution. In any case Muslims from outside should not be imported into *mohallas* of Delhi.

3. In these circumstances I would suggest that the matter had better be discussed by the Cabinet before any further action is taken to implement the proposal....

Yours Sincerely
Vallabhbhai Patel

New Delhi, 22 November 1947

LETTER TO GOVIND MALAVIYA

My Dear Govind,

...The point that you have raised in your letter about those who have in the past worked for, or had sympathy for, Pakistan choosing to stay in India for future service has not escaped our attention. Such people will be given no option. I have noticed in my experience during the last 10 months that the Muslim personnel of the services are thoroughly disloyal to Government, and it was impossible to run any administration efficiently or even tolerably fairly. Their full energy was concentrated in disruptive activities inside the organisation. There was no discipline, and they were not afraid of doing anything contrary to rules. We have therefore taken care to see that all such elements in the services go over to Pakistan.

After 15 August, the service rules and regulations will be strictly enforced and no disloyalty will be tolerated. The oath of loyalty to the Indian Government will first be administered to all, and anyone found to have any other sympathy or loyalty with any outside agency or organisation will have to leave service. You may therefore rest assured that proper action will be taken to see that all such people are weeded out from here.

Yours Sincerely
Vallabhbhai Patel

New Delhi, 7 July 1947

LETTER TO BALDEV SINGH

My dear Baldev Singh,

...I understood from you that the question of defence of the frontier was engaging the attention of the Commander-in-Chief. I feel that the Sikhs and Hindus of the East Punjab are very considerably, and for good reasons, exercised over this problem and we should take immediate action to allay their anxiety. The matter, as far as I see, can brook no delay. I hear that the Pakistan Government have made arrangements to settle Frontier Pathans within a belt of the territory near the Indian border. This in itself shows that we should be extremely vigilant. If necessary, you can seek early orders of the Cabinet on this problem.

2. In the meantime, the Provincial Government is organising a National Volunteer Corps and a sort of local militia. In the public meeting at Amritsar I myself made it clear that the Central Government would not hesitate to supply arms if people knew how to utilise them

on the right lines. I feel that there is no getting away from ensuring local co-operation in the defence of the frontier and the only way to do so is in the first place to give the reliable element of this population the means to defend themselves and to demonstrate to them that we are making the necessary preparations....

Yours sincerely,
Vallabhbhai Patel

1 October 1947

LETTER TO A. E. PORTER*

My dear Porter,

... Yes, many things, some almost cataclysmic, have happened since you left India but thank God we have survived the storm and have turned the corner. At one time it seemed that we would be completely overwhelmed but the people stood firm and four-square and we managed to hold them together. We are now settling down and hope shortly to take up the threads of rehabilitation and reconstruction which seemed almost to have snapped.

The disturbances in the Punjab did not come as a surprise to me. The poison of hate spread by the League had its inevitable reaction. The cleavage between the two communities had become wider and wider ever since the policy of the Conservative Government had put a premium on intransigence and obstinacy. We had hoped that the shock of freedom would evoke a healthy reaction. It was a risk and a grave risk, but we felt—and I think rightly so—that that risk was worth taking, since the stakes were freedom and domination.

I had also hoped that the partition would be throughout regarded as a friendly and brotherly arrangement giving scope for all communities in both the dominions to seek their own salvation and their own prosperity, but, unfortunately, elements which meant differently asserted themselves almost all over Western Pakistan and lawlessness overtook

*Porter was ICS and secretary, Home Department, during the term of the Interim Government in 1946–47.

Eastern Punjab. This engendered suspicions, bitterness and ill-will with the result that the relations between the two dominions became strained almost to a breaking point. Junagadh and Kashmir provided further bones of contention which increased estrangement.... Unless the Pakistan Government have the courage to disown the elements who have replaced the rule of law by the rule of brute force and are bent upon forcing a decision to their way of thinking, I feel that the situation is full of dangerous possibilities.... I have never spared myself in explaining to the people here and abroad that we genuinely mean friendship and prosperity for the new State of Pakistan and that we ourselves do not wish to force a union, though true to our convictions we feel that a union is inevitable. On the other hand, we would welcome a friendly reunion whenever there is a genuine desire amongst our brethren in Pakistan to return to us....

Yours sincerely,
Vallabhbhai Patel

19 December 1947

LETTER TO DR GOKULCHAND NARANG

Dear Friend,

... I am sorry to say that your letters make very painful reading. You seem to believe that we do not know what is happening in the Frontier or in the Punjab, or that we do not care for what is happening there. If that is your belief, it is futile for us to try to convince you otherwise. If you think that our vacating this place from the Central Government would be of help to the Hindu community, we are prepared to do so. Your having no confidence in us is understandable, but your prejudice against the Congress is so great that no Congressman would be able to convince you that they are capable of discharging their duty towards the great Hindu community or the brave Sikh community as well as any Indian....

You are labouring under a misapprehension that the Central Government has got powers which are not being exercised in this crisis. You also feel that we are not in touch with events that are happening in the Punjab and that we get our information only from the newspapers.

You must know that there is what is called the Intelligence Department of the Government of India. There is also the Military Intelligence Service. There is, therefore, nothing which is not known to us, and of which you are aware.

Both my colleagues had come there in consultation with me and they have done what was possible for them to do. We are also doing what is possible at this end, but you cannot ignore the fact that under the present Constitution that has been functioning the provinces are more or less independent and therefore the controlling authority in emergencies is the Governor and the Viceroy.

You have not understood correctly my speech at Meerut or at other places. I still stand by that, but that speech does not indicate that I am going to provide swords for the Hindus in the Frontier or in the Punjab or in any other minority areas. My advice to them was to be prepared to defend their lives, property and the honour of their womenfolk. After all, when the third party is going to disappear, in the transitional period, trouble is bound to arise, and the unfortunate people residing in the minority areas have to bear the brunt. They must be prepared to face the consequences. It is no use demoralising them by simply raising cries or throwing blame on others. That would not help them at all....

When I was at Poona, I had seen a letter addressed by you to Gandhiji in very offensive terms, and since then we had come to the conclusion that no useful purpose would be served by carrying on any correspondence with you. You hold very clear ideas about us, and perhaps you don't think that we know our duties and responsibilities. Excuse me, therefore, if I thought it right not to respond to your letters in order again to hear from you in not very pleasant terms.

I can only assure you again that without your reminding us of our duties, we are fully conscious of them and are doing what is humanly possible for us to do.

Yours Sincerely
Vallabhbhai Patel

25 March 1947

CREATING THE RIGHT ATMOSPHERE

Due to Mahatmaji's fast, I came here with a heavy heart. But, today, that heavy load has been lifted off my mind as the Father of the Nation has agreed to end the agony of his heart. That is all to the good. But we must reflect upon as to why such fasts became necessary. The world is at a loss to know what failings of the Indian people could have impelled this great man to undergo so much of self-imposed suffering! I hope this fast will be a lesson to the Governments and people to discharge country's affairs in a right manner....

The Government is fed up with handling the industrial unrest in Bombay, Kanpur, Ahmedabad, and Calcutta, etc., when they have to attend to far bigger problems such as Kashmir, Junagadh and Hyderabad, etc. Refugees from Karachi are crying for help and for sufficient transport to migrate to India immediately. I appeal to Bombay to sympathize with the Sindh refugees and endeavour to absorb them in society. The Sindhis who have now come over to India have left behind them some 400 to 500 crores worth of property!...

We cannot, however, compensate this loss by asking more Muslims to quit India. We can be compensated only by negotiation and agreed settlement between the two Dominions. Such a settlement will have to be reached sooner or later. But in order to reach such a settlement, the right atmosphere would have to be created. It was to create such an atmosphere that Mahatma Gandhi undertook his fast. It remains to be seen how far the object aimed at could be achieved.

Bombay, 18 January 1948

WE MUST CREATE AN ATMOSPHERE IN WHICH EVERYONE CAN LIVE IN CONFIDENCE AND SECURITY

We have thus accomplished so much. Many criticized us saying that it is a Congress Government and is favourable to Muslims. Those who think on these lines have now seen what we could do. Take the example of Hyderabad. You know that so long as a mango is unripe it tastes sour. But when it ripens, it falls to ground of its own accord and tastes sweet. That is what actually happened about Hyderabad.

You can now taste its sweetness whereas formerly your teeth would have been blunted by its sourness. Do they imagine that when we took over the reins of Government from princes it was only because we wanted to occupy a chair and order things about? We are not such traitors as they imagine us to be. We have not assumed powers to advance the cause of Muslims at the expense of Hindus. To be Hindus is not their [RSS–Hindu Mahasabha people's] monopoly. We are also Hindus. We do not believe in killing our opponents as some of our critics do. They say it was a revolver from Gwalior which was used in killing Gandhiji. The mere suggestion that it came from Gwalior is a matter of shame to Gwalior. Those who believe in that way can never succeed in ruling over India. If they have any such ambitions, they must first undergo a mental reformation. Mere bodily strength is not enough.... It is nobody's individual concern to deal with disloyal Muslims. They must be treated as your own brothers. If you think that you can go on constantly troubling loyal Muslims because they happen to be Muslims, then our freedom is not worthwhile. We must create an atmosphere in which everyone can live in confidence and security.

Gwalior, 4 November 1948

WHY SHOULD NOT A MEMBER OF ANY COMMUNITY BE THE PRIME MINISTER OF THIS COUNTRY?

There is no place here for those who claim separate representation. Separate representation, when it was introduced in this unfortunate country, was introduced not by the demand of those who claim to have made those demands, but as Maulana Mohammad Ali once said, it was a 'command performance' that has fulfilled its task and we have all enjoyed the fruits of it! Let us now, for the first time, have a change of chapter in the history of this country and have a 'consent performance'. I want the consent of this House and the consent of all the minorities to change the course of history. I hope and trust that the step that we are taking today is the step which will change the face, the history and the character of our country...

For a community to think that its interests are different from that of the country in which it lives, is a great mistake. Assuming that we agreed today to the reservation of seats, I would consider myself to be the greatest enemy of the Muslim community because of the consequences of that step in a secular and democratic State. You have a separate interest. Here is a Ministry or a Government based on joint responsibility, where people who do not trust us, or who do not trust the majority cannot obviously come into the Government itself. Accordingly, you will have no share in the Government. You will exclude yourselves and remain perpetually in a minority. What advantage will you gain? You perhaps still think that there will be some third power who will use its influence to put the minority against the majority and compel the majority to take one or two Ministers according to the proportion of the population. It is a wrong idea. That conception in your mind which has worked for many years must be washed off altogether. Here we are a free country; here we are a sovereign State; here we are a sovereign Assembly; here we are moulding our future according to our own free will....

I remember that the gentlemen who moved the motion here last time, in August 1947, when asking for separate electorates, I believe, said that the Muslims today were a very strong, well-knit and a well-organized minority. Very good! A minority that could force the partition of the country is not a minority at all. Why do you think that you are a minority? If you are a strong, well-knit and well-organized minority, why do you want to claim safeguards, why do you want to claim privileges? It was all right when there was a third party; but that is all over. That dream is a mad dream and it should be forgotten altogether.

Never think about that and do not imagine that anybody will come here to hold the scales and manipulate them continuously. All that is gone. So the future of a minority, any minority, is to trust the majority. ...It will be a misfortune to this country if the majority does not realize its own responsibility. If I were a member of a minority community I would forget that I belong to a minority community. Why should not a member of any community be the Prime Minister of this country? Why should not Mr Nagappa, who today challenges the brahmin be so. I am glad to hear that the ownership of 20 acres of land does not entitle him to be a scheduled caste man. 'That is my privilege;' he said, 'because I am born a scheduled caste man. You have first to be born in the scheduled caste.' It gladdened my heart immensely that that young man had the courage to come before the House and claim the privilege of being born in the scheduled caste. It is not a dishonour; he has an honourable place in this country. I want every scheduled caste man to feel that he is superior to a brahmin; or, let us say: I want every scheduled caste man and the brahmin to forget that he is a scheduled caste man or a brahmin respectively and that they are all equal and the same....

Now the other case is that of the Sikhs. I have always held the Sikh community in considerable respect, regard and admiration. I have been their friend even though sometimes they disclaimed me. On this occasion also, I did advise them that if they insisted, I would give it to them and induce the Committee to agree. But I do feel that this is not in their interests. It is for them to decide. I leave it to them. To ask for this concession for the scheduled caste Sikhs does not reflect credit on the Sikh community. They are not people who keep *kirpans*. They are a different lot. But to keep a kirpan or a sword and to entertain fear is inconsistent. This may react to your cause. I do not grudge this concession to the Sikhs. I will ask the Sikhs to take control of the country and rule. They may be able to rule because they have the capacity, they have the resources and they have also the necessary courage. In any field, either agriculture, engineering or the army, i.e., in any walk of life, you have proved your mettle. Why do you think low of yourself? That is why I am asking the Scheduled Castes also to forget that they are Scheduled Castes. Although it is difficult for them to forget it, it is not difficult for the Sikhs to do so. Therefore, when you acknowledge with gratefulness the concession that we have given, I am grateful to you.

In this country, we want an atmosphere of peace and harmony now not of suspicion but of trust. We want to grow. India today is suffering from want of blood. It is completely anaemic. Unless you put blood into its veins, even if we quarrel about concessions or reservations, we may get nothing. We have to build up this country on solid foundations. As I told you, I was trembling on the day I was appointed as Chairman of this Committee, but I felt proud and today also I feel proud and I hope the House will feel proud that we are able to bring about almost unanimity in removing the past blots in our Constitution (Hear, Hear) and to lay, with the grace of God and with the blessings of the Almighty, the foundations of a true secular democratic State, where everybody has an equal chance.

Let God give us the wisdom and the courage to do the right thing to all manner of people.

26 May 1949

THE ASSASSINATION OF MAHATMA GANDHI

My heart is full of grief and sorrow! I do not know what to say to you. What happened today is a matter of grief and shame.

I went to see Mahatmaji today at four o'clock in the afternoon and was with him for an hour. At five, he took out his watch and told me that it was time for his prayers; and, as he walked towards the prayer-ground, I left Birla House for my place. As soon as I arrived at my house, I was given the ghastly news.

On going back to Birla House immediately, I saw him after the tragedy. His face had the same calm and serene expression. Kindness and forgiveness were writ large on his face.

Of late, Gandhiji was dissatisfied with the state of affairs in the country. The fast which he undertook recently was an outcome of it. How good would it have been if he had laid down his life during that fast! But he had work to do and he survived it. A bomb was thrown on him by a misguided youth, the other day, and he escaped that also but today his life could not be spared for us.

The occasion today is for grief and not anger. Anger is sure to make us forget the great teachings which Gandhiji preached all his life. We did not take his advice during his life and let it not be said that we did not follow him even after his death. That will be a great blot on our name.

Whatever may we feel, we must not forget that now is the test for us. We must stand firmly and solidly without any division in our ranks. The burden which of late India has been called upon to bear is a tremendous one. It would have broken our backs if we had not the support of that great man. That support has now gone. But Gandhiji will still be with us always because his teachings and noble ideals will always be before us. Tomorrow at 4 p.m. his body will turn into ashes but his soul will be with us for all times to come because it is eternal.

What could not be achieved during his lifetime may be fulfilled now! This ghastly tragedy may startle the conscience of the young men of India and make them alive to their duty. Do not lose heart. Stand together and complete the work started by Mahatma Gandhi.

30 January 1948

AN APPEAL FOR PEACE

I am much distressed to find that in some places, particularly in the Province of Bombay and in Kolhapur State, some misguided members of the public have indulged in acts of goondaism against members of the Hindu Mahasabha and the Rashtriya Swayam Sevak Sangh and their offices. Some minor incidents are reported to have occurred in Delhi also. We shall prove ourselves unworthy of Gandhiji's teachings and his trust in us if we yield to feelings of anger and revenge. I should like to assure the members of the public that the Government are fully alive to their responsibilities in bringing to book those who are guilty of this dastardly crime. They would leave no stone unturned to unearth any conspiracy that might have preceded this most tragic and cruel outrage.

It behoves the public, however, to leave this task to the Government and not to take the law in their own hands even in the face of gravest provocation. I hope they will heed the advice I gave in my broadcast on January 30th and avoid letting anger get the better of their judgement. Any outbreak of violence on this occasion would be most unbecoming and would be quite contrary to the lifelong teachings of our great and revered leader whose loss we all mourn.

I would appeal to all sections of the people to keep calm and peaceful and to let each one of us settle down as quickly as we can to our normal tasks. Let them allow the law to take its course and not resort to the unlawful acts of private revenge or public outbursts of frenzy.

2 February 1948

I AM ONE WITH THE PRIME MINISTER ON ALL NATIONAL ISSUES

I am one with the Prime Minister on all national issues. For over a quarter of a century, both of us sat at the feet of our Master and struggled together for the Freedom of India. So far, we have no pronounced differences and it is unthinkable today that when the Mahatma is no more, we would quarrel.

The Socialists say that I have failed to protect the Mahatma. I deny the charge by giving details of the numerous security arrangements that were taken to protect Mahatma Gandhi so far as human foresight could provide.

Before the bomb incident [on 20 January], the Birla House was entirely ringed by armed guards. After the bomb incident, there was a Police Officer in almost every room. I knew Mahatma Gandhi did not like it and he had several arguments with me.

Finally, Gandhiji gave way but sternly insisted that in no circumstances should I permit the search of people who would come to attend the prayers.

He had almost a premonition-for he had said that if anybody wanted to assassinate him, he could do so at the prayer meeting. God's Will be done! So there was no question of the Police searching any one coming to join the prayer congregation.

Nevertheless, there were 30 plain-clothed Police Officers who mingled in the prayer gathering on the day of Gandhiji's assassination. The assassin is said to have knelt down before Mahatma Gandhi; and, as he rose, whipped out a pistol and fired before any one could apprehend him. This was a calamitous misfortune which could not be guarded against.

I strongly repudiate any differences with the Prime Minister. The present Cabinet functions on the principle of joint responsibility. Thus the Prime Minister has ipso facto the resignation of all the members of the Cabinet at all times in his pocket. As a self-respecting man, I would not think of continuing even for a minute in the Government, if I have the least suspicion that I do not enjoy the confidence of my leader.

The Socialist Party were offered seats on the Congress Working Committee. They refused. They were then offered seats in the Central Government. They refused. I then made an offer to hand over one province to them to carry on their experiments without let or hindrance. They refused. And today they exploited the greatest misfortune and calamity of the Nation for party ends....

4 February 1948

LETTER TO JAWAHARLAL NEHRU

My dear Jawaharlal,

...

I have kept myself almost in daily touch with the progress of the investigation regarding Bapu's assassination case. I devote a large part of my evening to discussing with Sanjevi the day's progress and giving instructions to him on any points that arise. All the main accused have given long and detailed statements of their activities. In one case, the statement extends to ninety typed pages. From their statements, it is quite clear that no part of the conspiracy took place in Delhi. The centres of activity were Poona, Bombay, Ahmednagar and Gwalior.... It also clearly emerges from these statements that the RSS was not involved in it at all. It was a fanatical wing of the Hindu Mahasabha directly under Savarkar that [hatched] the conspiracy and saw it through. It also appears that the conspiracy was limited to some ten men, of whom all except two have been got hold of. Every bit of these statements is being carefully checked up and verified and scrutinised, and where necessary, followed up. Sanjevi devotes a considerable time every' day to it. Senior officers of Bombay and GP are in charge of the investigation. Delhi police hardly comes in the picture.

Of course, it is impossible for us at this stage to publicise any of these things or to say anything publicly about what is being done to unearth the conspiracy. Every item of information that is being communicated to us through sources, known and unknown, real, anonymous or pseudonymous, is being investigated. More than 90 per cent of these have been found to be just imagination. Most of these have been directed to the activities of RSS men in various centres. We have followed this up, and except vague allegations that sweets were distributed or joy was expressed, hardly anything of substance has been found in them.

After having dealt with these matters at first hand and discussed these matters in detail with Sanjevi and other officers…. I have come to the conclusion that the conspiracy of Bapu's assassination was not so wide as is generally assumed, but was restricted to a handful of men who have been his enemies for a very considerable time—the antipathy can be traced right to the time when Bapu went for his talks with Jinnah, when Godse went on a fast and some others of the conspirators went to Wardha to prevent him [Bapu] from going. Of course, his assassination was welcomed by those of the RSS and the Mahasabha who were strongly opposed to his way of thinking and to his policy. But beyond this, I do not think it is possible, on the evidence which has come before us, to implicate any other members of the RSS or the Hindu Mahasabha. The RSS have undoubtedly other sins and crimes to answer for, but not for this one….

As regards the RSS in Delhi, I am not aware of any prominent men or active workers whom we have left out. We hear all sorts of reports from somebody or the other regarding a certain person being an active member or not. In some cases, on such reports, arrests were made, and we soon found representations coming from Congressmen themselves testifying to their Congress sympathies and anti-RSS views. We had to release them. In other cases on arrests of RSS people being made on similar information, both we and the Provincial Governments are being accused of rounding up innocent people. In the case of a secret organisation like the RSS which has no records of membership, no registers, etc., securing of authentic information whether a particular individual is an active worker or not is rendered a very difficult task. Nevertheless, I am assured that practically all the important workers of RSS in Delhi have been rounded up. Indeed, some knowledgeable people tell me that we have rounded up more than necessary. I have already asked Provincial Governments, including Delhi, to let us know what has been the result of these arrests, how many have been arrested, how many have been released, what has been revealed in searches, etc. As soon as these reports come in, we shall have to consider our next step. If there are any key men who are still at large, I should like to know their names, so that we can follow them up.

I quite realise that police and the local authorities who arc in Delhi or elsewhere have an appreciable number of RSS sympathisers. Here again, however, the difficulty is to locate the men. Whenever I have received the least information about the names, and particulars of any RSS men in Government service, I have communicated them to Sanjevi or Mehra. In some cases, Government servants in Delhi have already been arrested for RSS activities. Delhi's quota of RSS arrests compares favourably with that of any other place or province. I doubt, therefore, whether the accusation can be substantiated that Delhi police or local authorities have been inactive on account of RSS sympathies. However, I shall again have a discussion with Mehra on the particular problems which you have mentioned and see what further action could be taken.

Yours Sincerely
Vallabhbhai Patel

27 February 1948

LETTER TO SYAMA PRASAD MOOKERJEE

My dear Syama Prasad,

...

2. As regards Savarkar, the Advocate-General of Bombay, who is in charge of the case, and other legal advisers and investigating officers met me at a conference in Delhi before I came here. I told them, quite clearly, that the question of inclusion of Savarkar must be approached purely from a legal and judicial standpoint and political considerations should not be imported into the matter. My instructions were quite definite and beyond doubt and I am sure they will be acted upon. I have also told them that, if they come to the view that Savarkar should be included, the papers should be placed before me before action is taken....

3. I quite agree with you that the Hindu Mahasabha, as an organisation, was not concerned in the conspiracy that led to Gandhiji's murder; but at the same time, we cannot shut our eyes to the fact that an appreciable number of the members of the Mahasabha gloated over the tragedy and distributed sweets. On this matter, reliable reports have come to us from all parts of the country. Further, militant communalism, which was preached until only a few months ago by many spokesmen of the Mahasabha, including men like Mahant Digbijoy Nath, Prof. Ram Singh and Deshpande, could not but be regarded as a danger to public security. The same would apply to the RSS, with the additional danger inherent in an organisation run in secret on military or semi-military lines. Nevertheless, we have already decided upon a policy of gradual releases and more than 50 per cent of those originally detained have already been released in accordance with that policy. It could perhaps be safely said now that a large majority of those who continue to be detained, consists of men whose release would be a danger to public security or would lead to a resuscitation of the activities which we have banned. In the remaining three months, however, it may be possible, if the situation in the country remains satisfactory, to space out their releases. I should add that we have already received rather disquieting reports of the revival of those activities in some form or the other. In any case, as you probably know, none of the detained persons can be kept for a period longer than six months. I shall, however, see what further steps we can take to improve the present atmosphere in the country....

With kindest regards,

Yours Sincerely
Vallabhbhai Patel

6 May 1948

LETTER TO SYAMA PRASAD MOOKERJEE

My Dear Syama Prasad,

... As regards the RSS and the Hindu Mahasabha, the case relating to Gandhiji's murder is sub judice and I should not like to say anything about the participation of the two organisations, but our reports do confirm that, as a result of the activities of these two bodies, particularly the former, an atmosphere was created in the country in which such a ghastly tragedy became possible. There is no doubt in my mind that the extreme section of the Hindu Mahasabha was involved in this conspiracy. The activities of the RSS constituted a clear threat to the existence of Government and the State. Our reports show that those activities, despite the ban, have not died down. Indeed, as time has marched on, the RSS circles are becoming more defiant and are indulging in their subversive activities in an increasing measure. The number or persons arrested is not large; it is just above 500 throughout India. This would show that generally only those are in detention whose release is prejudicial to security. Almost all of them would be due for automatic release next month or so when the period of six months for which it is possible to keep under the various public safety measures will have expired. It is not necessary or desirable to anticipate that event by a fortnight or three weeks. The Premiers are fully alive to the necessity of diverting the enthusiasm and zeal of these persons into more useful channels. I am sure they will take steps to that end.

As regards Communists, here again, both we and the Provincial Governments realise the extent and dangers of the problem and have reached certain decisions how best to tackle it.

As regards Muslims, I entirely agree with you as to the dangerous possibilities inherent in the presence in India of a section of disloyal elements. Here also, we are taking such measures as we can consistent with the needs of security and the secular nature of our State....

Yours Sincerely
Vallabhbhai Patel

New Delhi, 18 July 1948

LETTER TO SYAMA PRASAD MOOKERJEE

My dear Dr. Syama Prasad,

... It is quite clear now that the Hindu Sabhas are being mobilised for the purpose of collecting subscription (for the Defence Fund.) It is futile, therefore, to argue that the Hindu Mahasabha is not officially concerned with it. It was open to the friends and well-wishers of Mr. Savarkar to organise separate agencies for the purpose of collecting funds. If the official organisation of the Hindu Mahasabha is being utilised for this purpose, there can be only one inference, namely, that the Hindu Mahasabha is in it. After what you had written to me last time, this has come to me as a great surprise.

Yours Sincerely
Vallabhbhai Patel

10 September 1948

LETTER TO M. S. GOLWALKAR

Bhai Shri Golwalkar,

Received your letter dated 11th August. Jawaharlal has also sent me your letter of the same date. You are very well aware of my views about the RSS. I have expressed those thoughts at Jaipur in December last and at Lucknow in January. The people had welcomed those views. I had hoped that your people also would accept them. But they appear to have had no effect on RSS persons, nor was there any change in their programmes. There can be no doubt that the RSS did service to the Hindu society. In the areas where there was the need for help and organisation, the young men of the RSS protected women and children and strove much for their sake. No person of understanding could have a word of objection regarding that. But the objectionable part arose when they, burning with revenge, began attacking Mussalmans. Organising the Hindus and helping them is one thing but going in for revenge for its sufferings on innocent and helpless men, women and children is quite another thing.

Apart from this, their opposition to the Congress, that too of such virulence, disregarding all considerations of personality, decency or decorum, created a kind of unrest among the people. All their speeches were full of communal poison. It was not necessary to spread poison in order to enthuse the Hindus and organise for their protection. As a final result of that poison, the country had to suffer the sacrifice of the invaluable life of Gandhiji. Even an iota of the sympathy of the Government or of the people no more remained for the RSS. In fact opposition grew. Opposition turned more severe, when the RSS men expressed and joy and distributed sweets after Gandhiji's death. Under these conditions it became inevitable for the Government to take action against the RSS.

Since then, over six months have elapsed. We had hoped that after this lapse of time, with full and proper consideration the RSS persons would come to the right path. But from the reports that come to me, it is evident that attempts to put fresh life into their same old activities are afoot. I once again ask you to give your thought to my Jaipur and Lucknow speeches and accept the path I had indicated for the RSS. I am quite certain that therein lies the good of the RSS and of the country and moving on that path we can join hands in achieving the welfare of our country. Of course, you are aware that we are passing through delicate times. It is the duty of every one from the highest to the lowliest in the country to contribute his mite, in whatever way possible, to the service of the country. In this delicate hour there is no place for party conflicts and old quarrels. I am thoroughly convinced that the RSS men can carry on their patriotic endeavour only by joining the Congress and not by keeping separate or by opposing. I am glad that you have been released. I hope that you will arrive at proper decision after due consideration of what I have said above. With regard to the restrictions imposed upon you I am in correspondence with the C.P. Government. I shall let you know after receiving their reply.

Yours,
(Sd.) Vallabhbhai Patel Offers Vande Mataram

New Delhi, 11 September 1948

LETTER TO M. S. GOLWALKAR

Bhai Shri Golwalkar,

...

2. From the reply which I had given to your letter, you will

appreciate the whole situation. It is in consultation with all the Provinces that action has been taken against the Sangh. Only recently, the suggestions of the Provinces were again taken. But their opinion is still the same, that the notification imposing ban on the Sangh cannot be withdrawn. You are aware that our own men are there in all the Provincial Ministries. When it is the unanimous opinion of all of them that the notification be kept in force, then there must be some defect in the organisation itself. No one has any animosity against the organisation. If even then their opinion is like this, there must surely be some real basis for it.

3. After viewing all the things my only suggestion to you is that the Sangh should be brought to adopt fresh lines of technique and policy. That new technique and new policy can be only according to the rules of the Congress. If there is enthusiasm among the youth or the students it cannot be that it should be expressed in aggression and violence. There are other beneficial paths on which youth and students can be taken, to which I personally and the Government will offer heartiest sympathies....

Yours
Vallabhbhai Patel

New Delhi, 26 September 1948

LETTER TO JAWAHARLAL NEHRU

My dear Jawaharlal

...

6. I had a talk with Golwalkar the day before yesterday when he was here to see me. They seem to be in a chastened mood and their sense of discipline is still very strong. I had made it quite clear that if he came to Delhi there should be no demonstrations, to receive him at the station, there were three to four thousand people who received him in silence. Nobody said a word and no demonstration was made. They all obeyed the dictates of the Guru [Golwalkar] implicitly. I am beginning to think as to how long under a democratic set-up we can justify restrictions on this organisation, if their unlawful activities are

abjured by them. I have made my views quite clear to Golwalkar, viz. that the Sangh will have to change its entire outlook and its programme before Provincial Governments could be satisfied that these activities would cease to be a menace to the peace and tranquillity of India. I also drew his attention to the reports which we are receiving regarding the secret activities of RSS men....

Yours,
Vallabhbhai Patel

New Delhi, 19 October 1948

HINDUISM CAN NEVER BE IN DANGER IN INDIA

Do not be led away that Hinduism is in danger. Hinduism can never be in danger in India. Have we not produced men of religion in the past who spread religion and culture all over India? What did Shankaracharya do? When he died, how young he was! But did he raise the cry that Hinduism was in danger? Religion is a matter between man and his Maker. If you forget your citizenship and talk of religion, it is a cloak. Therefore, when I hear some people talking about Hinduism in danger, I feel that they are going a wrong way. Do not indulge in scare-mongering for selfish ends. Do not employ wrong methods for catching votes or forming the parties. It is a very dangerous game. After all, we too want to serve our own people.

Ernakulam, 13 May 1949

LETTER TO JAWAHARLAL NEHRU

My dear Jawaharlal,

I have now received the correspondence which has passed between Ramdas [Gandhi, Gandhi's son] and Godse as also a copy of his letter to you. I adhere to my previous view that he should not see Godse. As it is, there is every likelihood of an attempt being made to treat him as a martyr. The discussion which Ramdas proposes to have would invest the last days of Godse with a certain amount of glory. To me, it appears somewhat quixotic that any attempt should be made to convince a man who has done such a dastardly crime and takes pride in it. Ramdas is not equal to him at all.

Yours Sincerely
Vallabhbhai Patel

Camp Dehradun, 16 June 1949

LETTER TO JAWAHARLAL NEHRU

My dear Jawaharlal,

… Golwalker came and called on me today. I had a general talk with him, explaining to him what the pitfalls were which the RSS should avoid in the interests not only of itself, but of the country at large. I particularly emphasised completely eschewing destructive methods and adopting a constructive role, and warned him against the suicidal policy of the Savarkar group, of which Godse was the exponent. I found him quite receptive and full of understanding. I have a feeling that he will not give us any trouble and will now adapt himself to the new requirements.

Yours Sincerely
Vallabhbhai Patel

Bombay, 9 August 1949

LETTER TO JAWAHARLAL NEHRU

My dear Jawaharlal

… Our difficulty in regard to Master Tara Singh is that he is a fanatic and will not change. There is no doubt that he commands some influence among the Sikhs. We have been able to solve the Sikh problem in so far as their political demands are concerned. This, I think, was possible only because Master Tara Singh was not there to influence the Sikhs otherwise. I feel it would be a mistake and would probably lead to trouble if we released him before the Sikh problem was settled. It is only when all these matters have been finally settled and we have taken an undertaking from the Sikh leaders that they have no other demands to make that it would be proper to release Master Tara Singh. We can then and only then take whatever risk is involved. I followed the same policy in the case of Golwalkar. It was only after I had made him agree to a satisfactory constitution for the RSS and got some assurances and undertakings in regard to the Sangh policy for the future that I thought it safe to release him….

Yours Sincerely
Vallabhbhai Patel

17 July 1949

LETTER TO G. B. PANT

The Prime Minister has already sent to you a telegram expressing his concern over the developments in Ayodhya. I spoke to you about it in Lucknow. I feel that the controversy has been raised at a most inopportune time both from the point of view of the country at large and of your own province in particular. The wider communal issues have only been recently resolved to the mutual satisfaction of the various communities. So far as Muslims are concerned, they are just settling down to their new loyalties. We can reasonably say that the first shock of partition and the resultant uncertainties are just beginning to be over and that it is unlikely that there would be any transfer of loyalties on a mass scale. In your own province, the communal problem has always been a difficult one. I think it has been one of the outstanding achievements of your administration that, despite many upsetting factors, communal relations have generally improved very considerably since 1946. We have our own difficulties in the UP organisationally and administratively as a result of group formations. It would be most unfortunate if we allowed any group advantage to be made on this issue. On all these grounds, therefore, I feel that the issue is one which should be resolved amicably in a spirit of mutual toleration and goodwill between the two communities. I realise there is a great deal of sentiment behind the move which has taken place. At the same time, such matters can only be resolved peacefully if we take the willing consent of the Muslim community with us. There can be no question of resolving such disputes by force. In that case, the forces of law and order will have to maintain peace at all costs. If, therefore, peaceful and persuasive methods are to be followed, any unilateral action based on an attitude of aggression or coercion cannot be countenanced. I am therefore quite convinced that the matter should not be made such a live issue and that the present inopportune controversies should be resolved by peaceful [methods] and accomplished facts should not be allowed to stand in the way of an amicable settlement. I hope your efforts in this direction will meet with success.

Yours Sincerely
Vallabhbhai Patel

9 January 1950

SECTION VI

PRINCELY STATES AND INTEGRATION*

*The official process of the integration of princely states began in June 1947, when Sardar Patel took charge of the newly formed Department of States. He had started lobbying the rulers much before the announcement. Out of more than 560 princely states (barring those adjoining Pakistan) all but three of the states (Jammu and Kashmir, Junagadh, and Hyderabad) signed the instrument of accession with India by the time of Independence.

SECTION VI

PRINCELY STATES AND INTEGRATION

WESTERN CIVILIZATION IS THE ROOT CAUSE OF THE UNREST IN THE WORLD

The people of the princely states need to awaken their selves. They can no longer say that 'We are not the subjects of the British Government. Are we? What do we have to do with this movement?' Can anyone from the princely states say that he is not concerned with [what happened in] Jallianwala Bagh? Who can say that the religion of the Muslims residing in the princely states is different from that of the Muslims staying in the British territory? Both are sailing in the same boat. Fortunately, their awakening has begun. Kathiawad Rajakiya Parishad [Kathiawad Political Conference] is proof of that awakening. The people of the princely states should adopt the self-purification part of our movement vigorously. It will not pose any difficulty for them. They should greet the swadeshi movement. [They should] abandon contempt for the untouchables, give up liquor. They should contribute to the membership of Congress and the Swarajya Fund. We do not expect anything more from them as of now. Some of the kings are worshippers of Western civilization. They fear the spinning wheel would take the country one hundred and fifty years back in the time. They cannot see that Western civilization is the root cause of the unrest of the world. The Western civilization, which has caused the distress between the ruler and the ruled, destruction of big empires, annihilation of the earth by colliding great kingdoms, conflict between the owners and the workers, is built on satanic weapons and material. As the raging cyclone of civilization is gripping the world, Hindustan is the only country that intends to save itself and the whole world if possible, by standing firm against it….

Bharuch, Gujarat, 31 May/1 June 1921

THE PRINCELY STATES HAVE NO REASON TO BE WARY OF THE INDEPENDENT HINDUSTAN

The condition of the princely states is awkward and saddening. No institution in the world is as strange as the states. Their dependence has no limits even if they are known as states. There are many big and small states in Kathiawad alone. The Empire has installed a guard on them. Nothing escapes his eyes. The safety and wisdom of the state are considered in obeying the wishes of the guard. Once upon a time, there must have been agreements between the states and the Empire to consolidate the power of the latter. To fall back on those agreements is akin to a sinking man trying to stay afloat holding a blade of grass. The fact that the states have to hire lawyers spending lakhs of rupees just to interpret old agreements shows the saddening condition of the states. Their claim of friendship with the Empire is claiming too much remaining at the humble position. Can there be a friendship between the lion and the fox? Rulers of many states go to Europe every year. Has any of them been accorded the reception or the felicitation? The area of some of the states is not less than Afghanistan. When the Amir of Afghan toured Europe last year, he was given a reception by all the countries. Everyone wanted to befriend him. What is the reason behind it? The fact is that the princely states are not safe, The Kings are in a state of fear. It is not natural. Because the condition of their state is not normal. The adage that the king's happiness lies in the happiness of the people and people's problems become the king's problems is not observed.

The states remaining in such an artificial condition have the power to harass their populace endlessly. But the real state power does not lie in extracting desired taxes by harassing the state's population or issuing death sentences. The real state power is in protecting the population against all the powers of the world. Not a single princely state, or even if they form a group, has such state power. The long-time dependence has resulted in the vanishing duties of the state. The populace has become soulless, dull, and poor. It is wrong to believe that only Kings are responsible for such a saddening state of affairs. All big and small plants have withered in the canopy of a huge tree of the Empire. They have turned lifeless and almost dead. The anarchy seen in the princely states is the reflection of the anarchy that prevailed in the Empire.

The kings can do much in such a state of limbo. They can extend responsible government to their people to make a weak state strong. It is safer for the states to side with the people rather than taking shelter under the empire. The days of uncontrolled state power have come to an end in such a revolutionary time. Hindustan is a single country. The state's policy cannot be separate for British Hindustan and princely states...The population of British Hindustan has become restless for independence. No one can stop the progress of a populace that has grown impatient for independence.... Notwithstanding the differences in the type of self-rule or independence, it is undisputed that the current system of rule in the British Hindustan will undergo important changes. It has to indirectly affect the population of the princely states. The states will be committing a grave mistake if they would just keep on beating the drums of loyalty. They will have to come to the right path compulsorily after losing a chance to do it voluntarily.... Those states who have sensed the changing times and started establishing public institutions have lost nothing. The princely states have no reason to distrust their people.... Fear causes distrust. People's trust is a symbol of the state's fearlessness. It should be remembered that the people are not for the state, but the state is for the people.

The states' safety and dignity lay in adjusting to the changing times as the day of reconstruction of the governing system come closer.... The place of princely states and the changes needed in their present governance have been accommodated in a scheme drafted by the leaders of all parties of the nation and endorsed by Congress. Most of the makers of the scheme have a favourable approach towards the princely states.... None of them are opponents of the princely states. It is worth giving serious thought to the scheme instead of opposing or keeping away from it. The scheme is designed with the scope for reasonable changes. Such changes can be formulated after discussing them with the makers of the scheme. The princely states will not get strong, but will only become weaker by seeking external help or intervention instead of taking a straight path according to my limited understanding. The princely states have no reason to be wary of the independent Hindustan. They will only get stronger. The interests of the princely states and the people of Hindustan are not mutually opposite. The strength of the one lies in the strength of the other.

Kings are not owners but trustees of the state treasury. The wealth should be spent mostly for the welfare of the people. An expenditure befitting the status of the King is permissible, but there should be a limit to it. The amount of personal expenditure of the King and the definition of personal expenditure should be decided and honestly implemented. The prosperity of the state does not lie in the increasing wealth. Some states are flush with the capital in such a way that their administration can run just from the income of the interest. Such states should reduce the burden of their population. Some are investing in property abroad. A limit to the private property of the state should also be decided.

The hobby of visiting Europe is on the rise among the Kings. The Kings with enjoying centralization of power have no right to go abroad leaving their state even for a day. It causes heavy wastage of the funds of their poor population and is in no way advantageous to the Kings personally. They come back instead with such vices that make them laughing stock in the eyes of the world. Some of the Kings do not like to live in this country at all. When they are compelled to return occasionally, family feuds take place and the queen has to rush to the throne of Delhi to complain about her husband's misdeeds. If such kings want to indulge in unlimited sensual pleasures, they must abandon the throne. The kings must stop wandering abroad for the sake of the prestige of their royal family.

Cruel policy of the [British] government has ruined the farmers of British India. Princely states have copied the policy and made it even merciless. It has resulted in further misery for the farmers of Kathiawad.... Foreign rulers have a different point of view. Their administration cost is high. They have to employ their countrymen with fat salaries. They have to maintain a huge army incurring heavy expenditure. The princely states have no reason to copy it. They do not have to maintain an army. They cannot even if they wish to. The income of the state depends largely on the farmers. They are the feeders of the state. The state that ruins such farmers digs out its base.

The condition of Kathiwad's railway is like a prostitute who has got no husband but only consumers.... Different partner states manage it separately. It causes great inconvenience to the travelers and the merchants.... A committee comprising of the representatives of the partner states, non-partner states, and the people that serve their respective interests should be formed. An independent president should be appointed for effective administration.... The condition of trunk roads has deteriorated gravely after their administration was handled to the princely states.... All states have arbitrarily created a web of octroi duties.... The kings can improve the situation if they wish.

The biggest sin of the British policies has been to destroy the only cottage industry of India tactfully. Before the establishment of the English rule, the country was producing enough for local consumption and was providing cloth worth lakhs of rupees to foreign countries.... All this cloth was made of hand-spun cotton and hand-weaving. Crores of people were getting employment right in their homes without any investment. Their employment is finished. No other profession can give employment to the bulk of these people. The Princely States could have saved their population from this had they wished. Kathiawad is a great place for Khadi. It produces enough cotton.... Lakhs of rupees can be saved by preventing the sale of foreign cloth in Kathiawad. Khadi should get a proud position in the palaces and the institutions of Princely States at least in the interest of the state....

Drinking is prohibited in the religions of both communities—Hindu and Muslims. It is a sin to imitate other states in the matter of excise duty on liquor and to sell and spread the liquor. It does not befit the Princely States. Some states in Kathiawad have set an example by prohibiting liquor....

The untouchables face more hardships in Kathiawad.... It is the state's duty to protect the weak.... The untouchables should have the right to study in public schools, to use the water from public wells and ponds, to rest in public places. They should not be treated as untouchables in the princely court. The sorrow of these people can end easily if the kings wish to do so.

The states might have many shortcomings. But to look at the problems of the states would not do any good to the people. Those tolerating the tyranny help the state getting more oppressive. It is people's duty to stand against oppression. The population that forgets its duty has fewer rights to look at the shortcomings of the state. It is people's right to depose the tyrannical king.... The state cannot do anything against the wish of powerful people. Patience and heavy restraint must be exercised where the population is not awakened and fearless. Getting impatient and hasty might harm people's cause.

There is no trace of public opinion in the Princely States. One might hold Kings or the people or the situation responsible for it. But the fact is people are not able even to complain about their sorrow.

Morbi, 30/31 March 1929

INDIA NEEDS TO INTROSPECT

...There is not a single princely state in India that can not be controlled if its populace knows how to get their right.

Some say the people of Baroda are not fit for a responsible government. ...I believe the most unfit people also have the right to govern and they can govern according to their wishes.

India needs to introspect. Big states are vying to participate in the Central government. If they do not extend that kind of autonomy in their states, they have no right to be part of the central government after British-governed India attains independence. Congress has given that notice to the rulers and the British government too.

...Many in the princely states wish that the states should be abolished. People like me and Gandhiji are dreaming of old times and hope that the rulers will make the dreams of Ram Rajya of old times true. It is also the policy of Congress. It will be friendly with the rulers if possible.

...Many rulers have been claiming that they are ready to give the responsibility [to the people]. But the huge British empire is a hurdle for that. The Dewan of Travancore clearly stated that the paramount power is against granting administration to the people. When the question was raised in Parliament, the straightforward reply was that paramount power had no objection and rulers can grant responsible government to the people if they wish so.

...In the published report of the Butler Committee, paragraphs 41 and 42 unambiguously state that if the majority of the people of a state ask for responsible government, they must get it. There is no need to fight or give up or sacrifice anything for it. ...British government should declare that it will not support the state in the situation of unrest.

...Congress claims that it will not remain a mute spectator if the people of any state, fighting for independence, are oppressed. Congress will support the people. The rulers must understand that no one can separate the people of British India from the people of princely states.

...The rulers should understand that their safety lies not in running here and there, but in securing the love and confidence of their people. They must grant responsible government for that.

Bhadaran, Gujarat, 29 October 1938

A FRAUGHT SITUATION

Human memory is proverbially short. Meeting in October 1949, we are apt to forget the magnitude of the problem which confronted us in August 1947. As the honourable members are aware, the so-called lapse of paramountcy* was a part of the Plan announced on June 3, 1947, which was accepted by the Congress. We had agreed to this arrangement in the same manner as we agreed to the partition of India. We accepted it because we had no option to act otherwise. While there was recognition in the various announcements of the British Government of the fundamental fact that each State should link up its future with Dominion with which it was geographically contiguous, the Indian Independence Act released the States from all their obligations to the British Crown. In their various authoritative pronouncements, the British spokesmen recognized that with the lapse of paramountcy, technically and legally, the States would become independent. They even conceded that theoretically the States were free to link their future with whichever Dominion they liked; although, in saying so, they referred to certain geographical compulsions, which could not be evaded. The situation was indeed fraught with immeasurable potentialities of disruption for some of the rulers did wish to exercise their technical right to declare independence and some others to join the neighbouring Dominion. If the rulers had exercised

*This refers to the fact that from 15 August 1947, owing to the terms of the 3 June plan, all agreements and treaties between the princely states and the British government would lapse, effectively making the former independent states.

their right in such an unpatriotic manner, they could have found considerable support from influential elements hostile to the interests of this country.

It was against this unpropitious background that the Government of India invited the rulers of the States to accede on three subjects of Defence, External Affairs and Communications. At the time the proposal was put forward to the rulers, an assurance was given to them that they would retain the status quo except for accession on these subjects. It had been made clear to them that this accession did not also imply any financial liability on the part of the States and that there was no intention either to encroach on the internal autonomy or the sovereignty of the States or to fetter their discretion in respect of their acceptance of the new Constitution of India. These commitments had to be borne in mind when the States Ministry approached the rulers for the integration of their States. There was nothing to compel or induce the rulers to merge the identity of their States. Any use of force would have not only been against our professed principles but would have also caused serious repercussions. If the rulers had elected to stay out, they would have continued to draw the heavy civil lists which they were drawing before; and, in a large number of cases, they could have continued to enjoy unrestricted use of the State revenues. The minimum which we could offer to them as quid pro quo for parting with their ruling powers was to guarantee to them privy purses and certain privileges on a reasonable and defined basis. The privy purse settlements are, therefore, in the nature of consideration for the surrender by the rulers of all their ruling powers and also for the dissolution of the States as separate units. We would do well to remember that the British Government spent enormous amounts in respect of the Maharatta settlements alone. We are ourselves honouring the commitments of the British Government in respect of the pensions of those rulers who helped them in consolidating their Empire. Need we cavil then at the small—I purposely use the word small—price we have paid for the bloodless revolution which has affected the destinies of millions of our people.

The capacity for mischief and trouble on the part of the rulers if the settlement with them would not have been reached on a negotiated basis was far greater than could be imagined at this stage. Let us do justice to them; let us place ourselves in their position and then assess the value of their sacrifice. The rulers have now discharged their part of the obligations by transferring all ruling powers and by agreeing to the integration of their States. The main part of our obligation under these agreements is to ensure that the guarantees given by us in respect of privy purses are fully implemented. Our failure to do so would be a breach of faith and seriously prejudice the stabilization of the new order.

12 October 1949

HYDERABAD

My dear Lord Mountbatten,

I have been thinking very seriously about the Hyderabad position and I wish to let Your Excellency know my mind before you meet the [Nizam's] delegation.

2. I see no alternative but to insist on the Nizam's accession to the Dominion of India. The least variations in the instrument of accession or arrangement regarding the State's association with the Dominion in regard to the three subjects would not only expose me to the charge of breach of faith with the States that have already joined the Dominion, but would create the impression that advantage lay in holding out rather than coming in and that while no special merit attached to accession, a beneficial position could be secured by keeping out. This is bound to have most unfortunate consequences in our future negotiations for accession to the Union.

3. We have also to recognise that the State has not sent any representatives to the Indian Constituent Assembly, although mere representation of a State in the Constituent Assembly did not commit it to accession to the Union. Popular demand for such representation has been systematically stifled. The affairs of the State, at least in regard to the constitutional association with the Indian Dominion, are being conducted in utter disregard of the sympathies and natural inclination of the majority community in the State. On the other

hand, the minority which is the ruling class is allowed to have more or less its own way and that way clearly is of coercion and violent agitation. I have authentic information that the recent activities of the Ittehad-ul-Mussalmeen are designed almost to create a feeling of terror amongst the non-Muslim population, so that its agitation in favour of the independence of Hyderabad with possible alliance with Pakistan should flourish. It is a militant organisation with an intensely communal appeal and there are indications that it receives active support from responsible Muslims, both inside and outside Government. Indeed there are what seem to be fairly reliable reports that it is being sponsored by HEH himself. I have also had very reliable reports from Hyderabad that the period of two months, which we have agreed to give to the State to make up its mind, is being utilised for preparations rather than for negotiations. The publication of the Nizam's letter of 8 August, the *firmans* issued relating to 15 August, and the events in the State on that day and since then seem to be designed with the sole object of establishing an independent status, as soon as possible, so that at the end of this stipulated period of two months we should be faced with facts either accomplished or as nearly accomplished as possible.

4. In these circumstances, I am convinced that it would neither be proper nor politic for us to agree to any arrangement other than the instrument of accession already settled between us and the other States. If the intentions of His Exalted Highness are bona fide and friendly, and if he is minded to translate the true expression, the will, and the interests of his people into action, there is no doubt at all that he should without hesitation adopt the course which all other States have chosen. As Your Excellency is aware, among those States there are some Muslim rulers, who, in their sympathies apart from those of their subjects, are not differently placed from His Exalted Highness.

5. If, however, the Nizam's Government are still unable to decide their course in the only right direction in which it lies. His Exalted Highness must agree to submit the issue to the judgment of his people and abide by their decision. We, on our side, will be content to accept whatever might be the result of such a referendum and should be

prepared to include Berar in the plans for referendum.

6. There is, however, one thing which is quite clear and should be beyond dispute and that is that a decision on the issue cannot, in my judgment, be postponed any longer.

Yours Sincerely
Vallabhbhai Patel

24 August 1947

LETTER TO JAWAHARLAL NEHRU

My dear Jawaharlal,

I have received your long letter in which you have dealt at length inter alia with Hyderabad. V. P. [Menon] has also come and told me the latest developments in the negotiations with Laik Ali and Monckton. I must frankly say that I was sorely disappointed that even after so much profitless discussion with so many Hyderabad delegations, we are still thinking of producing formulas for their acceptance. (For all practical purposes, it matters little whether the formula is produced by H.E. or V.P.)

2. We have done our best to solve this problem by peaceful means and in an amicable spirit. It was with this intention that we entered into a one-year's standstill agreement. At that time we were given to understand that before the year would be out, the twin problems of accession and responsible government would have been satisfactorily settled. But as we now know, even while the negotiations were going on, the Hyderabad Government were acting in complete breach of the letter and spirit of the agreement that was being negotiated. They have never ceased to assert their sovereignty and independence, even though it must be quite plain to anyone, dispassionately studying that agreement, that both these attributes have been taken away by the standstill agreement. They have fostered and encouraged a militant organisation which is both fascist and brutal in its character and activities and which is a serious menace to law and order not only in Hyderabad, but also in the surrounding Indian Dominion territories. They have perpetrated tragedies upon tragedies on the neighbouring villages in our territory,

and the Hyderabad Government have always either denied or minimised their occurrence. That organisation is in power and calls the tune. In the face of all these, I feel very strongly that a stage has come when we should tell them quite frankly that nothing short of unqualified acceptance of accession and of introduction of undiluted responsible government would be acceptable to us. That, of course, does not preclude an acceptable interim arrangement anticipating and facilitating introduction of responsible government and acceptable to the people of Hyderabad.

3. I would not, therefore, like to waste any more time on devising formulas, but would present the delegation with a brief letter containing the above-mentioned conclusions on behalf of the Government of India. They would then know where we stand and we would be able to follow whatever course of action we consider appropriate. I am also quite averse to delaying action on our part. I am quite definite that such delay would only place us in a worse and not more favourable position, both politically and militarily....

Yours,
Vallabhbhai Patel

June 1948

THERE SHOULD BE NO VACILLATION

My dear Gadgil,

...I am rather worried about Hyderabad. This is the time when we should take firm and definite action. There should be no vacillation; and the more public the action is the greater effect it will have on the morale of our people both here and in Hyderabad and will convince our opponents that we mean business. We should, therefore, go ahead with determination and vigour in applying the economic sanctions as well as in dealing effectively with border and other incidents. There should be no lack of definiteness or strength about our actions. If, even now, we relax, we shall not only be doing a disservice to the country, but would be digging our own grave. About this I am quite clear. We should also put our military in a state of preparedness for all eventualities. It is no use taking a complacent attitude on these questions....

Yours Sincerely
Vallabhbhai Patel

Dehradun, 21 June 1948

A DEMOCRATIC APPROACH

My dear Henderson

...I am glad you have referred to Kashmir and Hyderabad. In both the matters we have been throughout guided by the advice of Lord Mountbatten and our approach is, contrary to what others misrepresent, entirely democratic. We are prepared to be judged by democratic standards, but unfortunately prejudiced correspondents from your country and America deliberately misrepresent our attitude and make it out as if we are indulging in coercive tactics. Unfortunately, it is my experience that the attitude of an average Englishman in India is instinctively against us. There are some honourable exceptions, but those exceptions are rare. I myself felt that we should never have gone to the UNO and if we had taken timely action when we went to the UNO we could have settled the whole case much more quickly and satisfactorily from our point of view, whereas at the UNO not only has the dispute been prolonged but the merits of our case have been completely lost in the interaction of power politics. I should like to say at once that we were so terribly disappointed [at] the attitude of your delegation. Lord Mountbatten helped us to his best capacity, but it was, we maintain, the attitude of Noel-Baker that tilted the balance against us. But for his lead, I doubt if the USA and some other powers would have gone against us.

As regards Hyderabad, I am glad to say the attitude of your Government is more helpful. We are getting reports of smuggling of arms into Hyderabad by some interested Britishers who are private citizens. I fully realise your difficulty in controlling these non-official activities; at the same time, it is such activities which make our task of promoting genuine understanding and co-operation between India and the rest of the Commonwealth most difficult. I wish something could be done to propagate amongst the British public in England that, if they want India's goodwill, they must make capital out of what is left and not fritter it away by these prejudicial activities....

Yours Sincerely
Vallabhbhai Patel

Dehradun, 3 July 1948

A SETTLEMENT WITH HYDERABAD

For over a year now we have been attempting to come to a satisfactory settlement with the Government of Hyderabad. In November last our efforts led to a standstill agreement for one year. We hoped that this would be followed soon by a final and satisfactory settlement. Our view has all along been that the only satisfactory settlement would be for Hyderabad to accept an honourable partnership with the Indian Union, with autonomy in every respect as hitherto enjoyed, with the natural exception in matters concerning public security and foreign affairs. As regards internal government, our view has been that it is inconceivable to permit in the modern age and in the heart of India, which is pulsating with a new freedom, a territory to be indefinitely under autocratic rule and its people without enjoyment of that civic freedom and responsibility which they see exercised all around by the people of India.

Our attempt at a settlement, which so often came near to success, ended unfortunately in failure. The reason for this was obvious to us. There are forces at work which are determined not to allow any agreement to be reached between Hyderabad and the Indian Union, and which have progressively gained strength in Hyderabad and seem now completely to control the Government of the State. Irregular armies have been allowed to grow up; arms and ammunition are being smuggled in from abroad, a process in which foreign adventures are taking a prominent part. The private armies have become more and more aggressive and brutal, and have established a reign of terror. The repercussions of this on the border areas of the Union, and in India generally, have created a far more serious and urgent problem than even the state of political uncertainty. A full account of Razakar activities will take long. I shall give three typical incidents and a few figures.

A village inside the State offered stout resistance to these gangsters and it was put to the sword and burnt when resistance became impossible owing to the exhaustion of ammunition. The brave headman, under whose leadership the village resisted, was decapitated and his head carried about on a pole.

A large party of villagers which had fled in bullock carts in search of a haven of safety against the attacks of the Razakars was brutally attacked and the women abducted.

A train was held up, the passengers looted and a number of coaches burnt.

The House is aware of the attacks on our troops seeking to enter Indian territory enclaves within the State, and of Razakar incursions into our own villages along the border.

In this provocative campaign of violence conducted by the Razakars, 71 villages have been attacked inside the State, 140 incursions have occurred into our territory, 325 persons have been killed, 12 trains attacked, and a crore and a half worth of property looted. The latest act of aggression is the occupation of our buildings in Aurangabad and Jhalna cantonments, forcibly ejecting our watchmen.

The House will agree that we cannot permit such atrocities to continue to be perpetrated with impunity. No one is more conscious than myself of the dangers to India situated as it is today of launching on any action that may ultimately lead to military operations. The heavy task of reconstruction and development is before us calling for immediate attention, and it would be an undoubted waste of opportunity and resources to spend them on unproductive activities, whatever the provocation. I feel also very poignantly that it would be a sad contradiction of the ideals and the principles to which we have repeatedly pledged ourselves right from the beginning to the termination of our struggle for freedom from foreign rule, to launch on anything like armed intervention, but our enemies seem determined to take advantage of this ideological difficulty of ours. We cannot let our attachment to peace ruin the future of India or of those territories that fall by geographical connection within that description. The campaign of murder, arson and loot going on in Hyderabad rouses communal passion in India and jeopardizes the peace of the Dominion. The so-called lapse of paramountcy cannot alter the organic inter-relation of Hyderabad and India, and the mutual obligations of the one to the other.

We have been patient and forbearing. We have tried to act on the principle that no effort should be spared at any time to avoid conflict. At the present moment the dominant issue is not a settlement of the political relationship between India and Hyderabad, but that of public security. All other questions have become secondary, for peace and order are essential for the consideration of other questions. We feel that internal security and a sense of confidence can only be secured at this stage if our troops are stationed at Secunderabad as they used to be before August 1947. It is only this that can, with minimum conflict, secure a termination of the terrorist activities of private armies so necessary for any advance in the direction of peace. We are therefore intimating the Nizam accordingly.

THE PROBLEM OF HYDERABAD

We are all following with interest and admiration the performance of our armies in Hyderabad. They have already made speedy and notable advances towards their objective at a minimum cost of human life and destruction of property. For this, they deserve our full praise and congratulations. I should also like to thank all those—princes and people alike—who have sent me voluntary offers of help and personal service in the present operations against Hyderabad.

The problem of Hyderabad has been commanding public attention for more than a year. In the face of constant provocations, numerous disturbing incidents and heart-rending atrocities perpetrated by well-armed Razakars and Nizam's Police. and Military forces on innocent men, women and children on both sides of the border, the Indian Police have behaved with commendable patience and heartening trust and confidence in the assurances given by the Government that appropriate steps will be taken at the opportune moment and that if a surgical operation was considered necessary, it would be undertaken with all the speed and skill required and at a minimum loss of flesh, and blood.

That operation is now on, after Government have exhausted all other possibilities of alternative treatment. That the country has borne patiently with us during all this critical and delicate periods is a tribute to its essentially peace-loving and basically tolerant nature.

But the most outstanding evidence of the steadfastness and sense of discipline of the people is the manner in which they have falsified the prophets who presaged widespread and bloody communal disorders in the country the moment we raised even our little finger against the mailed fist of Hyderabad.

I should like to congratulate both Muslims and non-Muslims on the warm and unanimous support they have given to their Government in the action which they have had to take against Hyderabad.

The way in which all sections of the Muslim community have rushed to express their approval of that action has been particularly gratifying. There has been no single untoward incident throughout the country and with the co-operation and support of all sections of the people, we have succeeded in preserving the peace when we most needed it, although our enemies wished and hoped otherwise.

To the people of Hyderabad who have undergone so much misery and suffering during the past several months, I should like to send a word of comfort and good cheer. They have now the consolation that their agony will shortly be over and that they would be enabled ere long to take their due and honoured place in Indian polity.

16 September 1948

LEAVE US ALONE

...When people talk of aggression on Hyderabad, they either deliberately misrepresent the thing for whatever motives they may have or they do not understand what aggression is. How can we have aggression on our own people? What is Hyderabad? Is the Nizam Hyderabad? If the people of Hyderabad is Hyderabad it is part of India. The British people still think that Hyderabad is a British preserve. It is one year,** yet they do not understand that they have no claim here. And I trust that this will be the last debate in Parliament in

** Since achievement of Independence.

which reference is made about India's business. Otherwise, we do not want to be forced into friendship. If friendship is not wanted, we have self-respect enough to stand aloof against the whole world. Because if violence is the order of the world, and we have not got sufficient organized violence, we have enough non-violence by which we know how to die. But we know how to preserve our self-respect. Therefore, I wish we have no more sermons from people who still believe that they are trustees here—the trustees of the world. They must know that they had enough mismanagements in all parts of the world. They must now leave us alone.

1 October 1948

LETTER TO THE NIZAM OF HYDERABAD

Dear Exalted Highness,

I should have written to you earlier, but unfortunately I have been plunged in work ever since my return and have hardly any time to myself.

...

2. I was very glad to meet you and to make your acquaintance. As I have written to General Chaudhuri, it was very reassuring to find Hyderabad settling down to recent changes so well.

3. I was also happy to learn that Your Exalted Highness had adapted yourself so readily to changed conditions. As I told Your Exalted Highness, while error is a human failing and divine injunctions all point to forgetting and forgiving, it is the duty of human beings to contribute their share to this process by sincere repentance and by employing the period that is left in discharging their duties to their people and to their God. I should once more like to repeat that advice which, I can assure Your Exalted Highness, is in all sincerity intended to be friendly.

With kind regards

Yours Sincerely
Vallabhbhai Patel

New Delhi, 4 March 1949

THE CONSTITUTIONAL POSITION OF HYDERABAD

...I wish to remove certain doubts about the exact constitutional position of the Hyderabad State and its relations with the Centre. I said yesterday and I want to repeat it today that so far as the Chief Minister and the other Ministers are concerned they are appointed by a *firman* of the Nizam and not by us. After the Police Action the House is aware of the hostile atmosphere in the State where the services were composed of people who had to be placed in restraint or detention and one of them, the principal man, has escaped. In those circumstances, when the whole machinery of the State was such as to make it difficult to put the administration under proper control, we had to give the State trained and experienced officers who would exercise their functions with responsibility. To this State, Mr. Vellodit, a very senior officer, has been given on loan and His Exalted Highness has appointed him as his Chief. The other officer, next to him, Mr. Bakhle is also a very senior officer of the Bombay Government. He is an honest, upright, straightforward and a very able man of high repute. This officer is a Home Minister in charge of law and order. Under him is the Inspector-General of Police to look after the police administration.

If after the Police Action it had been thought necessary for us to treat the State as a conquered State there was nothing to prevent us. If we had found it necessary to remove the Nizam there was nothing to prevent us. But we did not do so because the Nizam himself said that he had been prisoner and that the Indian Government had released him from his prison and his bondage. We had nothing to doubt his statement and everything to support his statement that a clique of conspirators who ruled the State for their own purposes in a fanatical manner had kept the Nizam a prisoner. That was why we could not settle the question of the State's accession. So, when we found the position to be so, we treated him with all the courtesy due to him. And up to now he has been kept in a different position and status and he is today in the position of a Governor of a Province....

New Delhi, 7/8 March 1949

KASHMIR

My Dear Prime Minister,

I am addressing this letter to you after a long time with a heavy sense of responsibility….

You are aware that on 15 August, India, though divided, will be completely free, and you also know that by this time a vast majority of States have joined the Constituent Assembly of India. I realise the peculiar difficulties of Kashmir, but looking to its history and its traditions, it has, in my opinion, no other choice [but to join Indian Union]….

Yours Sincerely
Vallabhbhai Patel

3 July 1947

LETTER TO MAHARAJA HARI SINGH

My Dear Maharaja Sahib,

… Is it necessary to assure you that in your domestic affairs the Congress has no intention whatever of interfering? If it had not been so, the Constituent Assembly would not have been able to attract a vast majority of Princes who have joined it, and I have no doubt that the rest will also join with very few exceptions who have no choice owing to peculiar circumstances, for instance Bhawalpur, Kalat, etc. In the Negotiating Committee, your Prime Minister was present, and our decisions were unanimous in the four meetings that he attended….

I fully appreciate the difficult and delicate situation in which your State has been placed, but as a sincere friend and well-wisher of the State, I wish to assure you that the interest of Kashmir lies in joining the Indian Union and its Constituent Assembly without any delay. Its past history and traditions demand it, and all India looks up to you and expects you to take that decision. Eighty per cent of India is on this side. The States that have cast their lot with the Constituent Assembly have been convinced that their safety lies in standing together with India.

I was greatly disappointed when His Excellency the Viceroy returned without having a full and frank discussion with you on that fatal [fateful] Sunday, when you had given an appointment which could not be kept because of your sudden attack of cholic pain. He had invited you to be his guest at Delhi, and in that also he was disappointed….

May I take the liberty of suggesting that it would be better if you even now come to Delhi, when you will certainly be his guest? We want an opportunity of having a frank and free discussion with you in an atmosphere of freedom, and I have no doubt that all your doubts and suspicions…will completely disappear. In Free India, you cannot isolate yourself, and you must make friends with the leaders of Free India who want to be friends with you.

Yours Sincerely
Vallabhbhai Patel

3 July 1947

LETTER TO N. GOPALSWAMI AYYANGAR

My Dear Gopalswami,

We have not met since you left for the UNO, and after your return I was told that you would some day run up to Mussoorie. But you were all very busy, and hence we had no opportunity to meet.

…

2. I have followed the Kashmir proceedings of the UNO, with considerable surprise and pain. I thought things were straightened before you left, but it seems we are almost where we were before you left. It is difficult to follow British diplomacy in this affair. However, for good or evil, we are in it and we must do our best.

3. The military position is none too good, and I am afraid our military resources are strained to the uttermost. How long we are to carry on this unfortunate affair, it is difficult to foresee.

4. On the civil side, the relations between the Maharaja and Sheikh Abdullah have not improved in spite of several efforts on my part…. It would be desirable if you and Menon would go there for a couple

of days and try to bring about agreement between the two.... It is not possible to continue the present state of tension without serious detriment to the Kashmir cause.

Yours Sincerely
Vallabhbhai Patel

Dehradun, 4 June 1948

LETTER TO JAWAHARLAL NEHRU

My Dear Jawaharlal,

I was surprised to read this morning an account of the Press conference which Sheikh Mohammed Abdullah is reported to have held here yesterday....

It is rather odd that he should have found the venue of a Press conference to ventilate his alleged grievance against the Maharaja. No one should know better than he that the Maharaja is not in a position to resist the demands of the popular Ministry. We, the Maharaja and Sheikh Mohammed Abdullah himself came to a settlement last March. That settlement has not only been faithfully adhered to by the Maharaja but, in certain respects, he has acquiesced in departures from that settlement to the advantage of Sheikh Mohammed Abdullah and his Ministry.... [I] refer in particular to the position regarding the reserved subjects of which the jagirdars form one. I am not aware of any single instance—at least Sheikh Sahib has not brought it to my notice—in which the Maharaja has obstructed or resisted any of the popular reforms. As a constitutional head, he may have asked for reconsideration in one or two matters, but this could hardly be treated as the subject of a grievance. It is undignified and constitutionally improper for a Prime Minister to attack the constitutional head of his administration, knowing full well that the latter is not in a position to defend himself or to retaliate. On top of it, to insinuate that he is trying to retain power, or that he has strong friends in India or that he could buy friends is, in my opinion, to say the least, most unfortunate.

Sheikh Sahib also refers to the Hindu fanaticism of the East Punjab. This again is a generalisation which, I hope, Sheikh Sahib in calmer moments will regret. It certainly is a most unfortunate attack on a neighbouring province of the Dominion to which his State has acceded.

I hope Sheikh Sahib realises that nobody has been more accommodating to him than the Government of India and none has extended to him greater understanding and sympathy in his struggle than the people of India. In spite of the fact that he has departed from an accepted position from time to time, we have tried our best to put pressure on the Maharaja and make him concede the position which he has taken up […] I hope you will succeed in impressing upon him the mistake he has made. We shall have gained something if at least it is not repeated. I thought I would let you have my reactions so that if an opportunity arises you might speak to him some time. I am sending herewith a copy of my letter to Sheikh Sahib.

Yours Sincerely
Vallabhbhai Patel

New Delhi, 30 September 1948

LETTER TO JAWAHARLAL NEHRU

My dear Jawaharlal,

… I have seen Attlee's reply to our approach in regard to the possibility of Pakistan's attack on Kashmir. It is a disappointing reply and in some ways rather makes matters worse in that Pakistan will now come to know of this approach. I am afraid we can rule out any help and co-operation from Britain in settling this point. Indeed, it seems that they are determined not to disturb British military officers who are in Pakistan.

Dehradun, 9 July 1949

LETTER TO DR JOHN MATHAI

My Dear Dr. John Mathai,

I believe the question of arrears of privy purse of His Highness the Maharaja of Kashmir is pending with your Ministry. We have fixed his privy purse at 15 lakhs, out of which 6 lakhs would be paid by the Jammu & Kashmir Government and 9 lakhs by us. The Maharaja has not received any privy purse during, I believe, the whole of last year. This was because Sheikh Sahib said that he could not afford to pay anything more than 6 lakhs, whereas the Maharaja used to be entitled to something like 20–21 lakhs or more. I am sure you will realise the difficulty of the Maharaja's position. He has been putting his trust in us and has always deferred to our views every time that the Sheikh Sahib has been making demands on him. I feel that it would be a breach of faith on our part if we could not give him an amount which we felt was the minimum necessary according to the standards which we have applied to other Princes. Indeed, if we fixed his privy purse on the basis of the scales applied to other Princes, his privy purse would be much higher. I hope, therefore, that in these circumstances you will kindly see your way to apply the existing arrangement with retrospective effect and sanction the additional payment of Rs. 9 lakhs for last year as well. This is a commitment which I feel we should honour. Where crores are being spent on Kashmir, I think we should not mind these few lakhs.

Yours Sincerely
Vallabhbhai Patel

Bombay, 3 September 1949

LETTER TO N. GOPALASWAMI AYYANGAR

My Dear Gopalswami,

… I find there are some substantial changes over the original draft, particularly in regard to the applicability of fundamental rights and directive principles of State policy. You can yourself realise the anomaly of the State becoming part of India and at the same time not recognising any of these provisions.

I do not at all like any change after our party has approved of the whole arrangement in the presence of Sheikh Sahib himself. Whenever Sheikh Sahib wishes to back out, he always confronts us with his duty to the people. Of course, he owes no duty to India or to the Indian Government, or even on a personal basis, to you and the Prime

Minister who have gone all out to accommodate him.

In these circumstances, any question of my approval does not arise. If you feel it is the right thing to do, you can go ahead with it.

Yours Sincerely
Vallabhbhai Patel

New Delhi, 16 October 1949

LETTER TO JAWAHARLAL NEHRU

My dear Jawaharlal,

There was some difficulty about the provision relating to Kashmir. Sheikh Sahib went back on the agreement which he had reached with you in regard to the provision relating to Kashmir. He insisted on certain changes of a fundamental character which would exclude in their application to Kashmir the provisions relating to citizenship and fundamental rights and make it necessary in all these matters as well as others not covered by the accession to three subjects to seek the concurrence of the State Government which is sought to define as the Maharaja acting on the advice of the Council of Ministers appointed under the proclamation of 8 March 1948. After a great deal of discussion, I could persuade the party to accept all the changes except the last one, which was modified so as to cover not merely the first Ministry so appointed but any subsequent Ministries which may be appointed under that proclamation. Sheikh Sahib has not reconciled himself to this change, but we could not accommodate him in this matter and the provision was passed through the House as we had modified. After this he wrote a letter to Gopalaswami Ayvangar threatening to resign from the membership of the Constituent Assembly. Gopalaswami has replied asking him to defer his decision until you returned.

Yours Sincerely
Vallabhbhai Patel

New Delhi, 3 November 1949

LETTER TO JAWAHARLAL NEHRU

I am getting rather worried about Kashmir, particularly the attitude of Sheikh Sahib, his failure to deal with the Communist infiltration in the State, and the dissensions in the National Conference. I have had a talk with P. C. Chaudhuri [Secretary, Ministry of Information & Broadcasting] From what he tells me it appears that both the National Conference and Sheikh Sahib are losing their hold on the people of the Valley and are becoming somewhat unpopular. At the same time, it appears that there is a marked appreciation of what we have done for the Valley though they naturally feel that they deserve more. In such circumstances and in the world situation today, I agree with you that a plebiscite is unreal. Not only that, it would be positively dangerous because my own feeling is that once the talk starts, the non-Muslims in Jammu and Kashmir would start feeling uneasy and we might be faced with an exodus to India. This would be an additional point to emphasise in respect of our stand that the conditions preliminary to plebiscite should be fully and effectively fulfilled before we can talk of it.

Yours Sincerely
Vallabhbhai Patel

Dehradun, 3 July 1950

THE INTEGRATION OF JUNAGADH

...You know how the Nawab of Junagadh had left the State without a shot being fired. The trouble had been brought upon the Nawab's head by the wrong advice which he received from the people who were bent upon mischief and by the machinations of the Pakistan Government itself.

Pakistan had no business to meddle with Junagadh. When we accepted partition, we did so in the hope of a final settlement of a brotherly dispute. We felt that by satisfying the obstinate demand of a brother, who had been a part of the joint family, we would bring peace to both of us and prosperity to all. But hardly had partition been effected when the Punjab disturbances engulfed us. Nevertheless, we took particular care to avoid creating any obstacles in the way of

Pakistan's relationship with the States with whom such relationship was quite natural. We did not attempt to seduce any of their States into our fold. But it was they who throughout made it a business to create difficulties and obstacles for us as much and as often as possible.

Rampur, which was the first to declare its accession to the Indian Dominion, witnessed the first fruits of Pakistan's malevolence. We met this challenge resolutely and the resistance collapsed. Then they sought a foothold in Junagadh. We warned them, we begged of them, we reason with them, but obstinacy was not conquered. We could not be blind to the consequences which this interference with our affairs entailed, and with the affairs of the States which had acceded to us long before they took the final plunge into Junagadh. It was with this idea of safeguarding the rights of the acceding States and the peace of Kathiawar that we had to take precautionary measures and send troops to Manavadar, Mangrol and Babariawad.

Even then we had no intention of marching our troops into Junagadh territory, but then the 'Provisional Government' led by Mr. Samaldas Gandhi took a hand. They took village after village and reached Kutyana. It was then that the advisers of the Nawab, who had already fled, realized that the game was up. They left, leaving the people, who had financed them, in utter predicament.

The Dewan's decision to hand over the administration to the Indian Dominion was reached after Major Harvey Jones had been denied assistance by the Pakistan Government and after the Council and the people had been taken into consultation. It was no hasty decision but a calculated move to accept the inevitable. The Dewan informed the Pakistan Government of what he was doing. We waited for 24 hours to see how Pakistan would react. But there was no response whatsoever. We then decided to march in order not only to preserve the peace in Junagadh but also to forestall its adverse repercussions in the whole of Kathiawar.

I emphatically repudiated Pakistan's contention that the Dewan had no authority to take the action that he did. He had the assent of the Nawab of Junagadh and the backing of the people. What other authority under any conception of sovereignty did the Dewan need in support of his action?

It was, however, Pakistan's practice to use all sorts of devices in order to call in question anything that the Indian Dominion did. They would cry or use threats; sometimes they would blow hot and sometimes cold.

The Dewan in a more congenial atmosphere in Karachi suddenly realized that he had not handed over the administration completely to the Indian Dominion. But his letter is crystal clear and he cannot expect us to hand over the State on a plate after all the misdeeds of himself and his other officers and their desertion of the people. We have said more than once that the final arbiters on this issue are the people and it is by their verdict that we shall be guided. I can assure everybody that the verdict would be a real verdict ascertained in a truly democratic manner. We cannot imitate the methods which Pakistan utilised in forcing a decision in Kashmir.

On the general question of responsible Government in the States, I must say that as one who has done more than anyone else to preserve the true right of the Princes, I feel the Princes can survive only as trustees of the people.

Let them not heed any false or fraudulent advice which interested persons engaged in the pursuit of selfish ends might offer them. Instead, let them carry the people with them. Princes and people belong to one family and their best and mutual interest lies in remaining as a family rather than behaving as foes. But at the same time it is the duty of the people to prove themselves worthy of the great responsibility which a democratic regime entails. Remember how Cochin had seen recently the farthest advance yet made on the road to responsible Government but how, despite the full co-operation of the ruler, the responsible Government in the State came to grief.

...Finally, I feel I should make it clear to you all that there is no question of India being unable to face up to the threats which have been held out. Pakistan's actions are probably prompted by the feeling that India is in trouble and therefore fomentation of trouble in the States would make matters worse.

I assure you that we are not going to let the grass grow under our feet. Even if all these troubles come at the same time, we have got resources which would enable us to stand up to all of them at the same time. If they are anxious to challenge us, we would be ready to accept it. Let no State have evil designs on us or dream of extending its hegemony. Let them not entertain the fond hope of any Jatistan or Rajasthan or Sikhistan. If they persist, all these dreamers will soon be disillusioned. Instead, let them realise which way their true interest lies. I bear Pakistan no ill-will; I wish them godspeed; let them only leave us to pursue our own salvation and stop meddling with our affairs even in places like far-off Tripura. We shall then each settle down to our respective destiny. May be after we have become prosperous, they themselves will awaken to the need for reunion in the best interests of both. It is neither our business nor our intention to force a reunion. We only wish to be left alone so that both can live in peace and prosperity, happiness and harmony.

Rajkot, 13 November 1947

MYSORE STATE

Dear Friend,

I have received your letter of 21 January.

I do not understand what is your stand regarding the demand for responsible government in Mysore. This is an old demand which has so often been repeated by the Mysore Congress and its representatives in the Assembly that no exception can be taken by anybody to such a demand. The words 'wherein sovereignty vests in the people' added to the 'demand for responsible government' are superfluous, and its addition in the principal demand makes no change in the meaning.

Your inference that these words would mean ending the Princely Order is only unjustified. Sovereignty in England vests in the people of England and not in His Majesty the King. It is a constitutional phrase and its meaning is clear. No man in his senses in the modern world believes that sovereignty vests in any single individual, whether he be a prince or a monarch, or a Czar or a Hitler.

Responsible administration means nothing. What is wanted is responsible government in the Indian States, and any attempt to draw difference between responsible government and responsible administration is bound to create suspicion. Therefore, I would advise you to join the demand for responsible government with the Mysore Congress; and it you make a unanimous demand of that nature from the Legislature, I am prepared to advise the Mysore Congress to drop the words to which you object about the vesting of sovereignty in the people. Even without your admission in that behalf, sovereignty is not going to vest anywhere else. I do not understand this kind of quibbling. Let us tackle this problem in a more practical manner. If Mysore, which has been one of the most advanced States in India, gibes even at this stage in granting the long overdue demand of the Congress for responsible government, you may take it that the State will have to face serious troubles in the near future. Nothing in the world can prevent the rapidly marching forces of progress, and it is wise to recognise the writing on the wall.

Yours Sincerely
Vallabhbhai Patel

2 February 1947

THE ACCESSION OF BHOPAL

My dear Nawab Sahib,

Many thanks for your personal letter of 26 August 1947.

...

2. I am deeply touched by its transparent sincerity and cordial tone, and I can assure you that I warmly reciprocate the same.

3. Quite candidly, I do not look upon the accession of your State to the Indian Dominion as either a victory for us or a defeat for you. It is only right and propriety which have triumphed in the end, and in that triumph you and I have played our respective roles. You deserve full credit for having recognised the soundness of the position and for the courage, the honesty and the boldness of having given up your earlier stand, which, according to us, was entirely antagonistic to the interests as much of India as of your own State.

4. I have noted with particular pleasure your assurance of support to the Dominion Government in combating disloyal elements irrespective

of caste, creed or religion, and your offer of loyal and faithful friendship. During the last few months, it had been a great disappointment and regret to me that your undoubted talents and abilities were not at the country's disposal in the critical times through which we were passing, and I, therefore, particularly value this assurance of co-operation and friendship. No Government can tolerate even for a moment subversive influences and activities, and you can rest assured that we, on our part, realise that the sooner we get control over these the better.

5. I am looking forward to meeting Your Highness when you happen to come to Delhi and to talk over our many problems and difficulties pertaining not only to the new relationship between the States and the Dominion, but also the present situation in the country and the part which the States should play in the general advancement of the country.

Yours Sincerely
Vallabhbhai Patel

1 September 1947

LETTER TO G. B. PANT

My Dear Pantji,

… Some of the Princes, particularly the smaller ones, have begun to feel that power is slipping from the Union Government's hands and they think that now is the opportunity for them to revert to pre-British days. Bharatpur is one of them and we have to handle it carefully. I am glad you have sent me the leaflet published under the signature of Dhruva Singh. I have also got a report from Shankar Prasad from Ajmer quoting chapter and verse about raids and dacoities organised and committed by gangs of Jats under the leadership of Bharatpur's brother. I am collecting facts about Bharatpur's maladministration and misconduct during these troubled times and if I get sufficient evidence I propose to set an example so that others may take heed of our action.

Yours Sincerely
Vallabhbhai Patel

New Delhi, 23 October 1947

LETTER TO JAWAHARLAL NEHRU

My dear Jawaharlal,

I have seen the minutes and decisions of the Cabinet meeting held on Saturday, 6 August 1949, relating to the amendments proposed by us for incorporation in the new Constitution.... I am rather upset by the decisions relating to the privy purse payments, guarantees in respect of rights and privileges given to the rulers and regarding entries in the Legislative.... What I learnt from Vellodi about the trend of discussions in the Cabinet not only distressed me, but filled me with apprehensions and anxiety. I could not imagine that, after such repeated discussions over the question of privy purse, after our taking approval from the Cabinet to the many proposals for merger and integration which we put forward to the Cabinet from time to time and after solemn agreements having been reached between the Governor-General and the Rulers on these matters, there should have been so much misapprehension and even ignorance. Every decision and every policy that we have pursued in regard to States has not only been approved but acclaimed by the Assembly whenever any matter concerning the States has come up. It is, therefore, difficult for me to understand that my Cabinet colleagues should shirk the responsibility which devolves on them to ensure that all these agreements and arrangements are fully honoured not only by ourselves but by successor Governments and that they should regard a constitutional guarantee in regard to the continuance of privy purse as being unpopular in the Assembly.

2. ...During the last Budget session, we circulated a memorandum covering practically the whole field of our arrangements with the Rulers and the States and we specially dealt therein with the question of privy purse, pointing out the savings which we had effected as a result of these settlements. The covenants between the Rulers and the Governor-General have been placed on the table of the House. As far as I remember, there was seldom any reference to the privy purse settlements except probably a passing one. These arrangements were generally applauded as eminently satisfactory ones. Frankly speaking, therefore I cannot understand the fears regarding their acceptance by the Assembly.

3. As regards the privy purse, I have said a number of times in the Assembly, and we have made it clear in our published documents that the privy purse fixed by us makes a reduction of several crores in the expenditure which used to fall on the revenues of these States, i.e. the Civil List and other allowances of Rulers. We have also to remember that the total expenditure on privy purse running to about 2 or 3 crores is comparatively an insignificant price to pay for the consolidation and unity of India which we have achieved. We have entered into solemn undertakings and agreement with the Princes about the privy purse, and I do not think that we can, in good conscience, leave it to future Parliaments to do as they like with these amounts. These are commitments which have been consecrated by the signature of the Head of the State on behalf of the people of India with the full approval of the Cabinet, and it is our moral duty to ensure that these commitments arc fully honoured both now and in future. This can only be possible if we guarantee these payments under the constitutional provisions. Any other alternative would not be satisfactory and would not satisfy those who have accepted in good faith our pledges and our promises. We are, therefore, in honour bound to include these guarantees in the Constitution.

4. As regards the privileges and tights conceded to the Rulers, these are again part of the same commitments and cany the same moral obligation on our part. I think it would be correct to say that the Princes attach considerable significance to these rights and privileges. It is a question of self-respect and honour for them, and I do not think that having taken from them everything else that mattered, we should show any niggardly attitude in these matters.

5. You will recall that we had given the Rulers our assurances that they could continue to remain as they were except for accession of three subjects. There was, therefore, nothing to compel or induce them to merge their identity. If they had chosen to keep out of these arrangements, they could have continued to draw the heavy Civil Lists they used to draw before and in a large number of cases the Rulers could have enjoyed unrestricted use of their State revenues. Few people have an idea of the numerous ways in which they had squandered away the revenues of the State. There were, in fact, in

a large number of cases, no limits to their privy purse and if they had continued to rule a few years more they would have squandered away a considerable amount of the country's wealth. There were a few honourable exceptions, but you could count them on the tip of your fingers. Thus the capacity for mischief on the part of the Rulers in this respect was far greater than one could imagine. Even now the amount of harm that could be caused to the country by going back on our solemn promises would be very substantial. You may also be aware that in the Deccan States even under the award of Dr. Rajendra Prasad, Dr. Pattabhi Sitaramayya and Shri Shankarrao Deo, the scales of privy purse were more liberal than ours. In many cases where the Civil Lists were fixed under agreements between Rulers and the representatives of the people, the amounts settled were higher than those which we have now given. Lastly, even the amounts which we have settled, where they exceed 10 lakhs are liable to be reduced to the latter figure after the life time of the present incumbents.

6. We have also to consider these two matters from another point of view. Under the draft Constitution, agreements reached with Rulers prior to the coming into force of the new Constitution would not be justiciable. The covenants under which we have guaranteed the privy purse and the rights and privileges of Rulers will not, therefore, be within the jurisdiction of the Supreme Court. They will be subject virtually to the rule of Paramountcy, to which they are subject now. In these circumstances, a constitutional guarantee is the only thing that can provide some sort of a safeguard for the Princes. The only alternative would be to make these agreements justiciable. But if we did so, you and I, and even successor Governments, will have a perpetual cause for regret. I would, therefore, once more urge upon you and my Cabinet colleagues to reconsider the matter and to accept our proposals which had been reached in full agreement with the Drafting Committee. If the Chairman of the Drafting Committee or any of my colleagues feels any hesitation in sponsoring these proposals before the Constituent Assembly, I am quite prepared to interrupt my stay in Bombay and to come to Delhi merely for the sake of sponsoring these proposals. I consider it a matter of faith and honour, and I feel it would be moral cowardice on my part if I refrained from discharging this obligation.

7. Regarding the Indian State Forces, it would not be proper to make a transitional provision, again because the provision in the covenants are by no means transitional. What we hope to do is gradually to persuade the Princes to integrate their forces fully with the Indian Army. Even within the course of one or two years, we have succeeded in substantially reducing the position of the Princes in relation to the State Forces. In another one or two stages, we may be able to integrate them fully, but for obvious reasons it is not possible for us to say so. Otherwise, we would be charged with breach of faith. Making a transitional provision, such as the Cabinet has suggested, would bring about the same position which we wish to avoid, namely, the Princes will feel that we are departing from the arrangements which had been solemnly agreed to in the covenants, and even from now on, we are contemplating their termination in the period of transition. On the other hand, it would be much more appropriate to retain the item in the list in accordance with the provisions of the covenants, and subsequently allow it in actual practice to fall into desuetude. If the pace is as fast as we expect, it may even be possible to do away with this entry under the easier means of amendments to the Constitution provided for the first five years.

8. I hope you will appreciate the depth of feeling and the mental strain under which I have written this letter. I would be grateful If you would kindly read it to my Cabinet colleagues so that they may be able to appreciate the same. In the meantime, I am asking Menon to prepare a detailed note relating to these three matters and request the Cabinet to reconsider their attitude on these matters.

Yours Sincerely
Vallabhbhai Patel

Bombay, 9 August 1949

SECTION VII

NEHRU AND OTHER COLLEAGUES

LETTER TO SUBHAS CHANDRA BOSE

My Dear Subhas,

Your cable about the remains of my brother being embarked by the S. S. Narkunda from Marseilles dated 26th instant was received here by me this morning and I also learn that you have informed our friends in Bombay. You can well understand that I can do nothing or be of very little use from my place here but I am sure our friends in Bombay will make all arrangements for the reception of his body and Mr Gordhanbhai [Patel] will get all information about it at Aden.

You must have received my last letter thanking you for the wonderful assistance you have rendered him. My heart is too full and I cannot thank you adequately. I know that you have worked very hard against great odds, but it was destined that you should be his real brother in his last days and I should be here helpless to render any assistance or be of any use at such a time. At times from the reports that were received I was hopeful but God's will is done. I can well imagine your own disappointment and the terrific strain on your poor health, and I hope and pray that in spite of your having overstrained yourself you will soon recover your original strength so as to be back amongst us soon.

I am awaiting the arrival of Mr Gordhanbhai Patel, who I hope will be allowed to have an interview with me. You may be aware that I can see no one except blood relations without the special permission of Government. I have already asked for permission to see him. He will be able to give me first hand information about all that happened there as well as about your own health for which I am very anxious.

Please do write to me all about your health and about your activities.

Yours sincerely,
Vallabhbhai

Central Prison, Nasik Road, 28 October 1933

PANDIT JAWAHARLAL NEHRU IS ONE OF THE GREATEST LEADERS OF MODERN INDIA

Dear Friend,

…I understand that Pandit Jawaharlal Nehru is himself coming there as a messenger of peace to bring about honourable settlement of this vexed question. After all, he is also a Hindu and that a Kashmiri Hindu, and he is one of our foremost patriots and one of the greatest leaders of modern India. He is, as all human beings are, liable to err. But all his actions are governed by considerations of highest patriotism. Therefore you need not be afraid of him or his actions. Let us hope this unfortunate trouble in Kashmir will end soon and it will leave no bitterness behind.

Yours Sincerely
Vallabhbhai Patel

THE ATMOSPHERE IS FULL OF VIOLENCE

My Dear Mishraji,

… I have received numerous complaints about the formation of the new Working Committee by our new President [Nehru], and I fully appreciate the depth of feeling amongst comrades who have worked with us for so many years and who are upset by the revolutionary change in the personnel. I am therefore not surprised at the unrestrained manner in which you have expressed yourself in your letter.

Though the President has been elected for the fourth time, he often acts with childlike innocence, which puts us all in great difficulties quite unexpectedly. You have good reasons to be angry but we must not allow our anger to get the better of ourselves. We are passing through a critical period and our life's work may either yield successful results or our hopes may all be dashed to pieces by sheer foolishness on our part and the cup which is full of nectar and which is very near our lips may drop down from our hands before we can taste even a drop of it. The situation is full of perplexities and difficulties, but on such occasion seasoned soldiers have to hold their feet firmly and tightly on the ground and brave the tumult and storm through which the country is passing.

You may perhaps be thinking that I must have been consulted. Many Congressmen also think so. But you will be surprised that when I was informed of the new personnel, I pressed for being relieved of the burden. I cannot write to you all in a letter, because it would be unwise, but I feel as much that our cause has been injured at a critical juncture. I cannot afford to get out of it because it would be injuring our cause.

He has done many things recently which have caused us great embarrassment. His action in Kashmir, his interference in the Sikh election to the Constituent Assembly, his Press Conference immediately after the AICC are all acts of emotional insanity and it puts tremendous strain on us to set matters right. But in spite of all his innocent indiscretions, he has unparalleled enthusiasm and a burning passion for freedom which make him restless and drive him to a pitch of impatience where he forgets himself. All his actions are governed by a supreme consideration of reaching the cherished goal with electric speed. His mind has been exhausted by overwork and strain. He feels lonely and he acts emotionally and we have to bear with him in the circumstances. Opposition sometimes drives him mad, as he is impatient. His present action is also the result of a burning desire to take the younger elements with him and although in doing so he has committed a grave mistake he will not hesitate to rectify it when he realises the grave injustice he has done to others and to the organisation.

You may, however, rest assured that so long as one of us is inside the group that governs the policy of the Congress, the straight and steady march of the ship will not be interrupted. You are right when you say that the atmosphere is full of violence. You must be reading Harijan, wherein you will find that there can be no greater condemnation of the present-day hypocrisy, tomfoolery and mad race for power politics. You have seen that the Madras Ministry is formed and functioning against Gandhiji's advice. Who could have thought of its possibility before 1942? And yet these people claim or profess to belong to the Gandhian school.

The mad race for going into the Constituent Assembly has caused him [Gandhiji] considerable pain and he has come out with his heart's agony in an article in which he compares these people's jail-going with that of thieves and robbers. These people are also Congressmen of the Gandhian school. The underground variety of Congressmen, who call themselves 'Augusters', think that they created the August revolution. Like a dog walking under a fully loaded cart, they feel that the whole load is on their shoulders and they are dragging the whole cart. However, in a world full of violence and immorality resulting from the aftermath of the war, India cannot be isolated. But individuals who are conscious of their surroundings must stand firmly and resist all temptations so as to keep the torch burning.

I have written to you at length in order that you may derive some consolation by getting [an] inkling of my own mind and also with a hope that this passing phase of our political life will not upset you so much as to deviate from our chosen path.

Yours Sincerely
Vallabhbhai Patel

New Delhi, 29 July 1946

TO ERR IS HUMAN

My dear Sir C. R. Reddy,

… You do not agree with my defence of Pandit Nehru. But you will please appreciate the fact that in defending him, I am defending the organisation of which I am a loyal and humble soldier. You must have seen the resolution which the Working Committee has passed at Wardha and I think you will agree that our President* has shown great statesmanship and risen to the occasion in drafting this resolution.

---

*Nehru, after being appointed Congress president in July 1946, sought explicit assurance that Viceroy Wavell would function only as a figurehead, saying that the Congress would be wholly unable to cooperate without such an assurance. Later on in the Working Committee's meeting at Wardha on 8 August, the committee under the presidentship of Nehru, accepted the Viceroy's proposal to join the Interim Government even though the assurance sought by Nehru was not given. It was Patel's stand to accept the proposal. (Gandhi, *Patel: A Life*).

If he had erred on a previous occasion on this subject, he had made ample amends. To err is human, but to accept one's error is something much greater....

Yours Sincerely
Vallabhbhai Patel

New Delhi, 16 August 1946

THE SITUATION IN KASHMIR IS DIFFICULT

...The situation in Kashmir is difficult and delicate and Pandit Nehru himself has realised that some of his early statements were not based on accurate information, and hence he has not hesitated to rectify the errors publicly. You know, he is a Kashmiri Pandit and he would naturally feel tor them more than any other leader would do. But by nature and training, he is a democrat. His sympathies are always with the underdog. In Kashmir, there is Muslim majority and a large majority of them are comparatively very poor. The Kashmiri Pandits and the Hindus form a very small proportion of the population, and as they are comparatively better off, the poorer majority which is getting conscious, is trying to assert itself and the conflict of interests is creating a situation in which the minority finds itself in an unenviable position and lives in a state of perpetual insecurity and fear, resulting in demoralisation. The State being a Hindu State, situated in Muslim surroundings, finds itself in a very delicate and difficult position to take strong action against revolt or lawlessness, as such action at once disturbs the communal atmosphere outside, apart from its repercussions inside the State. The extreme poverty and illiteracy of the masses present an unpleasant picture to a foreign visitor and the State is generally represented outside as extremely irresponsible and unprogressive.

Sheikh Abdullah is supposed to be very popular and his association with Pandit Nehru has been regarded as sufficient guarantee of his being against any separatist movement. Evidently, his present stand appears to be capable of double interpretation and perhaps inconsistent with the policy of the States Peoples' Conference and therefore contrary to Pandit Nehru's views on this matter.

Pandit Nehru has left for Kashmir this morning and it is hoped that this unfortunate and regrettable movement will end in an honourable settlement and restore peace and harmony in Kashmir.

Yours Sincerely
Vallabhbhai Patel

19 June 1946

THE CONGRESS IS NOT OPPOSED TO ANY PRINCE IN INDIA

My Dear Maharaja Sahib,

…I am sorry to find that there is considerable misapprehension in your mind about the Congress. Allow me to assure Your Highness that the Congress is not only not your enemy, as you happen to believe, but there are in the Congress many strong supporters of your State. As an organisation, the Congress is not opposed to any Prince in India. It has no quarrel with the States. It is true that recent events resulting in the arrest of Pandit Jawaharlal Nehru and the continued detention of Sheikh Abdullah have created a feeling of great dissatisfaction amongst many Congressmen who wish well of your State. Pandit Jawaharlal Nehru belongs to Kashmir. He is proud of it, and rest assured he can never be your enemy.…

Yours Sincerely
Vallabhbhai Patel

3 July 1947

OUR COMBINATION IS UNBREAKABLE

My dear Jawaharlal,

Many thanks for your letter of the 1st instant. Our attachment and affection for each other and our comradeship for an unbroken period of nearly thirty years admit of no formalities. My services will be at your disposal, I hope, for the rest of my life and you will have unquestioned loyalty and devotion from me in the cause for which no man in India has sacrificed as much as you have done. Our combination is unbreakable and therein lies our strength. I thank you for the sentiments expressed in your letter.

Yours sincerely,
Vallabhbhai Patel

3 August 1947

LETTER TO LORD MOUNTBATTEN

My dear Lord Mountbatten,

Many thanks for your very kind letter of 14 August. I am overwhelmed by the personal references to me and by the generous terms in which you have referred to such assistance to you as I have been able to render in the very difficult and complicated task which was entrusted to you by His Majesty's Government.

You were good enough to call me a stern realist and it is as such that I make bold to say that, when the history of the six months of your Viceroyalty comes to be written, it cannot but accord to you the major share of the credit for the manner in which the manifold difficult tasks have been accomplished and for the transformation which has been made in Indo-British relationship during these fateful months. India and Indians have always been quick to respond to understanding and sympathy. Both Britain and India must congratulate each other that in you they at last found one so abounding in these virtues, essentially a man of speed and action, frank and painstaking and genuinely sincere and anxious to deliver the goods. The only regret of ours is, and of the future historian will be, that we should have had the benefit of your wise counsel and the privilege of your able guidance at a much earlier date.

I personally have a great deal to thank you for. It is possible I have taxed your patience and consideration severely during the last few months of great mental stress and strain, but I have always found in you a ready response which has often dispelled the clouds of anxiety and concern. In fact, what you have achieved in the way of friendship and goodwill merely emphasises what the long line of your predecessors have missed as a result of studied aloofness and failure to take into confidence leaders of public opinion.

I am also grateful to you for the kind thought which prompted you to send me your photograph as a souvenir of our collaboration during these historic times. I shall always prize it as such.

May I add a word of gratefulness to Her Excellency for the humanitarian service which she has rendered to India at a time when it was sorely needed? Her keen insight into human psychology and vigilant interest in the removal of human suffering and misery have touched the hearts of thousands with whom she has come in contact.

Yours sincerely,
Vallabhbhai Patel

16 August 1947

LETTER TO JAWAHARLAL NEHRU

My Dear Jawaharlal,

...

3. Para 19 of [Dwarkanath] Kachru's* letter has a fling which is obviously aimed at me. I do not think that anything which could have been done for Kashmir has been left undone by me; nor am I aware of any difference between you and me on matters of policy relating to Kashmir. Still it is most unfortunate that persons down below should think that there is a gulf between us. It is also distressing to me.

Yours Sincerely
Vallabhbhai Patel

8 October 1947

THE PRIME MINISTER HAS NO OVERRIDING POWERS OVER HIS COLLEAGUES

I have carefully read Jawaharlal's note sent to you, a copy of which was sent to me.

...

*Kachru was the secretary of All India States People's Conference.

2. There is no disagreement on the existence of temperamental differences and different outlook on economic matters and those affecting Hindu–Muslim relations. Both of us, however, place the interests of the country above these personal differences and, aided by mutual regard, respect and love for each other, have co-operated in a common endeavour. Through our joint efforts we have weathered many a storm that beset us and despite such differences we have got over one of the most critical phases in the history of any country or any government. It is painful and rather tragic to reflect that we cannot carry this any further, but I fully realise the strength of feeling and conviction behind the Prime Minister's stand as regards his own position.

3. I have tried my best to appreciate what he says on that subject, but howsoever much I have tried to understand it on the twin basis of democracy and Cabinet responsibility, I have found myself unable to agree with his conception of the Prime Minister's duties and functions. That conception, if accepted, would raise the Prime Minister to the position of a virtual dictator, for he claims 'full freedom to act when and how he chooses.' This in my opinion is wholly opposed to democratic and Cabinet system of government.

4. The Prime Minister's position, according to my conception, is certainly pre-eminent; he is first among equals. But he has no overriding powers over his colleagues; if he had any, a Cabinet and Cabinet responsibility would be superfluous. In my view the Prime Minister, as the leader of the party and the head of the whole administration, is inevitably concerned that Cabinet decisions are effective and that there is no conflict between one Ministry and another. But the entire responsibility for implementing the policy of Government rests upon the Ministers and Ministries under them which are concerned with the subject matter of the Cabinet decisions. He has accordingly the right to ask for information from the Minister concerned as well as the right to consult and advise on the lines of policy to be adopted and even the manner in which the policy is to be implemented. But the responsibility for the implementation of the policy must be that of the Ministry concerned and of the Minister in charge, and the Prime Minister should influence action by way of consultation with

and advice to the Minister. I feel sure that this position of the Prime Minister not only fully safeguards his pre-eminence and makes him an effective head of the Administration but is also fully in accord with democratic principles and rules of ministerial and Cabinet responsibility. This is also, as far as I have been able to ascertain, in accord with the UK practice.

5. The incident of Iengar's visit to Ajmer was not the immediate cause of the whole matter coming to a head. If the Prime Minister will recall, it was on the issue of Gopalaswami's telegram to the East Punjab Government authorising the loan of motor vehicles to the Kashmir State that he gave expression to his view that Gopalaswami should be given full latitude in helping in Kashmir matters and took a stand which meant that the States Ministry should virtually submit not only to the Prime Minister personally dealing with issues arising out of the Kashmir situation (this was already in force) but also to other Ministers having a finger in the pie while the Ministry which was normally concerned should be at best a repository of information as and when it was given.

6. Nor is Iengar's visit the only matter in which I had to point out to the Prime Minister the inadvisability of a course which he had taken without even consulting me. Several occasions in the past few months—since 15 August—have given rise to similar correspondence. In some the Prime Minister had extended to me the courtesy of informing me beforehand of the action he intended to take and I had tendered my advice in favour of or against the proposed course of action as seemed to me appropriate. If even the tendering of advice or the pointing out of the inadvisability of a course of action or the submission that a particular matter fell within my responsibility proves irksome or irritating to the Prime Minister and interferes with the exercise of his functions, the position is one which is wholly inconsistent with a democratic system of government.

7. As regards Iengar's visit to Ajmer, I regret I am unable to share the Prime Minister's view of its nature or its consequences. Iengar went to Ajmer, inspected various places, received deputations and conferred with officials and non-officials; the public mind is bound to associate it with an inquisition. The Chief Commissioner took it in that light

and stated that the public also felt it as such. It was not that I did not want anyone to go. When the Prime Minister mentioned to me that he wanted to go, I promptly agreed that he should go. I did not come to know of Iengar's visit in substitution of the Prime Minister's until after Iengar had returned. I should have been glad to deputise for the Prime Minister if he had asked me; as I wrote to him, any other Minister could have been asked to go. But to send an official was, in my submission, hardly likely to be interpreted otherwise than in the manner in which it was taken by the public and the Chief Commissioner. The question is not whether the Prime Minister was entitled to take this step or not or whether he is not to be the judge of the propriety of the action but whether I, as a Minister, was wrong in pointing out to him the inadvisability of the course he had taken and the probable consequences it entailed.

8. A reference has also been made to the functioning of the States Ministry. I cannot recall any one instance in which I have taken any decision of major policy without the approval or confirmation of my colleagues. The only instance in which I anticipated a Cabinet decision was that of the merger of Orissa and Chhattisgarh States; subsequent confirmation of my action practically without discussion upholds my judgment in anticipating it. The matter was obviously such that the postponement of the decisive act would have been fraught with serious consequences and would have let slip an opportunity which would have perhaps recurred only after considerable patience, toil and trouble to all concerned.

9. The Prime Minister has also referred to his preference for leaving office if mutual accommodation cannot be secured. I maintain, however, that if anybody has to go, it should be myself. I have long passed the age of active service. The Prime Minister is the acknowledged leader of the country and is comparatively young; he has established an international position of pre-eminence for himself. I have no doubt that the choice between him and myself should be resolved in his favour. There is, therefore, no question of his quitting office.

January 1948

LETTER TO JAWAHARLAL NEHRU

My dear Jawaharlal,

I enclose herewith two Press cuttings, one from the Statesman of today [in the 'Letters to the Editor' column] and another from a well-known Communist whose speech is reported in the Madras Mail. Of course they do not know that my resignation is already there. I had written again to Bapu when I left for Bombay on the last occasion but his unexpected death has left the matter in the air.

Statesman's contention takes a constitutional stand and I think he [the correspondent] is right. This is an additional reason for my resignation. Your yesterday's speech has also reinforced the need for such as obvious failure. I do not wish to do anything to embarrass you at this critical juncture, but when there is a public demand, a challenge which is obviously justified, I feel 1 must once again request you to help me.

Yours Sincerely
Vallabhbhai Patel

3 February 1948

LETTER TO JAWAHARLAL NEHRU

My dear Jawaharlal,

I am deeply touched, indeed overwhelmed, by the affection and warmth of your letter of 3 February. I fully and heartily reciprocate the sentiments you have so feelingly expressed.

We both have been lifelong comrades in a common cause. The paramount interests of our country and our mutual love and regard, transcending such differences of outlook and temperament as existed, have held us together. Both of us have stuck passionately to our respective points of view or methods of work; still we have always sustained a unity of heart which has stood many a stress and strain and which has enabled us to function jointly both in the Congress and in the Government.

Recent events had made me very unhappy and 1 had written to

Bapu when I was going to Bombay appealing to him to relieve me, but his death changes everything and the crisis that has overtaken us must awaken in us a fresh realisation of how much we have achieved together and the need for further joint efforts in our grief-stricken country's interests.

I had the good fortune to have a last talk with him for over an hour just before his death and he communicated to me what had passed between you and him as well as his talk with H.E. [Lord Mountbatten]. He had also fixed an appointment to meet both of us the next day. His opinion also binds us both and I can assure you that I am fully resolved to approach my responsibilities and obligations in this spirit.

I agree with you that we must find more time for mutual consultations so that we can keep each other informed of, and in touch with, what is happening and we can thus resolve any points of difference that might arise.

We should also find an early opportunity to have a long talk and clear our minds of any doubts and difficulties that may be there. Continued harping on our differences in public or in private is bad for us, bad for the Services and bad for the country. The sooner we set this at rest once for all and clear the murky atmosphere the better.

Yours Sincerely
Vallabhbhai Patel

5 February 1948

TELEGRAM TO N. V. GADGIL

YOUR SON-IN-LAW HAS WIRED YOU CONTEMPLATE REMARRIAGE ON 1 MAY. I AM SURPRISED TO HEAR OF IT AND IF TRUE WOULD ADVISE YOU IN YOUR OWN INTEREST POSTPONE IT. I HAVE NO DOUBT THAT SUCH AN EVENT SO SOON WOULD CREATE CONSIDERABLE EMBARRASSMENT AND CAUSE CONSIDERABLE CRITICISM.

VALLABHBHAI
Camp Mussoorie, 9 May 1948

LETTER TO JAWAHARLAL NEHRU

My dear Jawaharlal,

Some of the recent speeches of Jai Prakash [Narayan] have been filling me with misgivings. The one about Hyderabad in which he tried to put the entire blame on the States Ministry and claimed that, if the Socialists had been allowed to function in their own way, things would have been settled long ago, was particularly vicious and mischievous. I would not have troubled you with this letter had it not been that you have been publicly praising him and been hailing him as the coming man. I feel that such irresponsible utterances and embarrassing attitude on his part hardly justify any faith in him. I have all along been of the view that if the future of India is in the hands of men like Jai Prakash, it would probably be a most unfortunate circumstance. Recent events and his attitude after Gandhiji's death bear out this view and I sincerely feel that it is time he was pulled up. I do not know whether you can succeed in putting him right, but if you feel that you can, it might be worth while trying. If he and his party can be brought round to some sober thinking and acting, it will be in the best interests of this country.

Yours Sincerely
Vallabhbhai Patel

Dehradun, 15 June 1949

I HAVE LEARNT FROM MAHATMA GANDHI TO HAVE FRIENDSHIP TOWARDS ALL

I appeal to the working-class not to be misled by interested parties. These parties tell the Labour that present Government is a capitalist Government. This is absurd. The leader of the present Government is no other than the first President of the Trade Union Congress.

Allegations are also made that Pandit Nehru does not wield enough power inside the Cabinet and that his Socialism is of no help to the working-class. It is further alleged that there are two parties in the Cabinet. All these statements are absolutely baseless.

The working of the present Cabinet is marked by perfect harmony. I have accepted Pandit Jawaharlal Nehru as my leader and my place will not be in the Cabinet if my actions do not have the approval of my leader or if they do not strengthen his hands.

I am always charged as being a friend of capitalists like Mr [G. D. Birla]. All that I wish to say is that I have learnt from Gandhiji never to have any personal property and in my opinion there is no better Socialism than this. I have also learnt from Mahatma Gandhi to have friendship towards all, rich or poor, great or humble. Thus, I can be friendly to labour, industrialists, princes, peasants and the zamindars alike and can persuade them with love to do the right thing.

Delhi, 3 October 1948

LETTER TO RAJENDRA PRASAD

My dear Rajen Babu,

...

3. ...I am sure it must have been farthest from Jawaharlal's mind to cause you any pain. You know how overworked he is and how busy his time is. In fact, my heart goes out to him in sympathy in the great and almost intolerable burden that he is carrying. One cannot, in these circumstances, expect him to weigh every word that he writes or, even at times, to realize the full import of what he is writing. In these circumstances, the subsequent letter which he has written acquires an importance of its own and explains to you fully how his mind was working and what led him to write to you. I am sure, you will accept that letter as finally disposing of the matter. Indeed, I am very glad to receive just now the further correspondence that has passed between him and you and to know that you have accepted that letter in the right spirit.

Camp Birla House, Bombay, 16 September 1949

THE GAME OF FAULT FINDING

My dear Bidhan,

I have seen your letter dated 1 December 1949.

I was distressed to find you writing to the Prime Minister like this. Had it been a personal letter or had you been talking to him, perhaps as an elder, you could afford all this liberty. But in an official communication to him as Prime Minister, I had expected that you would be deferential as is appropriate to the dignity of the high office that he holds as well as the office which you yourself occupy. Even if you felt strongly on this point, I am sure one can be strong and dignified at the same time.

…

3. I shall not comment on the merits of your proposal. I can only say this that yours is only one way of looking at it and that one way is not the only way of doing so. You have said some hard things about the way the Centre does things. I wish you had stuck to the principle which you yourself propound viz. 'I need not be intensely critical as criticism of others without accepting responsibilities for their task has no reality.' I am not quite sure that in the mutual game of fault-finding [we] would necessarily be on the losing side. However, that game is most distasteful to me and I do not propose to emulate the example of others.

Yours Sincerely
Vallabhbhai Patel

6 December 1949

LETTER TO JAWAHARLAL NEHRU

My dear Jawaharlal,

Thank you for your letter of 14 February 1950 with which you sent a copy of a letter which you have received from Jayaprakash Narayan.

It is of course the Socialists' game to propagate that you are more sympathetic than myself. They also leave no opportunity to appeal to you in that sense. Jayaprakash's letter is a piece of that activity. They do not seem to realise that you are as much cognisant and critical of their mischievous activities as I am.

Jayaprakash speaks in such extreme terms about what happened in Rewa. He, of course, ignores the fact that, as against two or three persons killed and about half a dozen wounded among the public, there were 38 policemen who were injured in what he terms as 'atrocity of the executive authority'. If our attitude has been correctly represented, viz. that the Congress Governments can do no harm and, if that attitude is going to destroy the Congress itself, nothing should please Jayaprakash Narayan more than that attitude, since, after all, it is his aim, as well as that of his party, to destroy the Congress.

As regards the Hind Kisan Panchayat about which he makes so much complaint, the position is that they wanted 1,000 gallons of petrol which the Chief Commissioner could not spare from the limited supplies which he obtains. At some inconvenience, however, he has made an allotment of 100 gallons. They wanted Government to supply them with tents, *shamianas*, *durries* and to let the invitees stay in State bungalows and houses. They also wanted the Government to arrange for supply of water from the wells (there is no pipe water supply in Rewa) at Government expense. Naturally, the Chief Commissioner could not do any of these things. After all, if they wanted all this, they might have put in an application asking the Government to hold the conference for them at its own expense. The Chief Commissioner has explained the position clearly in a Press Note, a copy of which I enclose.

Yours Sincerely
Vallabhbhai Patel

New Delhi, 20 February 1950

LETTER TO JAWAHARLAL NEHRU

My dear Jawaharlal,

My affectionate greetings on your birthday. Relations between us transcend formalities, and I need hardly say anything more than this: it is my fervent and heartfelt prayer that you may live long and well to lead the country through all difficulties and establish in it an era of peace, happiness and prosperity....

Yours Sincerely
Vallabhbhai Patel

14 November 1950

SECTION VIII

A PLAIN, BLUNT MAN

JAIL DIARY

Friday, 7-3-1930

The Deputy Superintendent of Police, Mr. Billimoria, brought me from Borsad to the Sabarmati jail where we arrived about 8 o'clock at night. He was deeply affected when he arrested me, and, indeed, when he left me at the jail he wept copiously. On the way, he showed me the utmost consideration. At night, I was kept in what is called a 'quarantine Ward'. There, I was given three blankets and I slept on them.

Saturday, 8-3-1930

On waking up, I saw prisoners all around me. They had formed a queue—of two in each row—in order to go to the latrine; there was only one latrine. After relieving yourself in one you went into another row for water. This was a totally new experience and I gave up the idea altogether. A big pot was placed out in the open for those who wanted to pass urine. Everyone was required to stand up while doing so. All the while there would be people moving about—prisoners, warders and policemen—so that I did not have the courage even for this. A warder cut for me a *datan* (small tender twig) from neighbouring neem tree and with it I brushed my teeth. I found that I knew some of the prisoners. Three had come only very recently from Jalalpur. The older residents assured me that I would not be here and that turned out to be true. At 9 o'clock, the warder made special arrangements for me for going to the toilet. In one latrine he had two pots placed. As all the others had finished this mor morning's task, I had it for a full half an hour to myself. Soon afterwards the Jailor and the Superintendent came and enquired if I wanted anything. I said I did not want anything as a favour, and I could not ask for anything as I did not know, exactly what I was entitled to. I learnt later that according to prison rules there was no provision for any special facilities being given to anyone. I then enquired if there was any difference in the treatment which would be meted out to an European prisoner, and I was informed that there was no difference at all. But when I enquired if the same facilities would be given to an Indian accustomed to a Western way of living as would be given to an European, I did not receive any satisfactory reply. I then asked for a copy of the Jail Manual but was told that, according to their regulations, they could not supply me with one. I therefore informed them that I would have to consider how to secure their compliance with my request. I was given the Bhagavad Gita, and the Tulsi Ramayana to read. This was all needed. At 10 o'clock, I was taken to the doctor. There were two doctors, both very young. They were so small in build that any prisoner would have been able to lift them bodily and run away with them. Such weak looking boys were deputed to attend to the medical requirements of 1,400 prisoners! My weight was found to be 146 lbs. and height 5'-5 1/2'. On my return I was taken to another barrack on the outside of which was inscribed 'Juvenile Habitual No. 12' but inside I found there were 5 old prisoners and one middle-aged sweeper. Of the five, one was a Chamar from Bodal, another a Baraiya from Katosan; the third was a wandering Sadhu from north India who had been arrested in Dakor; a fourth was a Bhaiya from Uttar Pradesh who had been arrested in Bombay, while the fifth was an old Muslim from north India. I was the sixth.... On top of all these was a Muslim policeman by name Lal Khan. And among these I was placed. The poor prisoners were anxious to look after me. The warders are shown some slight consideration in the matter of food as compared to the other prisoners. They were given wheat bread while the prisoners got bread made of jowar flour. The wanders were embarrassed on seeing me supplied with jowar bread. In the morning, we were offered a kind of porridge made of jowar flour mixed with water and salt. I refused this. The prisoners are given two meals; one, at 10 o'clock in the morning and the other, at 4 o'clock in the evening. I ate one roti with vegetable or dal at each meal. The prisoners are given two such rotis and dal or vegetable alternatively; both are duly weighed and are given in a fixed measure. I found I could manage with only one roti. When I was not in jail I had to go to the toilet four or five times, and, in spite of tempting the stomach with tea, cigarettes and all sorts of other things, it was with difficulty that my bowels used to move. Here I left everything to nature, and decided to go only once to the latrine. Not until the third day did I have a bowel movement. I rested as much as I could, both during the day and at night, and, in the interval, walked as much as I could. There was a very nice place in the park for a walk—it was clean and had three neem trees. The prisoners were very kind to me and would reserve one latrine for my exclusive use, and it was kept very neat and clean. There was also a water-tap nearby so that there was no difficulty about bathing except, of course, that it had to be in the open. I refused to make any special representation. One of the warders was deeply moved when he saw me eating jowari roti and pressed me to exchange it with his wheat bread. And while I thanked the kindly warder, I refused his offer as it would have been against the rules.

…

Friday, 11-4-1930

Woke up at 4 a.m. Prayers and other morning duties. Nine more prisoners, including Ramdas from Surat, joined us. Thus we were now 44. Commissioner Garret accompanied by the Superintendent, came at 10 o'clock to see us. The latter had been insistent that we stand in front of our rooms whenever anyone such as the Collector or Commissioner came to see us. I refused to comply with his request, and said that we were not going to agree to any condition which we felt was detrimental to our self-respect. We would, at the same time, not fail in politeness or good manners. In the course of discussion regarding food, I told him that we had no suggestions to make. We had come prepared to face the worst possible treatment, but we thought it only fair that the Government should tell us how much it had decided to spend on us per head. So long as we managed within that amount we should be allowed the liberty to make our own arrangements. If there was any objection to our being given this freedom of choice we would make no difficulty, but in that case we would only take from the amount fixed as much as we wanted and only that sum should be debited to our accounts. We did not wish to accept rations to which we were opposed, and which we could not use as we were anxious that there should be no wasteful expenditure. The Commissioner said that he would take up the matter with the Government. Then Mansukhlal and Kasturbhai came to see us. They were both in khadi clothes which suggested that the movement was progressing well. As the number of Satyagrahi prisoners had increased, one further ward was vacated and this we had at our disposal.

7 March 1930 to 22 April 1930

OBSCENE IMAGES ON TEMPLES

Dear Sir,

You are no doubt aware that the question of removing or at least effacing the nude and other obscene images on temples in our country has been exercising the minds of all decent men for a long time past. The presence of such figures in any place of public resort and particularly their exhibition in temples is most revolting and humiliating to the aesthetic sense of every pure-minded person. The sooner therefore our temples are rid of these obnoxious symbols of a morbid taste, the better for our religion, culture and art. Seth Jamnalalji informed me and the members of the Working Committee which recently met in Bombay, of his efforts in this behalf. It appears the priests of the temple of Sri Jagannath at Puri have agreed to get the particular images on that temple cemented over. I shall be glad to hear from you that the proposed effacement has been effected. I have no doubt you will move in the matter with promptness and see that the offensive features of the great Gopura and elsewhere in the Puri temple are obliterated forthwith. I wish that this process should be completed in good time before the ensuing Congress at Puri.

Yours Sincerely
President

14 November 1931

LETTER TO MAHATMA GANDHI

Revered Bapu,

…You had asked about my nose trouble, but the government had not taken any decision regarding it, and therefore I could not write to you….

I do not want to get operated on under any circumstances. There is a danger of damage. I do not want to get into any such trouble. Many people advise me, and I also believe that I should get operated on in Bombay by an expert. Dr. Ansari had recommended getting it done by Dr. T.O. Shah [...] I got 'Cotorise' done In last January. But I had to come here the very next day and there might likely be some damage due to the journey by car and the flow of wind during the time. Whatever may be the case, I do not want to take the risk by accepting the conditions imposed by the government. It is not proper to have a doctor from Bombay while staying at the Sassoon Hospital, Poona. A doctor from Bombay can not get the facilities he needs here. Who will bear the risk? The government wants to stay clear of any risk. You can understand this is happening as per the wish of IGP. He will arrange for my operation or give me the necessary facilities only when the government thinks the operation is inevitable. It is better to suffer till then. I have already suffered for one and a half years. I do not mind bearing it for some more time. But the operation can not be performed under such difficulties. If the government thinks there is a risk to my life, it will do whatever it can. If there is no risk, we must bear the pain. We have come here to suffer and we shall suffer. What is the big deal? I want you to be relieved. Nothing will happen to me.…

I request you not to write anything to the Government in this matter. There should be no agitation outside the jail too. It will be a shame if the news of my illness spreads out and I am sure you would not allow anything that discredits me.…

Vallabhbhai's Vandematram

Yeravada Mandir, 23 June 1933

LETTER TO HIS SON, DAHYABHAI PATEL

Chi. Dahyabhai,

…There is no meaning or gain in writing bitter letters to Gordhanbhai. He has been appointed as 'the executor'. Hence, he must take legal steps. He is not supposed to tell us anything.… He must ensure that he arranged to show a copy of the will to all the relatives of the deceased. But nobody came forward and objected. He will send the letter via a solicitor to achieve this. That is how it should be done. There is no reason for us to get angry at him for that.... You have got a copy of the will. Show it to Mangaldas [Pakwasa]. If there is anything to be said from the legal point of view, do write me and if not, it is futile to say anything.

...When the deceased trusted him and we try to say anything, we might be accused of selfishness and other false charges....

Bapu's blessings

Central Prison, Nasik Road, 17 February 1934

MY MOTHER DELIVERED FIVE STONES

Bhai Chhaganlal,

Received your letter dated 6.6.1934. It was written on the day you completed your 38 years. You are fortunate that you know your birthday with surety. I have to bluff about my age. When I have to state on oath, I say approximately. My mother delivered five stones. How those stones will turn out or what sort of person they will become in the future, nobody knew. So, nobody noted or remembered the day or the year of our birth....

Vallabhbhai's Vandan

Central Prison, Nasik Road, 2 July 1934

I HAVE CROSSED THE BARRIERS OF CASTE AND CREED

You know that I have crossed the barriers of caste and creed. So you cannot honour me as a person belonging to a particular caste. You should come out from the shackles of caste and creed to break the shackles of our slavery.

Karachi, 28 August 1938

LETTER TO NARHARI PARIKH*

Bhai Narhari,

...

Governor was to visit Jyoti Sangh, Gujarat Vidyapith, and Ashram. Then Mridula [Sarabhai] received a letter from the Collector, which she showed to me. It said the Governor cannot visit the buildings with the national flag. The collector sought a reply from Mridula. I told her to write that the Governor can cancel his visit. You should also have the same policy. Let them not come if they cannot tolerate the flag on our institutions.

...

Vallabhbhai's Vande Mataram

Bombay, 8 December 1939

FASTING SHOULD BE LEFT TO GREAT MEN LIKE GANDHIJI

Dear Friend,**

...

2. I do not understand the philosophy of fast, and it is not for ordinary men to use this weapon against anybody. Many people have tried it and failed. People do not take this seriously. Many of those who threaten fasting are not themselves serious, but fasting should be left to great men like Gandhiji.

---

*Narhari Parikh was a close associate of Gandhi. He wrote the first biography of Sardar Patel in two parts.

**The friend here is B. N. Saojee. He was the owner of a news service in Nagpur and threatened to fast unto death at Mahatma Gandhi's hut at Sewagram after his news service was blacklisted and he was not granted an interview by D. P. Mishra, minister of Information.

3. If you are going to fast for self-purification, there can be no objection. It will do good to you physically and mentally, but if it is intended against anybody else it will be considered as blackmail, pure and simple. You may do whatever you like.

Yours Sincerely
V. J. Patel

New Delhi, 14 November 1946

WE HAVE WON FREEDOM

Dear Shri Kasturbhai,

We have already received a good number of opinions from astrologers. But there is no unanimity as to their forecasts. If we will fix some other date for the transfer of power, there is no reason to believe that it will brighten the future of India. Formalities or no, by virtue of the Act of British Parliament, the sovereign power passes into our hands at the midnight hour between the 14th and the 15th of this month. What formalities will then take place are for the namesake only.

The celebrations will merely betoken our joy and enthusiasm. We shall all meet together on the 14th of night and shall say our last good-bye to the British Parliament at 12 o'clock. We have won freedom and it is a very significant event. Now the future of India lies in the hands of Indians alone. Who can say whether they will make or mar their future? Our lifework, in this context, has borne fruit. There are many hurdles to be removed as yet and there may be new ones ahead of us. So we must have fullest capacity and strength to surmount all of them. Verily, that would necessitate fullest co-operation from all quarters.

8 August 1947

THE BURDEN OF WORK HAS BECOME HEAVY

Revered Bapu,

I have to leave for Kathiawad at seven this morning. It is agonising beyond endurance to have to go away when you are fasting. But stern duty leaves no other course.

The sight of your anguish yesterday has made me disconsolate. It has set me furiously thinking.

The burden of work has become so heavy that I feel crushed under it. I now see that it would do no good to the country or to myself to carry on like this any more. It might even do harm.

Jawahar is even more burdened than I. His heart is heavy with grief. May be I have deteriorated with age and am no more any good as a comrade to stand by him, and lighten his burden. The Maulana (Azad) too is displeased with what I am doing and you have again and again to take up cudgels on my behalf. This also is intolerable to me.

In the circumstances, it will perhaps be good for me and for the country if you now let me go. I cannot do otherwise than I am doing. And if thereby I become burdensome to my lifelong colleagues and a source of distress to you and still I stick to office, it would mean—at least that is how I would feel—that I let the lust of power blind my eyes and so was unwilling to quit. You should quickly deliver me from this intolerable situation.

I know it is no time for argument while you are fasting. But since I can be of no help even in ending your fast, I do not know what else there is for me to do. I therefore earnestly beseech you to give up your fast and get this question settled soon.

It may help even remove the causes that have prompted your fast.

Yours Sincerely
Vallabhbhai Patel

13 January 1948

I HATE PROLONGED DISCUSSIONS

... I agree with your Vice-Chancellor that here came one and the sole leader of our Independence Movement, viz., Gandhiji. It was his austerity and his *tapasya* that brought us this gift of Freedom. I claim to be nothing more than an obedient soldier of him like the millions who obeyed his call. There was a time when everyone used to call me his blind follower, but both I and he knew that I followed him because our convictions tallied. I am not one given to debates and verbal disputes. I hate prolonged discussions. For several years, Gandhiji and I were in perfect agreement. Mostly, we agreed instinctively; but when the time for a big decision on the question of India's Independence came we differed. I felt that we had to take Independence there and then. We had, therefore, to agree to Partition. I came to this conclusion after a great deal of heart-searching and with a great deal of many bits and completely ruined. My experience of office of one year had convinced me that the way we were proceeding we were heading for disaster. Gandhiji felt that he could not agree with this conclusion. But he told me that if my heart bore testimony to the rightness of my convictions, I could go ahead. Our leader whom he nominated as his heir and successor [Jawaharlal Nehru] was with me. Gandhiji did not oppose us nor did he consent to what we thought was right and proper. Even today I do not repent for having come to that decision, though it was with a great wrench of the heart that we did so.

25 November 1948

A PLAIN, BLUNT MAN

I am grateful to you for the double honour you have done me by inviting me to address this distinguished gathering and by conferring on me the degree of Doctor of Laws. When I look back upon the long line of distinguished personalities and the galaxy of talents, who have addressed you in the past or who have been the recipients of your honorary degrees, I feel myself in strange company. I lay claim to no academic distinctions; whatever lessons I have learnt were taken in the great university of life. I lay no pretence to scholarship and I have never sored in high regions of arts or of science. My work has lain in the mud huts and in the fields and fallows of the humble peasant or the slums and drains of towns. In public life, I have not been a politician but like Mark Antony a plain blunt man! The distinction which you have conferred on me today I regard not as a tribute to any so-called qualities of head and heart but as a recognition of 'the common man'-men and women of 'the humbler clay' whom it has been my pleasure and privilege to serve.

27 November 1948

I DO NOT LIKE THE IDEA OF STARTING ANY COLLEGE OR ACADEMY AFTER ME OR AFTER MANIBEN

Dear friend

Thank you for your letter of 3 July 1950.

I do not like the idea of your starting any college or academy either after me or after Maniben. Please drop all your efforts in respect of these proposals.

...

Yours,
Vallabhbhai Patel

Dehradun, 6 July 1950

LETTER TO AJIT PRASAD

My Dear Ajit Prasad,

I learnt only this morning that, in regard to certain matters concerning his interest in the Electric Supply Company at Karachi, Dahyabhai has been approaching you or/and your Ministry with some proposals for exchange of property or shares, etc. While Dahyabhai's personal and business interests are his own affair and I have nothing to do with them—nor do I take any interest in them—it is impossible for me to prevent him from safeguarding or promoting those interests. All that I am interested in is to ensure that no consideration is extended to him because he happens to be my son. I would, therefore, like you to see that no such consideration is extended to him and if you or/and your Ministry have to deal with any of his requests or representations, it must be purely from the impersonal point of view and strictly on merits, it being clearly understood that I have nothing to do with them.

Yours Sincerely
Vallabhbhai Patel

22 August 1950

ACKNOWLEDGEMENTS

Aakar Patel (Bengaluru)
For introducing me to the English writing space.

Rama Lakshmi (*The Print*, New Delhi)
For encouragement.

Professor Tridip Suhurd (Ahmedabad)
For prompting me to accept this assignment.

Ramachandra Guha (Bengaluru)
For warm, informal support.

Dipak Soliya-Hetal Desai (Mumbai)
Kartik Shah (Ahmedabad)
Hasit Mehta-Limisha Mehta (Nadiad)
Aarti Nair (London)
Neesha Parikh (Melbourne)
For being my life force in their special ways.

Sonal-Aastha (Mahemdavad)
Biren-Kamini-Ishan Kothari (Vadodara)
Shachi-Siddharth-Saarth Sharma (Ushker Ramkund)
and
My late mother Smita Kothari (1939–2022)
For unconditional love and concrete support as a family.

Sabarmati Ashram Preservation and Memorial Trust (Ahmedabad)
For library support.

NOTES AND REFERENCES

I. 'I AM JUST A SOLDIER': THE FORMATIVE YEARS

RECOLLECTIONS: *Life and Work of Sardar Vallabhbhai Patel*, P. D. Saggi (ed.), Bombay: Overseas Publishing House, 1955, pp. i–iii.

IMITATING THE BRITISH: Speech given at Modasa, Gujarat, 29 March 1921; *Sardar Vallabhbhainaan Bhaashano*, Narhari Dwarikadas Parikh and Uttamchand Deepchand Shah (eds.), Ahmedabad: Navjivan, 1950, pp. 26–28.

BE FEARLESS: Speech given at Raas Village, Gujarat, 18 April 1918; *Sardar Vallabhbhainaan Bhaashano*, Parikh and Shah (eds.), pp. 3–4.

THE LONGER THE FIGHT, THE STIFFER THE TEST: A pamphlet, 1918; Narhari Parikh, *Sardar Vallabhbhai Patel, Vol. I*, Ahmedabad: Navjivan Publishing House, 1953, p. 85.

WHICH COUNTRY HAS ATTAINED FREEDOM EASILY?: Speech as the chairman of the reception committee at the Fourth Gujarat Political Conference, Ahmedabad, 17 August 1920; *Sardar Vallabhbhainaan Bhaashano*, Parikh and Shah (eds.), pp. 10–24.

BE COURAGEOUS: Speech given at Ahmedabad, 28 September 1920, *Sardar Vallabhbhainaan Bhaashano*, Parikh and Shah (eds.), pp. 24–26.

BREAK THE CHAINS OF SLAVERY: Speech given at Ahmedabad, 18 September 1921; *Sardar Vallabhbhainaan Bhaashano*, Parikh and Shah (eds.), pp. 42–43.

REAL LEADERSHIP LIES IN SERVICE: Speech as the chairman of the reception committee at the annual session of Congress in Ahmedabad, December 1921; *Sardar Vallabhbhainaan Bhaashano*, Parikh and Shah (eds.), p. 46.

MAHATMA GANDHI HAS LEFT ENORMOUS WEALTH FOR US: An appeal after Gandhi was awarded six years imprisonment in a sedition case, *Navjivan*, 26 March 1922, p. 238; *Sardar Vallabhbhainaan Bhaashano*, Parikh and Shah (eds.), pp. 54–55.

THE CAPACITY TO SUFFER AND TO SACRIFICE: An appeal in *Navjivan*, 19 November 1922, p. 93; *Sardar Vallabhbhainaan Bhaashano*, Parikh and Shah (eds.), pp. 58–60.

RULES FOR SWADESHI TROOPS: Rules announced by Patel as the President of Gujarat Provincial Congress, November 1922; *Navjivan*, 3 December 1922, p. 112. Some of the points were translated and published in Young India.

I AM JUST A SOLDIER: Speech at Gaya Congress Session, 25 December 1922; *Navjivan, Congress Session Special*, Issue No. 3, 28 December 1922, p. 2.

SACRIFICE FOR THE SAKE OF THE PLAN: Appeal to Gujaratis, June 1923; *Navjivan*, 1 July 1923, p. 345.

EVERY BATTLE NEEDS SOLDIERS AND FUNDS: An appeal, Ahmedabad, 20 July 1923; *Navjivan*, 22 July 1923, p. 369.

BE READY TO SUFFER MORE AND MORE TILL WE REACH OUR FINAL GOAL: A statement on the triumphant end of the Flag Satyagraha, 3 September 1923; *Young India*, 6 September 1923, pp. 297–99. In the same issue of *Young India*, C. Rajgopalachari, the editor, termed Vallabhbhai's statement as 'a magnificent document which would do credit to any true disciple of Mahatmaji'. He also remarked, 'We wish Mr. Vallabhbhai had magnanimously omitted the amusing reference to the Commissioner of Nagpur whom the inadvertent (or shall we say the more honest) "Statesman" has unwittingly betrayed. Not that he did not deserve to be exposed, but this great statement was no place for it.'

GREATNESS LIES IN GETTING BEATEN FOR THE SAKE OF DUTY: Address to Borsad Taluka Conference, 2 December 1923; *Navjivan*, Special Issue 4, 6 December 1923, pp. 7–8 in Parikh, *Sardar Vallabhbhai Patel Vol. I*, pp. 219–22.

OUR FIGHT IS NOT EVIL: Speech at Borsad after successful Satyagraha, 12 January 1924; *Navjivan*, Special Issue No. 6, 20 January 1924, pp. 3–5.

YOUR BATTLE IS BASED ON THE TRUTH: Speech before the resolution of the Bardoli Satyagraha, 12 February 1928; Mahadev Haribhai Desai, *Bardoli Satyagrahano Itihas* (History of Bardoli Satyagraha), Ahmedabad: Navjivan Prakashan Mandir, 1985, pp. 41–42.

SPEECH AT WANKANER: Desai, *Bardoli Satyagrahano Itihas*, pp. 48–50.

I WANT TO INOCULATE YOU WITH FEARLESSNESS: Speech; Mahadev Desai, *The Story of Bardoli*, Ahmedabad: Navjivan Press, 1929, p. 48.

THE GNAT NEED NOT FEAR THE ELEPHANT: Desai, *The Story of Bardoli*, p. 63.

BE PREPARED TO DIE FOR SELF-RESPECT: Desai, *The Story of Bardoli*, p. 64; Desai, *Bardoli Satyagrahano Itihas*, pp. 90–91.

OUR FIGHT IS AGAINST THE BIGWIGS: Desai, *Bardoli Satyagrahano Itihas*, pp. 107–108.

MAINTAIN YOUR CALM: Desai, *Bardoli Satyagrahano Itihas*, p. 118.

I DO NOT WANT TO REST: Desai, *Bardoli Satyagrahano Itihas*, p. 134.

ALL OF US ARE DISCIPLES OF THE SAME GURU: Speech after the settlement of Bardoli, *Young India*, 16 August 1928, p. 279.

WHAT WILL HAPPEN WHEN GANDHIJI IS GONE?: Speech after felicitation by the citizens of Ahmedabad, August 1928; *Sardar Vallabhbhainaan Bhaashano*, Parikh and Shah (eds.), pp. 167–68.

II. THE PARTY STRATEGIST

DISCIPLINARY ACTION: Press Statement; *The Collected Works of Sardar Vallabhbhai Patel, Vol. 4*, p. 177. Used by permission of Konark Publishers Pvt. Ltd, New Delhi.

ADOPTING THE CONGRESS NAME: Statement to Press regarding Pandit Malaviya's use of Prefix 'Congress'; *The Collected Works of Sardar Vallabhbhai Patel, Vol. 4*, p. 184. Used by permission of Konark Publishers Pvt. Ltd, New Delhi.

I AM NOT AFRAID OF MY OPPONENTS: Election Campaign Speech; *The Collected Works of Sardar Vallabhbhai Patel, Vol. 6*, pp. 91–95. Used by permission of Konark Publishers Pvt. Ltd, New Delhi.

THE CONGRESS PRESIDENT HAS NO DICTATORIAL POWERS: Statement; *The Collected Works of Sardar Vallabhbhai Patel, Vol. 6*, pp. 137–9. Used by permission of Konark Publishers Pvt. Ltd, New Delhi.

A LETTER TO SUBHAS BOSE: *The Collected Works of Sardar Vallabhbhai Patel, Vol. 8*, pp. 48–49. Used by permission of Konark Publishers Pvt. Ltd, New Delhi.

A LETTER TO JAWAHARLAL NEHRU: *The Collected Works of Sardar Vallabhbhai Patel, Vol. 8*, p. 50. Used by permission of Konark Publishers Pvt. Ltd, New Delhi.

A LETTER TO ACHARYA NARENDRA DEVA: *The Collected Works of Sardar Vallabhbhai Patel, Vol. 8*, p. 62. Used by permission of Konark Publishers Pvt. Ltd, New Delhi.

A LETTER TO B. G. KHER: *The Collected Works of Sardar Vallabhbhai Patel, Vol. 8*, p. 73. Used by permission of Konark Publishers Pvt. Ltd, New Delhi.

A LETTER TO SUBHAS CHANDRA BOSE: *The Collected Works of Sardar Vallabhbhai Patel, Vol. 8*, p. 80. Used by permission of Konark Publishers Pvt. Ltd, New Delhi.

A LETTER TO RAJENDRA PRASAD: *The Collected Works of Sardar Vallabhbhai Patel, Vol. 8*, pp. 122–23. Used by permission of Konark Publishers Pvt. Ltd, New Delhi.

GANDHIJI DOES NOT WISH THAT WE FOLLOW HIM BLINDLY: Speech at Gujarat Provincial Congress Committee; *The Collected Works of Sardar Vallabhbhai Patel, Vol. 8*, pp. 233–34. Used by permission of Konark Publishers Pvt. Ltd, New Delhi.

LETTER TO MAULANA AZAD (see p. 99): *Sardar Patel's Correspondence 1945–50, Vol. 2*, pp. 23–24.

LETTER TO MAULANA AZAD (see p. 99): *Sardar Patel's Correspondence 1945–50, Vol. 2*, p. 47.

LETTER TO JAWAHARLAL NEHRU: *Sardar Patel's Correspondence 1945–50, Vol. 2*, p. 68.

LETTER TO MAULANA AZAD: *Sardar Patel's Correspondence 1945–50, Vol. 2*, pp. 152–53.

LETTER TO V. V. GIRI (p. 102): *Sardar Patel's Correspondence 1945–50, Vol. 3*, pp. 8–9.

LETTER TO V. V. GIRI (p. 103): *Sardar Patel's Correspondence 1945–50, Vol. 3*, p. 33.

LETTER TO HAREKRISHNA MAHTAB: *Sardar Patel's Correspondence 1945–50, Vol. 3*, pp. 149–50.

LETTER TO FAAZKIAN NEBAL SINGH: Tata Workers' Union; *Sardar*

Patel's Correspondence 1945–50, Vol. 5, p. 97.

LETTER TO RAJENDRA PRASAD: *Sardar Patel's Correspondence 1945–50, Vol. 6*, pp. 426–27.

LETTER TO BASANT KUMAR DAS: *Sardar Patel's Correspondence 1945–50, Vol. 8*, p. 227.

LETTER TO RAFI AHMED KIDWAI (p. 107): Minister for Communications; *Sardar Patel's Correspondence 1945–50, Vol. 8*, pp. 559–60.

LETTER TO RAFI AHMED KIDWAI (pp. 107–108): Minister for Communications; *Sardar Patel's Correspondence 1945–50, Vol. 9*, pp. 315–16.

LETTER TO JAWAHARLAL NEHRU (p. 109): *Sardar Patel's Correspondence 1945–50, Vol. 10*, pp. 208–209.

LETTER TO JAWAHARLAL NEHRU (p. 110): *Sardar Patel's Correspondence 1945–50, Vol. 10*, pp. 218–20.

LETTER TO C. RAJAGOPALACHARI: *Sardar Patel's Correspondence 1945–50, Vol. 10*, p. 224.

LETTER TO JAWAHARLAL NEHRU: *Sardar Patel's Correspondence 1945–50, Vol. 10*, pp. 222–23.

III. SOCIAL ISSUES

THE DUTY OF THE HINDUS IS TO FULLY HELP THE MUSLIMS: Speech as the president of the Fifth Gujarat Political Conference; *Sardar Vallabhbhainaan Bhaashano*, Parikh and Shah (eds.), p. 36.

HINDU–MUSLIM UNITY: Speech as president of the Seventh Maharashtra Political Conference; *Sardar Vallabhbhainaan Bhaashano*, Parikh and Shah (eds.), p. 201.

DO NOT CRUSH YOUNG GIRLS: *Sardar Vallabhbhainaan Bhaashano*, Parikh and Shah (eds.), pp. 211–12.

WE ARE WALKING AT AN ANT'S PACE: *Sardar Vallabhbhainaan Bhaashano*, Parikh and Shah (eds.), pp. 172–75.

NATURE DOES NOT RECOGNIZE ANY DIFFERENCE BASED ON CASTE OR RELIGION: Allahabad Kisan conference; *The Collected Works of Sardar Vallabhbhai Patel Vol. 5*, pp. 81–91. Used by permission of Konark Publishers Pvt. Ltd, New Delhi.

WOMEN MUST GET THEIR RIGHTFUL PLACE: Speech at Jyoti Sangh; *Sardar Vallabhbhainaan Bhaashano*, Parikh and Shah (eds.), p. 370.

A GREAT MORAL REFORM: Speech at a public meeting, Mumbai, 1 August 1939; *Harijan Bandhu*, 6 August 1939, pp. 171–73; *The Collected Works of Sardar Vallabhbhai Patel Vol. 8*, pp. 142–45. Used by permission of Konark Publishers Pvt. Ltd, New Delhi.

A RURAL UNIVERSITY: Message on the inauguration of Birla Vishwakarma Vidyalaya, Vallabh Vidyanagar; *In Tune With The Millions Vol. I [Birth-Centenary Vol. II]*, Manibehn Vallabhbhai Patel and G. M. Nandurkar (eds.), Ahmedabad: Sardar Vallabhbhai Patel Smarak Bhavan, 1975, pp. 271–72.

A GREAT ACHIEVEMENT: Message for the Bombay's Prohibition Drive; *In Tune With The Millions Vol. II [Birth-Centenary Vol. III]*, Manibehn Vallabhbhai Patel and G. M. Nandurkar (eds.), Ahmedabad: Sardar Vallabhbhai Patel Smarak Bhavan, 1976, pp. 24–25.

IV. THE ADMINISTRATOR

LETTER TO GHAZNAFAR ALI: *Sardar Patel's Correspondence 1945–50, Vol. 4*, pp. 71–73.

LETTER TO LORD MOUNTBATTEN (p. 132): *Sardar Patel's Correspondence 1945–50, Vol. 4*, pp. 180–81.

LETTER TO LORD MOUNTBATTEN (p. 133): *Sardar Patel's Correspondence 1945–50, Vol. 4*, pp. 165–66.

LETTER TO DR. P.C. GHOSH: To chief minister, Bengal; *Sardar Patel's Correspondence 1945–50, Vol. 4*, pp. 168–69.

THE REFUGEE PROBLEM: Suggestions to the representatives of East Punjab and the Eastern Punjab States; *In Tune With The Millions Vol. I*, Patel and Nandurkar (eds.), pp. 130–32.

THE SALARIES OF THE MINISTERS: Note; *Sardar Patel's Correspondence 1945–50, Vol. 4*, pp. 443–44.

LETTER TO K. C. NEOGY: To minister for Relief and Rehabilitation; *Sardar Patel's Correspondence 1945–50, Vol. 4*, p. 437.

LETTER TO K. C. REDDY: To Chief Minister, Mysore State; *Sardar Patel's Correspondence 1945–50, Vol. 5*, p. 419.

LETTER TO JAWAHARLAL NEHRU (p. 140): *Sardar Patel's Correspondence 1945–50, Vol. 4*, p. 450.

LETTER TO JAWAHARLAL NEHRU (pp. 141–42): *Sardar Patel's Correspondence 1945–50, Vol. 6*, pp. 370–71.

LETTER TO JAWAHARLAL NEHRU (p. 142): Regarding acquiring the house of G. D. Birla; *Sardar Patel's Correspondence 1945–50, Vol. 6*, pp. 71–73.

LETTER TO THE PREMIERS OF STATES: To the chief ministers of states; *Sardar Patel's Correspondence 1945–50, Vol. 6*, pp. 439–45.

LETTER TO N. GOPALSWAMI AYYANGAR: *Sardar Patel's Correspondence 1945–50, Vol. 6*, pp. 483–84.

I HAVE NO AGGRESSIVE INTENTIONS AGAINST PAKISTAN: Speech at the Subject Committee of the Congress at Jaipur Session; *In Tune With the Millions Vol. I*, Patel and Nandurkar (eds.), p. 142.

SPEECH AT MADRAS: *In Tune With the Millions Vol. 2*, Patel and Nandurkar (eds.), pp. 5–7.

THE CIVIL SERVICES: Speech in the House; *In Tune With the Millions Vol. 2*, Patel and Nandurkar (eds.), pp. 111–21.

INDIAN COMMUNISTS: Speech at Ernakulam; *In Tune With the Millions Vol. 2*, Patel and Nandurkar (eds.), p. 100.

LETTER TO JAWAHARLAL NEHRU: *Sardar Patel's Correspondence 1945–50, Vol. 8*, pp. 136.

LETTER TO C. RAJAGOPALACHARI: To governor general of India; *Sardar Patel's Correspondence 1945–50, Vol. 8*, pp. 279–80.

THE QUESTION OF HINDI: Letter to K. M. Munshi, governor general of India; *Sardar Patel's Correspondence 1945–50, Vol. 8*, pp. 331–32.

I AGREED TO PARTITION AS A LAST RESORT: Speech in the House; *In Tune With the Millions Vol. 2*, Patel and Nandurkar (eds.), pp. 122–30.

NATIONAL LANGUAGE IS NOT FORMED BY FANATICISM: Letter to R. R. Diwakar, Minister of State, Information & Broadcasting; *Sardar Patel's Correspondence 1945–50, Vol. 8*, pp. 379–81.

WE MUST HAVE INDUSTRIALIZATION: Speech at Bombay; *In Tune With the Millions Vol. 2*, Patel and Nandurkar (eds.), p. 20.

LETTER TO JAWAHARLAL NEHRU: *Sardar Patel's Correspondence 1945–50, Vol. 10*, pp. 104–107.

LETTER TO MORARAJI DESAI: *Sardar Patel's Correspondence 1945–50, Vol. 9*, pp. 425–26.

LETTER TO RAMKRISHNA DALMIA: *The Collected Works of Sardar Vallabhbhai Patel Vol. 15*, pp. 134–35. Used by permission of Konark Publishers Pvt. Ltd, New Delhi.

LETTER TO JAWAHARLAL NEHRU (p. 176): *Sardar Patel's Correspondence 1945–50, Vol. 10*, pp. 335–41.

LETTER TO JAWAHARLAL NEHRU (p. 179): *Sardar Patel's Correspondence 1945–50, Vol. 10*, pp. 505–508.

V. COMMUNAL ISSUES

PROCESSION ATTACKED: Telegram to Gandhi; *The Collected Works of Sardar Vallabhbhai Patel Vol. 8*, p. 91. Used by permission of Konark Publishers Pvt. Ltd, New Delhi.

I DESIRE UNITY AMONG ALL COMMUNITIES: Speech at Bhavnagar; *Sardar Vallabhbhainaan Bhashano*, pp. 432–34.

LETTER TO RAJENDRA PRASAD (p. 186): *The Collected Works of Sardar Vallabhbhai Patel Vol. 8*, pp. 106–107. Used by permission of Konark Publishers Pvt. Ltd, New Delhi.

LETTER TO RAJENDRA PRASAD (p. 187): *The Collected Works of Sardar Vallabhbhai Patel Vol. 8*, p. 169. Used by permission of Konark Publishers Pvt. Ltd, New Delhi.

JINNAH'S UNFOUNDED ALLEGATIONS: Statement in Response to Jinnah's Allegations; *The Collected Works of Sardar Vallabhbhai Patel Vol. 8*, pp. 188–89. Used by permission of Konark Publishers Pvt. Ltd, New Delhi.

DIVIDE AND RULE: Letter to Dr V. K. John, Madras; *Sardar Patel's Correspondence 1945–50, Vol. 3*, p. 51.

LETTER TO DR MOHAMMAD ALAM: *Sardar Patel's Correspondence 1945–50, Vol. 3*, p. 83.

LETTER TO K. C. NEOGY: To leader of Congress in Bengal Legislative Assembly; *Sardar Patel's Correspondence 1945–50, Vol. 4*, pp. 39–40.

I DO NOT THINK IT WILL BE POSSIBLE TO CONSIDER HINDUSTAN AS A HINDU STATE: Letter to Brij Mohan Birla; *Sardar Patel's Correspondence 1945–50, Vol. 4*, pp. 56–57.

INDIA IS ONE AND INDIVISIBLE: *In Tune With The Millions Vol. I*, Patel and Nandurkar (eds.), pp. 3–7.

LETTER TO RAJENDRA PRASAD: To Minister for Food and Agriculture; *Sardar Patel's Correspondence 1945–50, Vol. 4*, pp. 338–40.

WAR OF THE JUNGLE: Speech; *In Tune With The Millions Vol. I*, Patel and Nandurkar (eds.), pp. 133–35.

I WANT HINDUS AND MUSLIMS TO FORGET THE PAST: Speech on the Integration of Junagadh; *The Collected Works of Sardar Vallabhbhai Patel Vol. 12*, pp. 229–31. Used by permission of Konark Publishers Pvt. Ltd, New Delhi.

THE DANGERS OF PREDOMINANTLY MUSLIM OR PREDOMINANTLY HINDU AREAS IN THE CITY: Letter to K. C. Neogy, Minister for Relief and Rehabilitation; *Sardar Patel's Correspondence 1945–50, Vol. 4*, p. 361.

LETTER TO GOVIND MALAVIYA: *Sardar Patel's Correspondence 1945–50, Vol. 4*, p. 413.

LETTER TO BALDEV SINGH: To Minister for Defence; *Sardar Patel's Correspondence 1945–50, Vol. 4*, pp. 516–17.

LETTER TO JAWAHARLAL NEHRU: *Sardar Patel's Correspondence 1945–50, Vol. 4*, p. 364

LETTER TO A. E. PORTER: *Sardar Patel's Correspondence 1945–50, Vol. 4*, pp. 505–506.

LETTER TO DR GOKULCHAND NARANG: To Hindu Mahasabha sympathiser, Lahore; *Sardar Patel's Correspondence 1945–50, Vol. 5*, pp. 284–86.

CREATING THE RIGHT ATMOSPHERE: Speech; *In Tune With The Millions Vol. I*, Patel and Nandurkar (eds.), pp. 20–22.

WE MUST CREATE AN ATMOSPHERE IN WHICH EVERYONE CAN LIVE IN CONFIDENCE AND SECURITY: Speech; *In Tune With The Millions Vol. I*, Patel and Nandurkar (eds.), pp. 51–53.

WHY SHOULD NOT A MEMBER OF ANY COMMUNITY BE THE PRIME MINISTER OF THIS COUNTRY?: Speech in the house as Chairman of the Advisory Committee on Minorities; *In Tune With The Millions Vol. II*, Patel and Nandurkar (eds.), pp. 153–61.

THE ASSASSINATION OF MAHATMA GANDHI: Address to the Nation after Gandhi's assassination; *In Tune With The Millions Vol. I*, Patel and Nandurkar (eds.), pp. 217–18.

AN APPEAL FOR PEACE: After Gandhi's assassination; *In Tune With The Millions Vol. I*, Patel and Nandurkar (eds.), pp. 217–18.

I AM ONE WITH THE PRIME MINISTER ON ALL NATIONAL ISSUES: Speech before the meeting of the Congress Legislature Party in Parliament; *In Tune With The Millions Vol. I*, Patel and Nandurkar (eds.), pp. 221–22.

LETTER TO JAWAHARLAL NEHRU: *Sardar Patel's Correspondence 1945–50, Vol. 6*, pp. 56–58.

LETTER TO SYAMA PRASAD MOOKERJEE (p. 213): To Minister for Industry and Supply; *Sardar Patel's Correspondence 1945–50, Vol. 6*, pp. 65–67.

LETTER TO SYAMA PRASAD MOOKERJEE (p. 214): *Sardar Patel's Correspondence 1945–50, Vol. 6*, pp. 323–24.

LETTER TO SYAMA PRASAD MOOKERJEE (p. 215): *Sardar Patel's Correspondence 1945–50, Vol. 6*, pp. 86–87.

LETTER TO M. S. GOLWALKAR (p. 216): *The Collected Works of Sardar Vallabhbhai Patel Vol. 14*, p. 288. Used by permission of Konark Publishers Pvt. Ltd, New Delhi.

LETTER TO M. S. GOLWALKAR (p. 217): *The Collected Works of Sardar Vallabhbhai Patel Vol. 14*, p. 289. Used by permission of Konark Publishers Pvt. Ltd, New Delhi.

LETTER TO JAWAHARLAL NEHRU: *Sardar Patel's Correspondence 1945–50, Vol. 7*, p. 261.

HINDUISM CAN NEVER BE IN DANGER IN INDIA: Speech; *In Tune With The Millions Vol. I*, Patel and Nandurkar (eds.), p. 100.

LETTER TO JAWAHARLAL NEHRU: *Sardar Patel's Correspondence 1945–50, Vol. 8*, p. 268.

LETTER TO JAWAHARLAL NEHRU: *Sardar Patel's Correspondence 1945–50, Vol. 8*, pp. 602–604.

LETTER TO JAWAHARLAL NEHRU: *Sardar Patel's Correspondence 1945–50, Vol. 9*, p. 146.

LETTER TO G. B. PANT: To Premier of United Province; *Sardar Patel's Correspondence 1945–50, Vol. 9*, pp. 310–11.

VI. PRINCELY STATES AND INTERGRATION

WESTERN CIVILIZATION IS THE ROOT CAUSE OF THE UNREST IN THE WORLD: Speech as the President of the Fifth Gujarat Political Conference; *Sardar Vallabhbhainaan Bhaashano*, Parikh and Shah (eds.), p. 39.

THE PRINCELY STATES HAVE NO REASON TO BE WARY OF THE INDEPENDENT HINDUSTAN Speech as the president of the fifth Kathiawad Political Conference; *Sardar Vallabhbhainaan Bhaashano*, Parikh and Shah (eds.), pp. 177–84.

INDIA NEEDS TO INTROSPECT: Speech; *Sardar Vallabhbhainaan Bhaashano*, Parikh and Shah (eds.), pp. 388–99.

A FRAUGHT SITUATION: A document read by K. M. Munshi in the Parliament on Sardar Patel's behalf; *In Tune With The Millions Vol. II*, Patel and Nandurkar (eds.), pp. 85–87.

HYDERABAD: Letter to Lord Mountbatten; Sel*ected Correspondence of Sardar Patel 1945–50, Vol. 7*, pp. 109–10.

LETTER TO JAWAHARLAL NEHRU: Draft; *Sardar Patel's Correspondence 1945–50, Vol. 7*, pp. 211–13.

THERE SHOULD BE NO VACILLATION: Letter to N. V. Gadgil, President of Congress Committee; *Sardar Patel's Correspondence 1945–50, Vol. 7*, p. 217.

A DEMOCRATIC APPROACH: Letter to Arthur Henderson, Under-Secretary of State for India in Attlee Government; Letter to N. V. Gadgil, President of Congress Committee; *Sardar Patel's Correspondence 1945–50, Vol. 7*, pp. 221–22.

A SETTLEMENT WITH HYDERABAD: A statement on Hyderabad in the Constituent Assembly; *Sardar Patel's Correspondence 1945–50, Vol. 7*, pp. 235–37.

THE PROBLEM OF HYDERABAD: *In Tune With the Millions Vol. 1*, Patel and Nandurkar (eds.), pp. 115–16.

LEAVE US ALONE: Speech before the officers and men of Royal Indian Air Force; *In Tune With the Millions Vol. 1*, p. 316.

LETTER TO THE NIZAM OF HYDERABAD: *Sardar Patel's Correspondence 1945–50, Vol. 7*, p. 310.

THE CONSTITUTIONAL POSITION OF HYDERABAD: Speech in Parliament on Hyderabad; *In Tune With the Millions Vol. 2*, Patel and Nandurkar (eds.), pp. 59–60.

KASHMIR: Letter to Ramchandra Kak, Prime Minister of Kashmir; *Sardar Patel's Correspondence 1945–50, Vol. 1*, p. 32.

LETTER TO MAHARAJA HARI SINGH: *Sardar Patel's Correspondence 1945–50, Vol. 1*, pp. 32–34.

LETTER TO N. GOPALSWAMI AYYANGAR: *Sardar Patel's Correspondence 1945–50, Vol. 1*, p. 199.

LETTER TO JAWAHARLAL NEHRU (p. 246): *Sardar Patel's Correspondence 1945–50, Vol. 1*, pp. 227–28.

LETTER TO JAWAHARLAL NEHRU (p. 247): *Sardar Patel's Correspondence 1945–50, Vol. 1*, p. 284.

LETTER TO Dr JOHN MATHAI: To Minister of Finance; *Sardar Patel's Correspondence 1945–50, Vol. 1*, p. 296.

LETTER TO N. GOPALASWAMI AYYANGAR: *Sardar Patel's Correspondence 1945–50, Vol. 1*, p. 305.

LETTER TO JAWAHARLAL NEHRU (p. 249): *Sardar Patel's Correspondence 1945–50, Vol. 1*, p. 310.

LETTER TO JAWAHARLAL NEHRU (p. 250): *Sardar Patel's Correspondence 1945–50, Vol. 1*, p. 317.

THE INTEGRATION OF JUNAGADH: Speech; *The Collected Works of Sardar Vallabhbhai Patel Vol. 12*, pp. 229–31. Used by permission of Konark Publishers Pvt. Ltd, New Delhi

MYSORE STATE: Letter to M. Sankar Lingegowda, Member of Assembly, Mysore; *Sardar Patel's Correspondence 1945–50, Vol. 5*, pp. 401–402.

THE ACCESSION OF BHOPAL: Letter to Nawab of Bhopal; *Sardar Patel's Correspondence 1945–50, Vol. 5*, pp. 362–63.

LETTER TO G. B. PANT: Chief Minister of United Province; *Sardar Patel's Correspondence 1945–50, Vol. 4*, pp. 430–31.

LETTER TO JAWAHARLAL NEHRU: *Sardar Patel's Correspondence 1945–50, Vol. 8*, pp. 597–601.

VII. NEHRU AND OTHER COLLEAGUES

LETTER TO SUBHAS CHANDRA BOSE: *The Collected Works of Sardar Vallabhbhai Patel Vol. 4*, pp. 60–61. Used by permission of Konark Publishers Pvt. Ltd, New Delhi.

PANDIT JAWAHARLAL NEHRU IS ONE OF THE GREATEST LEADERS OF MODERN INDIA: Letter to Pandit Jiyalal Kaul Jalali, retired assistant accountant general, Jammu and Kashmir; *Sardar Patel's Correspondence 1945–50, Vol. 1*, pp. 2–3.

THE ATMOSPHERE IS FULL OF VIOLENCE: Letter to D. P. Mishra, Minister of Industries; *Sardar Patel's Correspondence 1945–50, Vol. 3*, pp. 153–55.

TO ERR IS HUMAN: Letter to Sir C. R. Reddy, United Nationalist Party; *Sardar Patel's Correspondence 1945–50, Vol. 3*, p. 40.

THE SITUATION IN KASHMIR IS DIFFICULT: Letter to C. Parmeswaram, Srinagar; *Sardar Patel's Correspondence 1945–50, Vol. 1*, pp. 3–4.

THE CONGRESS IS NOT OPPOSED TO ANY PRINCE IN INDIA: Letter to Maharaja Hari Singh of Kashmir; *Sardar Patel's Correspondence 1945–50, Vol. 1*, pp. 32–33.

OUR COMBINATION IS UNBREAKABLE: *Sardar Patel's Correspondence 1945–50, Vol. 4*, p. 537.

LETTER TO LORD MOUNTBATTEN: *Sardar Patel's Correspondence 1945–50, Vol. 4*, pp. 552–53.

LETTER TO JAWAHARLAL NEHRU: *Sardar Patel's Correspondence 1945–50, Vol. 1*, p. 56.

THE PRIME MINISTER HAS NO OVERRIDING POWERS OVER HIS COLLEAGUES: A note to Gandhi regarding differences of opinion with

Jawaharlal Nehru; *Sardar Patel's Correspondence 1945–50, Vol. 6*, pp. 21–24.

LETTER TO JAWAHARLAL NEHRU (p. 274): *Sardar Patel's Correspondence 1945–50, Vol. 6*, pp. 27–28.

LETTER TO JAWAHARLAL NEHRU (pp. 274–75): Ibid., pp. 30–31.

TELEGRAM TO N. V. GADGIL: To the Minister for Works, Mines and Power; *Sardar Patel's Correspondence 1945–50, Vol. 6*, p. 376.

LETTER TO JAWAHARLAL NEHRU: *Sardar Patel's Correspondence 1945–50, Vol. 6*, p. 213.

I HAVE LEARNT FROM MAHATMA GANDHI TO HAVE FRIENDSHIP TOWARDS ALL: Speech at a Reception at Imperial Hotel, Delhi; *In Tune With the Millions Vol. 1*, Patel and Nandurkar (eds.), p. 258.

LETTER TO RAJENDRA PRASAD: To President of Constituent Assembly; *Sardar Patel's Correspondence 1945–50, Vol. 8*, pp. 206–209.

THE GAME OF FAULT FINDING: Letter to Bidhan Chandra Roy, Premier of West Bengal; *Sardar Patel's Correspondence 1945–50, Vol. 9*, p. 35.

LETTER TO JAWAHARLAL NEHRU (p. 278): *Sardar Patel's Correspondence 1945–50, Vol. 9*, pp. 410–11.

LETTER TO JAWAHARLAL NEHRU (p. 279): *Sardar Patel's Correspondence 1945–50, Vol. 9*, p. 290.

VIII. A PLAIN, BLUNT MAN

JAIL DIARY: Excerpts from Sardar Patel's jail diary; *Sardar Vallabhbhai Patel, Vol. II*, pp. 14–17, pp. 25–26.

OBSCENE IMAGES ON TEMPLES: Letter to the secretary, District Congress Committee, Puri; *The Collected Works of Sardar Vallabhbhai Patel Vol. 3*, pp. 252–53. Used by permission of Konark Publishers Pvt. Ltd, New Delhi.

LETTER TO MAHATMA GANDHI: *Sardarshrina Patro Vol. 4* (Letters of Sardar), Manibahen Vallabhbhai Patel and G. M. Nandurkar (eds.), 3rd edn, Ahmedabad: Sardar Vallabhbhai Patel Samrak Bhavan, 1981, pp. 283–84.

LETTER TO HIS SON, DAHYABHAI PATEL: Letter regarding Vitthalbhai Patel's will; *Sardarshrina Patro Vol. 3*, Patel and Nandurkar (eds.), p. 189.

MY MOTHER DELIVERED FIVE STONES: Letter to Chhaganlal; *Sardarshrina Patro Vol. 2*, Patel and Nandurkar (eds.), p. 177.

I HAVE CROSSED THE BARRIERS OF CASTE AND CREED: A speech responding to a welcome address given by the Patidars of Karachi; *The Collected Works of Sardar Vallabhbhai Patel Vol. 7*, p. 163. Used by permission of Konark Publishers Pvt. Ltd, New Delhi.

LETTER TO NARHARI PARIKH: *Sardarshrina Patro Vol. 3*, Patel and Nandurkar (eds.), p. 262.

FASTING SHOULD BE LEFT TO GREAT MEN LIKE GANDHIJI: Letter to B. N. Saojee, Nagpur; *Sardar Patel's Correspondence 1945–50, Vol. 3*, p. 158.

WE HAVE WON FREEDOM: Letter to Kasturbhai Lalbhai, a Gujarati industrialist; *The Collected Works of Sardar Vallabhbhai Patel Vol. 12*, p. 151. Used by permission of Konark Publishers Pvt. Ltd, New Delhi.

THE BURDEN OF WORK HAS BECOME HEAVY: Letter to Gandhi during his last fast; *Sardar Patel's Correspondence 1945–50, Vol. 6*, pp. 25–26.

I HATE PROLONGED DISCUSSIONS: Address to students of Benaras Hindu University; *In Tune With The Millions Vol. I*, Patel and Nandurkar (eds.), pp. 277–78.

A PLAIN, BLUNT MAN: Speech at Allahabad University on being conferred Doctor of Laws; *In Tune With The Millions Vol. I*, Patel and Nandurkar (eds.), p. 282.

I DO NOT LIKE THE IDEA OF STARTING ANY COLLEGE OR ACADEMY AFTER ME OR AFTER MANIBEN: Letter to P. Rangaswamy who wanted to start the Vallabhbhai Patel Academy of Applied Sciences at Banglore; *Sardar Patel's Correspondence 1945–50, Vol. 10*, p. 398.

LETTER TO AJIT PRASAD: To the Minister of State for Rehabilitation; *The Collected Works of Sardar Vallabhbhai Patel Vol. 15*, pp. 200–201. Used by permission of Konark Publishers Pvt. Ltd, New Delhi.

BIBLIOGRAPHY

Chopra, P. N. (ed.), *The Collected Works of Sardar Vallabhbhai Patel Vol. 1–15*, New Delhi: Konark Publishers Pvt Ltd, 1990–99.

Das, Durga (ed.), *Sardar Patel's Correspondence 1945–50, Vol. 1–10*, Ahmedabad: Navjivan Publishing House, 1971–74.

Desai, Mahadev Haribhai, *Bardoli Satyagrahano Itihas* (History of Bardoli Satyagraha), Ahmedabad: Navjivan Prakashan Mandir, Samvat 1985.

Desai, Mahadev, *The Story of Bardoli*, Ahmedabad: Navjivan Press, 1929.

Parikh, Narhari D. *Sardar Vallabhbhai Vol. 1* (Gujarati), Ahmedabad: Navjivan Publishing House, 1950, (English edn 1953).

Parikh, Narhari Dwarkadas, *Sardar Vallabhbhai Vol. 2* (Gujarati), Ahmedabad: Navjivan Publishing House, 1952 (English edn 1952).

Parikh, Narhari Dwarkadas and Shah, Uttamchand Deepchand (eds.), *Sardar Vallabhbhainaan Bhashano* (Speeches by Sardar Vallabhbhai), Ahmedabad: Navjivan Prakashan Mandir, 1949.

Patel, Manibahen Vallabhbhai and Nandurkar, G. M. (eds.), *Sardarshrina Patro* (Letters of Sardar), 3rd edn, Ahmedabad: Sardar Vallabhbhai Patel Samrak Bhavan, 1980.

Patel, Manibahen Vallabhbhai and Nandurkar, G. M. (eds.), *Sardarshrina Patro-2* (Letters of Sardar), 3rd edn, Ahmedabad: Sardar Vallabhbhai Patel Samrak Bhavan, 1981.

Patel, Manibahen Vallabhbhai and Nandurkar, G. M. (eds.), *Sardarshrina Patro-3* (Letters of Sardar), 3rd edn, Ahmedabad: Sardar Vallabhbhai Patel Samrak Bhavan, 1981.

Patel, Manibahen Vallabhbhai and Nandurkar, G. M. (eds.), *Sardarshrina Patro-4* (Letters of Sardar), 3rd edn, Ahmedabad: Sardar Vallabhbhai Patel Samrak Bhavan, 1981.

Patel, Manibahen Vallabhbhai and Nandurkar, G. M. (eds.), *Sardarshrina Patro-5* (Letters of Sardar), 2nd edn, Ahmedabad: Sardar Vallabhbhai Patel Samrak Bhavan, 1981.

Patel, Manibehn Vallabhbhai and Nandurkar G. M. (eds.), *In Tune With The Millions Vol. I [Birth-Centenary Vol. II]*, Ahmedabad: Sardar Vallabhbhai Patel Smarak Bhavan, 1975.

Patel, Manibehn Vallabhbhai and Nandurkar G. M. (eds.), *In Tune With The Millions Vol. II [Birth-Centenary Vol. III]*, Ahmedabad: Sardar Vallabhbhai Patel Smarak Bhavan, 1976.

Saggi, P. D., *Life and Work of Sardar Vallabhbhai Patel*, Bombay: Overseas Publishing House, 1955.